NATURAL RELIGION AND THE NATURE OF RELIGION

The Legacy of Deism

ROUTLEDGE RELIGIOUS STUDIES

Advisory Editor: Professor Stewart Sutherland, Principal,
King's College, University of London

NATURAL RELIGION AND THE NATURE OF RELIGION

The Legacy of Deism

Peter Byrne

ROUTLEDGE
LONDON AND NEW YORK

First published 1989
by Routledge
11 New Fetter Lane, London EC4P 4EE
29 West 35th Street, New York, NY 10001

© 1989 Peter Byrne

Disc conversion in 10/12 Baskerville by Columns of Reading
Printed in Great Britain by TJ Press (Padstow) Ltd, Padstow

British Library Cataloguing in Publication Data

Byrne, Peter, *1950–*
Natural religion and the nature of religion:
the legacy of deism
1. Deism. Theories, history
I. Title
211'.509

ISBN 0–415–04104–X

Library of Congress Cataloging in Publication Data

Byrne, Peter, 1950–
Natural religion and the nature of religion:
the legacy of deism
Peter Byrne.
p.   cm. – (Routledge religious studies)
Bibliography: p.
Includes index.
1. Deism – History. 2. Deism – Influence.
3. Natural theology – History. 4. Natural theology – Influence.
5. Religion – Study and teaching – History.
I. Title. II. Series.
BL2747.4.B97 1989
210 – dc19   88–36899

CONTENTS

Acknowledgements   vii

Preface   ix

1 THE CONCEPT OF NATURAL RELIGION   1

Natural and revealed religion   1
Natural theology, civil theology, and mythic theology   5
Natural and supernatural religion   7
Natural religion and natural religiousness   8
Religion and Christianity   11

2 HUMANISM AND RATIONALISM   22

Lord Herbert of Cherbury and religious humanism   22
John Locke on the nature and necessity of revelation   37

3 DEISM AND THE CASE FOR NATURAL RELIGION   52

Introduction   52
The doctrine of God   53
The doctrine of man   61
Religious certainty   70

4 DEISM AND THE CRITICISM OF RELIGION   79

Introduction   79
A general picture of the history of religions   82
The church   88
The bible   93

5 THE PROGRESS OF THE CONCEPT OF NATURAL
   RELIGION   111

   Introduction   111
   Hume on the natural religion of mankind   113
   Kant on the place of religion in history   128

6 RELIGION, ROMANTICISM, AND IDEALISM   141

   Introduction   141
   J.G. Herder on human nature and history   143
   The case against natural religion in Schleiermacher's Speeches   156
   Hegel on religion in history   166

7 NATURAL RELIGION AND THE SCIENCE OF
   RELIGION   181

   Introduction   181
   F. Max Mueller   183
   Natural religion in Tylor's Primitive Culture   196
   Conclusion   203

8 THE CONTEMPORARY STUDY OF RELIGIONS   207

   Introduction: the legacy of deism   207
   The concept of religion and the universality of religion 209
   Religion and human nature   226
   Naturalism and the history of religions   241

   Notes   256

   Works cited   260

   Index   266

ACKNOWLEDGEMENTS

I am grateful to the publisher's reader for useful comments on the first four chapters of this book, and to various colleagues who read or heard parts of it; in particular, Peter Clarke, Grace Jantzen, Stewart Sutherland, and Keith Ward.

I was given considerable help in typing early drafts of some of the material by Anne Boydell, Charlotte Byrne, and the late, much-missed Betty Wood.

Peter Byrne

PREFACE

The aim of this study is to offer students of religion and philosophy a series of linked, introductory essays on the concept of natural religion.

The concept of natural religion is a diverse and highly ramified one. The essays in this volume concentrate on one thread that has been important in the notion of natural religion in European thought. This is the link between the concept of natural religion and reflection on the nature of religion as a human phenomenon. This link in turn provides the opportunity to treat a number of other themes. One such theme is the emergence and development of the concept of religion itself. What is offered here does not amount to a history of the concept of religion, but the essays are written both in the belief that the concept of religion is one with a history which has been crucially shaped by important philosophical developments, and in the belief that unless we are aware of this history we cannot engage in useful discussion in the present about the concept of religion. Another theme is brought in via the subtitle of the book – the legacy of deism. The important philosophical developments associated with the history and emergence of the concept of religion can all be illustrated and discussed by reference to the notion of natural religion and, through that, to the ideas and influence of deistic thought of the Enlightenment. Again, the essays are not offered as a history of this theme (if this implies trying to tell a complete story) but are illustrative of some important aspects of deism and its legacy. The essays on natural religion in this book are thus illustrative of crucial questions about, and developments in, the concept of natural religion, while at the same time being a treatment of deism and its consequences.

To introduce these themes properly more needs to be said about the concept of religion, its history, and about the nature of deism.

Contemporary writers and thinkers on religion debate many aspects of the nature and significance of mankind's religious life. But their debates only have meaning if they have a common reference-point. The protagonists must share a concept of religion, which means holding some common beliefs about the thing they are investigating, even if they disagree about much else. Included in these common beliefs are those connected with the now widespread perception that religion is a global and historical phenomenon. This perception is part of our modern concept of religion because it is the precondition of the very possibility of the study of religion as we now know it – a general and historically orientated investigation into the religious life of mankind as a whole. These simple, underlying beliefs about the nature of religion are not without their ambiguities, as we shall note in Chapter 8 when discussing exactly how far religion can be viewed as a universal phenomenon in human culture and to what precise extent it can be seen as capable of historical description and explanation. Moreover, as we shall also see, opinions have differed and do differ over how religion is to be defined if its universal and historical character is to be perceived. Yet we do appear to have in these beliefs about the character of religion a common reference-point for the modern study of religion. This modern approach to religious phenomena (and with it the concept of religion that makes it possible) emerges relatively late in the history of European thought, and is not fully fledged until the latter half of the nineteenth century (Sharpe 1975:1). So we cannot take the global, historical approach to religion for granted; no more can we take for granted the apparently simple perspective that lies behind it.

Religion can exist in a society and human beings can engage in it without the perspective behind the modern concept of religion also existing in that society or being shared by those who engage in religion. The perspective on religion we are investigating is the result of detachment and reflection. Those who participate in or observe the life of religion in their culture will only see this life as one instance of a global and historical phenomenon if they are prepared to detach themselves from its present demands and reflect on its nature and existence after a certain fashion. They must be able in thought to isolate the religious life they participate in or observe as a distinct aspect of human culture. They must be prepared to recognize the beliefs and practices of other cultures as instances of this same, now generalized, aspect of all human culture. They must in addition be ready to realize that the phenomena encompassed in this aspect of social and personal life are historical realities, things which change and develop along with other aspects of human culture.

Because this perspective on religion cannot be taken for granted as an inevitable accompaniment of the existence of religion itself we can see that the concept of religion has a history. In presupposing acts of detachment from, and reflection about, the religious traditions of our society the concept can be given a beginning and its development illustrated and explored. Detachment from and reflection about dominant religious traditions are as old as Classical antiquity, and thus we could take the beginning of the concept of religion back to Greek and Roman philosophy (Sharpe 1975:2). However, it is easier to see the origins of the modern concept of religion in the European Enlightenment and the reaction to it, for it was the Enlightenment that marked the emergence in modern European culture of detachment from and reflection about inherited and established religious beliefs and practices. Concentrating on the Enlightenment and its consequences does not deny the importance of the Classical tradition. The Enlightenment can be characterized both by its development of habits of critical thought concerning existing customs and traditions and by its elevation of the thought of antiquity above that of traditional Christian theology:

> For the Enlightenment, then, the organized habit of criticism was the most far-reaching invention of classical antiquity. A solvent of custom, accepted explanations, and traditional institutions.
>
> (Gay 1967:121)

After an intervention of an age of superstition, the philosophers of the Enlightenment could celebrate their own as the second age of criticism consequent upon the criticism of custom and tradition established by Greek and Roman thinkers. The criticism of religion was of course one of the most important aspects of Enlightenment thought, for in detaching itself from and scrutinizing the traditional and customary basis of European society, the Enlightenment naturally found religious traditions and customs to be central to so much else. Religious ideas and practices were established ideas and practices, and much that was established was maintained and fostered by religion.

It is not my aim to add to the many detailed histories of the religious thought of the Enlightenment, but to seek instead to illustrate through a number of essays the theme of how its approach to religion in human life led to that perspective on religion so fundamental to our modern ways of conceiving of it. This theme is illustrated by reference to one single, if highly ramified, notion central to the Enlightenment's approach to religion and to later thinkers' reaction to that approach – the concept of natural religion.

Concentration on the notion of natural religion provides a good way of illustrating and introducing the philosophical issues relevant to our overall theme of the development and nature of the concept of religion. Among other things, we need to treat of such matters as the detachment from Christianity, the criticism of its presuppositions, the attempt to see it as an instance of a general aspect of human culture, the effort to see it as an historical phenomenon: all the important intellectual questions which surround the Enlightenment's engagement with the concept of religion can be explored by reference to its beliefs about natural religion. Moreover, the later reaction to and contemporary significance of the Enlightenment's treatment of religion as a human reality can be expounded through concentrating on how the concept of natural religion was developed and treated. Even those writers who come after the Enlightenment but crucially contribute to the development of the modern concept of religion can be seen as wrestling with problems created by the concept of natural religion. Finally, focusing discussion of the concept of religion via the notion of natural religion enables us to explore some of the main features of the Enlightenment's treatment of religion by discussion of texts of great clarity – the primary works of the more important English deists.

The legacy of deism mentioned in the subtitle to this study is the legacy of its thought, flowing from its concept of natural religion, about the nature of religion as a human phenomenon. Other facets of deism could be fastened on as bearing fruit for contemporary religious thought. We might look to it for insights into natural theology and the rational proof of the existence of God. In fact, we find that the deists tend to take rational theology for granted and add little to the arguments of natural theology. We might find greater fruit in their emphasis on morality above dogma in religion. Many aspects of the liberal theology that still enjoys wide appeal in religious life today are prefigured in their writings. I choose to fasten upon the implications of their thought for our understanding of the human reality of religion and hence for questions about method in the study of religion. There are a number of implications of deism in this field which are still of contemporary significance, as indicated in Chapters 7 and 8. One of the aims of this study is thus to show that there is something of contemporary, and not merely of antiquarian, interest in English deism.

Whom I take to be deists and what views I regard as characteristic of deism are indicated in Chapters 3 and 4. There in effect I identify 'deism' with the main teachings of Matthew Tindal's *Christianity as Old as the Creation* and use other English writers of the early eighteenth century in so far as they provide opinions and arguments which support or amplify a Tindal-like perspective on religion. This means taking deism to be defined initially by belief in the sufficiency of natural religion and the superfluousness of revealed religion. It must be said, however, that there is a degree of abstraction and stipulation in this definition. For Tindal was in no sense a spokesman for an organized group, and there is in fact a great variety of detailed opinion among the writers customarily awarded with the title 'deist'. The variety among those called 'deists' has led one recent commentator to speak of the 'elusiveness of deism' and to conclude that 'deism' should function only as a label of convenience for the historian of ideas rather than a precise term of analysis (Sullivan 1982:232).

The vagueness of 'deism' as a term for analysing the thought of radical critics of religion is something that was noted by eighteenth-century commentators on religious thought. Samuel Clarke in his *Discourse* on natural religion and revelation of 1738 found four distinct categories of religious philosophy that could be called 'deism' but his overall verdict is that 'There is now no such thing as a consistent scheme of deism' (Clarke 1738:607). The most thorough commentary on deism of the time, Leland's *View of the Principal Deistic Writers*, has similar difficulties in pinning down an agreed philosophy of religion for deism. Leland speaks of the 'several schemes' formed by those called deists having one common end 'viz, to set aside revelation, and to substitute mere natural religion, or which seems to have been the intention of some of them, no religion at all, in its room' (Leland 1757a:ii). The last clause of this quotation is important: the subject matter of Leland's lectures shows that at the time it was quite acceptable to use 'deist' to cover any writer perceived to have critical views on Christian revelation. So Leland writes on Hume, Hobbes, and Herbert, as well as the kind of author treated in Chapters 3 and 4 of the present study. We are interested in the emergence of a standpoint which offers on the one hand, a negative critique of claims for the uniqueness and divine character of any revealed religion (including Christianity), and, on the other, a positive affirmation that a religion founded on reason and nature is suffient for salvation. It is this perspective which has the interesting methodological implications we are concerned to trace. It can be found in Tindal's major work and it is also true that a number of other writers roughly contemporary with him (for example Chubb, Annet, Wollaston, Woolston, Collins, Toland, Middleton, and Blount) can be quarried for arguments and opinions that support this stance. It is legitimate to treat these writers as a group for the purposes of these essays in so far as they form a loose family, noted for its critical stance toward established faith and its rationalist temper. It is the absence of this latter feature which means that it is profitable to consider them as apart from Hume and, as I shall explain in Chapter 2, Lord Herbert of Cherbury. But it must be said that they are a loose sort of family. Some of the members are rather removed from the paradigm represented by Tindal's *Christianity as Old as the Creation*. Collins shows an inclination, in works such as *A Philosophical Enquiry into Human Liberty*, to materialism which gives him pronounced atheistic tendencies. Toland does not altogether close the door on revelation in *Christianity not Mysterious*, and in works such as the *Pantheisticon* displays an eccentric religious outlook all his own (a similar comment could be made about the thought of Thomas Woolston which we use in Chapter 4).

What in the end matters for the present study is that we can find in these writers arguments for a point of view on religion connected with the concept of natural religion and of great importance for the subsequent development of the Enlightenment's philosophy of religion and, through that, the later shape of modern thought about the nature of religion. This is what makes 'deism' a useful term of convenience for this book.

This book is an introduction to and illustration of philosophical themes connected with the development of the concept of religion, and cannot pretend to be an history of ideas in any full sense. Accordingly I have made as little reference as possible to scholarly secondary sources or debates about the details connected with the authors mentioned in this work. Footnotes have been consciously kept to an absolute minimum. I have tried to aid students by giving them clear expositions of authors' views that are related directly to the primary sources. For this same reason I have occasionally simplified and modernized spelling of eighteenth-century texts where it is in the interests of clarity to do so. Dates for the main authors discussed in the historical chapters of the book are given in the Index.

All references in the book are within the text, citing author's name and the date of the edition used. This information is amplified in the list of works cited at the close. Detailed reference is given to the page number of the work cited, except in a few cases where an alternative form of detailed reference is traditional and more usually found in the literature. So in *The City of God* reference is to Book and Chapter number; in Aquinas' *Summa Theologiae* to Part, Question, and Article; in his *Summa Contra Gentiles* to Book and Chapter; and in Locke's *Essay concerning Human Understanding* to Book, Chapter, and Section. English translations of foreign texts have been used throughout, except in the case of the writings of Herder. A number of his key works have not been fully translated into English, so I perforce have made reference to the standard German edition of his works. The passages quoted in Chapter 6 are translated by me.

1

THE CONCEPT OF NATURAL RELIGION

NATURAL AND REVEALED RELIGION

The concept of natural religion is not a unitary notion. Of the many senses of the phrase 'natural religion' to be found in philosophical thought four will occupy our attention as we trace the emergence of the concept of religion. Three can be brought out by considering the oppositions or distinctions in which 'natural religion' or the allied 'natural theology' can figure. These oppositions are: (1) natural religion (theology) versus revealed religion (theology); (2) natural theology versus civil and mythic theology; (3) natural religion versus supernatural religion. The fourth sense of 'natural religion' to be treated does not fit so easily into a pair of opposites, being used to refer to a natural human religiousness. All these modes of natural religion (theology) will be explored in sections of this chapter. In this section the first sense and contrast will be discussed.

The contrast between natural religion and revealed religion is likely to give the student a first aquaintance with the notion of natural religion. It is implicit in the title of Hume's celebrated *Dialogues concerning Natural Religion*. A student is likely to be told by way of explaining Hume's title that the natural religion mentioned is nothing more than an expanded version of the natural theology used by Christian apologists such as Aquinas. Natural theology contains a body of truths about God and his relationship to the world discoverable by the use of unaided human reason and is contrasted with a body of truths – revealed theology – discoverable only by reflection on God's special revelation in history. Cleanthes'

1

natural religion in Hume's *Dialogues* is Aquinas' natural theology writ large and can be explained through a similar contrast. It is, however, thought capable of enjoying an independence of revealed theology/religion not contemplated by Aquinas.

The readiness to explain this distinction between natural and revealed theology by reference to Aquinas receives an initial disappointment when we turn to the classic texts which are the source of the distinction, for in neither the *Summa Theologiae* nor the *Summa contra Gentiles* is the opposition drawn in these terms. Aquinas in fact tends to use 'natural theology' in the second sense to be explored in this chapter. The substance, if not the terminology, of the distinction between revealed and natural theology is certainly to be found in Aquinas:

> For certain things that are true about God wholly surpass the capability of human reason, for instance that God is three in one: while there are certain things to which even the natural reason can attain, for instance that God is one, and others like these, which even the philosophers proved demonstratively of God, being guided by the light of natural reason.
>
> (Aquinas 1924:I,3)

The distinction between these two sorts of truths is absorbed into a distinction between what theology or sacred science can demonstrate about God and what philosophy can demonstrate. The grounds of this distinction will be familiar and so need only the briefest mention here. Through the fact of the creation a general revelation of God's existence and his nature as first cause is accessible to reason from the character of the world around us. Other matters, relating to God-as-saviour, are dependent on grace and revelation for their discovery. Aquinas' reasons for not relying wholly on reason in the discovery of theological truth will likewise be familiar. Only a brief summary is required to enable the contrasting views of later writers, particularly the deists, to be brought out. This will facilitate some brief early comment on what needed to transpire for natural theology to expand into natural religion.

First, we note that Aquinas demands that special revelation exist as a second, better teacher of the truths about God-as-creator that natural theology deals in. For if the knowledge of God-as-creator were not reinforced in this way, then it would be enjoyed by only some, and by them only after a long lapse of time and with the admixture of many errors (Aquinas 1924:I,4). Natural theology is deficient then in the universality, ease and certainty with which it can make its branch of religious truth available. With expanded notions of the power of human reason the deists were to affirm precisely the opposite. The deeper reason why natural theology remains a mere part of religious thought for Aquinas is brought to light when we consider his remarks on the end of human life that is the goal of religion. When we are directed toward God-as-our-end we are essentially contemplating something beyond the discoveries of unaided human reason. This is not merely because our end is in a life to come, since deists were to contend that immortality was a discovery of the unaided intellect; it is rather that the mode of blessedness that is salvation is beyond discovery. For that goal consists in an unmediated vision of God's essence, a form of union through knowledge with him. So salvation is concerned with a kind of knowledge simply unavailable to the human reason (cf. Aquinas 1974:I*a*,1,1; I*a*,12,8; I*a*,12,11).

Expanded views on human reason will produce a different account of the balance between a revealed and a natural knowledge of God's existence and nature. But above all we will find a lowering or domestication of the notion of salvation, so that it points to merely the continuation of the kind of happiness known in this life. Then a mundane knowledge of human nature will enable us to know our destiny. It will be some such change in the relationship between salvation and human destiny that explains why it seems so obvious to many writers of the eighteenth century that unaided natural reason can produce all the important religious truths itself. By these means natural theology becomes expanded until it contains a sufficient account of God-as-creator and God-as-saviour on its own. Two things of great significance follow from this expansion: natural theology becomes enlarged into natural *religion*, and the distinction between natural theology and revealed theology becomes that between a chimera and a reality.

Natural theology becomes natural religion when it is thought of not merely as a body of truths about God, but as so extensive a body of truths that it can generate a religion on its own. It then becomes, in the terms of Samuel Johnson's *Dictionary* of 1755 not merely a 'science of things divine' but a 'system of divine faith and worship as opposite to others' (entries for 'Divinity/Theology' and

'Religion'). This expansion of natural theology into natural religion is assisted by the inclusion of a natural knowledge of morality into natural religion. Granted the premiss of the natural-law tradition that there is natural knowledge of the moral law, and the assumption that salvation consists in the securing of that happiness already contained within the best parts of human nature, then a sufficient account of what we must do to be saved will be present in ordinary human morality. Ordinary morality will contain all we need if we are to discover how human nature is to flourish and be blessed, and thus it will include a knowledge of our path to salvation. If this be added to the truths about God contained in natural theology (suitably expanded and grounded), we shall have a knowledge of God with an attendant account of how salvation is to be attained, or in other words 'a system of divine faith and worship as opposite to others'.

Now our fundamental contrast between revealed and natural theology can become a contrast between, on the one hand, Christianity or revealed religion and, on the other, natural religion or the religion of nature (see Morgan 1739:15). We have a distinction between two systems of faith and worship. For revealed theology brings with it a special system of divine worship through rites, sacraments and prayer – all said to have the authority of revelation. The contrast does not indeed have to be thought of as an opposition. A latitudinarian theologian can regard the system of revealed religion as a harmonious supplement to that of natural religion. But for many writers, as I shall illustrate, revealed religion can only suffer by comparison with natural. First, it is regarded as unnecessary and then only as a mass of superstition. For many Enlightenment critics of Christianity the meaning attached to 'natural theology/religion' which comes by contrasting it with 'revealed theology/religion' remains crucial in understanding the notion. But it is a contrast now containing but an echo of Aquinas' distinction between philosophy and sacred science. It is a distinction between a *supposed* set of divine truths specially communicated by God in history and a real system of truths available to all by the use of the unaided reason.

NATURAL THEOLOGY, CIVIL THEOLOGY, AND MYTHIC THEOLOGY

As I have pointed out, in the *Summa Theologiae* the phrase 'natural theology' is used in a sense different from that in the distinction 'revealed versus natural theology'. In his discussion of idolatry Aquinas lists three types of theology. Alongside natural theology there is also mythical theology and civil theology (Aquinas 1974:2a2ae,94,1). These phrases refer to three types of pagan thought and are also found in Books 6, 7, and 8 of Augustine's *City of God*. They are in turn borrowed by Augustine from Classical philosophy. Augustine preserves for us Varro's threefold classification of the types of human thought and theory about the gods known in the Classical world. Mythical (or fabulous) theology is that branch of human thought about the divine represented in the poets' tales of the gods. 'Civil theology' refers to the modes of thinking about the gods displayed in the civic temples and their ceremonies. Natural (or physical) theology, in contrast, does not belong to the public and the city but to the philosophers of paganism. It offers a philosophical commentary on the theology of poets and civic temples, and does so by seeking to interpret the better aspects of mythical and civil theology in terms of a philosophically demonstrated knowledge of the natural world. While Varro is reported by Augustine as dismissing the theology of poets and dramatists as mere superstition, some of the rites of the cities and their temples can be 'made pure by the interpretation which makes them symbolical of natural phenomena' (Augustine 1979: VI,8). The philosophical investigation of the natural world is given significance as discovering the operation of the gods in nature and is made the arbiter of what is valid in the temple-worship of the cities.

This use of 'natural theology' is important in the first instance because it was the original use of the phrase. In the history of thought natural theology was originally contrasted with civil, and only later with revealed (see Webb 1915:9). Some of the force 'natural theology' (and 'natural religion') gains from the contrasts Augustine describes remains with the phrase and later unites with the meaning it has through the contrast with revealed theology. This will be explained below when links are made between the various senses of 'natural religion', but for the present we need to note two further features of Varro's treatment of natural theology as reported in *The City of God*.

We should note first that the natural theology of Varro is crucially different in content from anything contemplated by Aquinas or used by the deists. Varro is reported as accepting the common philosophical opinion of his day that the world is animated and divine (Augustine 1979:VII,5). His theology is natural, not merely in starting from facts concerning the operation of the natural world, but in describing the divine operations of nature, considered as a god and as containing divine beings. Augustine describes this body of ideas very succinctly: 'Varro declares that the soul of the world and its manifestations are the true gods' (Augustine 1979:VII,5). This explains why Varro's interpretations of temple-rites are natural or physical in strong senses of those terms. They make the rites symbolic of such operations in nature as are worthy of being regarded as divine. Despite the obvious differences which must then exist between this natural theology and the natural religion of the Enlightenment, there are respects in which it could be assimilated by later writers. As we shall see in Chapter 2 some seventeenth-century writers thought this pantheistic and polytheistic natural theology could itself be interpreted as symbolic. They managed to see in it an indirect reference to a single, transcendant God. If pagan philosophy could salvage parts of civil temple-worship through naturalistic interpretation, some philosophers of later date thought that both could be saved by adding an extra layer of allegory. The true meaning of pagan natural theology thus ceased to be idolatrous: Augustine himself acknowledges that in the hands of the platonists pagan philosophy ceases to be so, since the platonists transcend the idea of God as a world-soul (Augustine 1979:VIII,1). Platonism thus represents a complication for Augustine's dismissal of pagan thought, but provides another opportunity to make positive connections between earlier and later varieties of natural theology.

The second feature of Varro's treatment of mythical, civic, and natural theology worthy of note is his readiness to admit that both mythic and civil varieties are human creations. The myths of the dramatists and poets contain much that is fantastic, and they are obviously fictions of human devising. Though the theology contained in the rites of the public temples is in a somewhat better state, it is equally a human creation. We cannot pretend that the rituals of the cities were actually founded by the gods themselves. The ceremonies of civil religion were founded by those responsible

6

for the creation of all the other institutions of the city. Human communities create their institutions, as a painter creates a picture. Civil religious institutions are a province of human affairs as a consequence (see Augustine 1979:VI,4 for the above points).

That man is the creator of pagan religion is a major point in the debate between paganism and Christian apologetics, and we shall return to it later. How far religion is humanly produced leads us on to the third sense of 'natural religion' to be distinguished and the final contrast in which it figures.

NATURAL AND SUPERNATURAL RELIGION

This sense of 'natural religion' is contained in remarks from F. Max Mueller's lectures on *Natural Religion* of 1889:

> These two religions [Judaism and Christianity] were considered, in Europe at least, as different in kind from all the rest, being classed as supernatural and revealed, in opposition to all other religions which were treated as non-revealed, as natural, and by some theologians even as inspired by the powers of evil.
>
> (Mueller 1889:51)

This distinction between natural religion and supernatural religion draws upon some of the strands in the previous two contrasts in which 'natural religion' and 'natural theology' have figured. It is a distinction concerning the origin and thus the explanation of modes of belief and worship in religion. Some have an origin that is human and mundane; others an origin and explanation that are divine and supernatural. A good illustration of the use of this distinction is to be found in E. B. Tylor's study of the religions of primitive peoples in his *Primitive Culture*. He announces the following methodological principle to be followed in their description and explanation:

> First as to the religious doctrines and practices examined, these are to be treated as belonging to theological systems devised by human reason, without supernatural aid or revelation; in other words as being developments of Natural Religion.
>
> (Tylor 1903a:427)

Primitive religion is thus to be treated entirely as a human phenomenon, the product of human mental powers alone. Whether

7

or not there are supernatural beings, they will not figure in the explanation of the existence and character of primitive religion.

Mueller's claim that the distinction, in point of origin and explanation, between supernatural and natural religions was for many centuries used to distinguish Judaism and Christianity from other faiths could be amply illustrated. We shall trace in Chapter 2 how Locke uses various arguments to show that Moses and Jesus deliver a divine religion, while other religious prophets do not. A similar use of Mueller's distinction is found in *The City of God*. Seizing upon Varro's admission that the theology of paganism has to be treated as a human affair, Augustine claims:

> Whereas it was not any terrestrial community that established true religion [Christianity]; it was true religion, without doubt, that established the Celestial City, and true religion is given to his true worshippers by the inspiration and teaching of the true God, the giver of eternal life.
>
> (Augustine 1979:VI,4)

Like Locke, Augustine appears to regard the religion of the Old and New Testaments as something that has a divine origin and explanation.

NATURAL RELIGION AND NATURAL RELIGIOUSNESS

The fourth sense of natural religion is best brought out after connections between the first three senses are made. These connections become plain when we consider how they are established in deistic thought.

The ruling assumption in deism is that natural religion (in its first sense of a religion of reason derived from reflection on nature) is the true religion. This true religion, including the elements of the naturally discoverable moral law, also stands as an instance of natural religion in Sense 3, being a religion having a human origin and explanation. Though a divine being is its object, it is not generated by that being but rather by mundane capacities of mind directed upon mundane facts. 'Natural religion' (or 'theology') in its second sense refers to a knowledge of divine things acquired by philosophical reflection and is contrasted with thought about the divine of poetic or civil origin. In this scheme of contrasts, the types of religion/theology distinguished may all be thought of as instances of natural religion in its third sense, all being examples of humanly produced thoughts and rituals. The connection between the third and first two senses of 'natural religion' can be made stronger if we again remind ourselves that on deistic assumptions the contrast between natural religion (Sense 1) and revealed religion is the contrast between a reality and a fiction. There was no certain revelation in history, so Christianity considered as a revealed religion was fabulous. Those aspects of its beliefs and worship that did not repeat natural religion could be seen as strictly analogous to the mythical and civil theologies of paganism which so embarrass Varro. Thus Thomas Morgan distinguishes between natural and 'positive, instituted, revealed religion' and of the latter says 'And to avoid circumlocution, I shall call this the political religion, or the religion of the hierarchy' (Morgan 1738:94). Morgan's remarks indicate how the stance pagan philosophers adopted toward the popular religion of their day, and the terms of criticism used to describe that religion, can be reused of Christianity. Once a thinker comes to see the contrast between natural religion (Sense 1) and revealed religion as that between true religion and false, then he is bound to regard all religion as natural religion in Sense 3. All religion must have a human origin and be explicable by reference to mundane powers and facts. This will be true of the philosopher's rational theology and morality: both are the product of unaided human reason. It will be true of what claims to go beyond these and to have the sanction of divine revelation: revealed theology and ritual is a poetic and civil creation. The elevation of natural religion (in Sense 1) to the status of *the* true religion entails a naturalistic stance upon all religion: it is not a naturalism which denies the existence of divine beings, but one which gives a human origin to all thought about the divine.

Given the assumption that all forms of religion are natural, in the sense of being humanly produced, then it seems to follow that there is a common origin to all of them in human nature. This allows the introduction of a fourth sense of 'natural religion' – the religion of human nature. This is a vague idea. It can be given content by tracing through some consequences of the thought that true religion is the product of human nature independent of revelation. It is natural to attach to this the belief that true religion is universal, consisting of a small number of key notions that are the common and permanent posession of humanity. (We shall see one of the key contentions in favour of a religion of reason and against a religion of revelation is that the former is universal and unchanging, while the latter is local and changing.) The basis for such a religion can then only be a universal and constant trait in human nature. The foundation of religion must be a property of human nature itself, and not merely of human beings in certain circumstances. An underlying property of human nature generates true religion. This human religiousness must undergird all religions that are not mere aberrations from true religion. 'Natural religion' can then be used to refer to this natural human religiousness and to the religious ideas or inclinations it gives rise to. This natural human religiousness can function as a general revelation in contrast to special revelation in history. An interesting consequence of this is that the history of religions, being the working-out of this natural human religiousness, becomes a form of revelation in its entirety.

This fourth sense of 'natural religion' has a contrast and opposite too. There can be forms of what passes for religion that are not the expression of man's natural religion, forms which represent the social forces overlaying and corrupting man's natural religiousness. For deistic thinkers the forces at work in the creation of civil and mythic theology would be ready candidates for these. Hence the institutional life and the imaginative life of mankind come to be opposed to his natural religiousness. This notion of an opposite to natural religiosity brings with it a final nuance in the notion of natural religion. We shall find authors trying to get at the character of this natural religiousness through the question 'What is the natural religion of mankind?' But answers to this question are easily linked to answers to the rather different question 'What was the original religion of mankind?' 'Natural religion' can come to have some of the meaning of 'original religion'. The link is easily understood, since it is tempting to suppose that the effects of human nature uncorrupted, and thus the fundamental traits of human nature, can be discerned by finding that original state of human life before the corrupting effects of sophisticated, social existence took hold. The clue to religion in human nature lies in the original religion of man. As we shall see in Chapter 6, the line of thought just advanced, linking natural religion and pre-social origins is open to very powerful objections, but that does not prevent it being influential.

RELIGION AND CHRISTIANITY

I have suggested in the foregoing that the elevation of natural religion (in my Sense 1) is historically important in the development of the modern concept of religion. We have seen that through the concept of natural religion there is room to stand back from Christianity and reflect upon its claims and origins. In particular, Christianity's uniqueness is one of the obvious and primary targets of the elevation of natural religion. Through this elevation Christianity's better aspects are likened to philosophical discoveries long known; its worst aspects are analogous to popular religion in other times and places. Within the concept of natural religion there is a tendency to see Christianity in historical terms, for Christianity must be viewed like all religion as a natural and human creation. Like all religions its foundation must lie in human nature.

In opposition to the above claims we must set Christianity's past attitudes toward its place in the religious life of mankind. These are summed up in this quotation from Augustine:

> This is the religion which contains the universal way for the liberation of the soul, since no soul can be freed by any other way. For this is, one may say, the royal road, which alone leads to that kingdom whose glory is not the tottering grandeur of the temporal, but the secure stability of the eternal.
>
> (Augustine 1979:X,32)

It is arguable that these traditional attitudes are essential to Christianity, even though modern apologists may seek to jettison them. Christianity as a form of proclamation and worship centred around the person of Christ would seem committed to preaching the necessity both of God's activity in Christ and of mankind's knowledge of that activity. These commitments are necessary if its distinctive vision of the achievement of salvation is to be upheld. It seems hard to have a Christ-centred religion which does not proclaim his necessity for salvation, and difficult to see how that necessity can be urged if non-Christ-centred forms of belief are allowed to contain valid paths to salvation. Augustine displays throughout *The City of God* one of the consequences of this scheme of ideas. If salvation centres upon what God has done in Christ,

11

then the events in which that work was being effected (for example, Christ's incarnation, passion, and resurrection) cannot simply be some events among others within human history. They must rather be the turning-points and culmination of that history. So these events and the religion which preserves and proclaims them are the very means by which history is to be interpreted. As being the meaning of history, they are part of human history in one sense, but not in another, for they are the work of God and thus are points where human history becomes enmeshed with the divine.

We have already seen that from within Christian theology it is customary to acknowledge the existence of some form of natural theology. Yet this natural knowledge of God presents both a dilemma and a problem to the Christian vision of history. The dilemma takes the following form. The more natural knowledge is played down, the more Christianity appears to be an abrupt intervention into human religious history. If no preparation for Christ's proclamation is allowed in the general history of thought, the more it appears to be a new and local disclosure and the more arbitrary and capricious the God behind it appears to be. Yet if its message is made more reasonable by being likened to ancient and long-known truths, it will seem far from unique. It will appear an unnecessary repetition of what the best minds have already taught. The accompanying problem is that Christianity seems bound to suffer by comparison with a naturally available knowledge of God and morality. For if God were going to effect the salvation of the whole of mankind, it would seem *a priori* much more reasonable to do so by way of a universal and naturally available knowledge of his character and existence than by way of anything so local and recent as the life of Jesus. Once the knowledge and service of God is brought under the perspective of a universal and caring providence, then a religion produced by natural reason seems infinitely preferable to one tied to specific historical events. This argument from God's perfect providence and justice was to seem to Enlightenment thinkers the most obvious and convincing for the superiority of natural religion over revealed.

Those who laid the basis for Christian apologetics were thus faced with a complex task in defending both the uniqueness of the revelation they articulated and its justice. They had to show that it had a universal intent, offering salvation to all men. They had to represent it as confirming what the wise had long since taught. At the same time, it had to appear as a decisive new addition to, or completion of, what had gone before, to the extent that what preceded it contained no sure path to salvation.

There are many apologetic schemes in Christian theology which attempt to meet the task described. I shall concentrate on just four key themes to be found in many versions of the attempt to defend the uniqueness of Christianity and the justice of God. (These four themes can be shown, I think, to be implicit in the origin of many of these schemes: Paul's remarks in Romans 1:18–23.) We should look for (1) the assertion that underlying the Christian proclamation there is a universally available knowledge of God; (2) the inadequacy, because of perversion, of this universal awareness of God; (3) the role of sin as the cause of this perversion and as the defence of God's justice in dealing with man; and (4) Christianity as a means for saving the whole of mankind in response to the inadequacy of an originally available means of knowing about God. Each of these is worth some comment, but the third I shall treat at greatest length because it is the particular target of defenders of natural religion in the Enlightenment.

Point (1) we have already met in the context of Aquinas' teaching on the possibility of a natural theology and a natural knowledge of the moral law. A natural knowledge of God was taken by many to be implied in Paul's statement about the heathen:

> For what can be known about God is plain to them, because God has shown it to them. Ever since the creation of the world his invisible nature, namely, his eternal power and deity, has been clearly perceived in the things that have been made.
>
> (Romans 1:19–20)

To this might be added the apparent endorsement of the universality of moral knowledge in Romans 2:13–16. Point (1) allows two valuable jobs to be done within apologetics. An explanation can be given of the existence of the best kinds of pagan anticipation of Christian truth, as in platonism, and it secures God's justice in taking the world to task if it has turned its back on him in embracing idolatry. The fact of idolatry brings in Point (2). Despite this universal knowledge, Paul berates the heathen for failing to honour God as he ought and for exchanging 'the glory of the immortal God for images resembling mortal man or birds or animals' (Romans 1:23). The universally available natural knowledge has proved inadequate in crucial respects as a means of approaching God. The inadequacy is shown in the example provided by Socrates, Plato, and their successors. For all their fine teaching they have had no impact upon the vile practices of idolatry described by Paul and they themselves remained involved with pagan forms of worship. The first of these charges amounts to belittling the impact platonism has had upon the general character of pagan thought. Augustine complains that, while Plato wrote down much of this knowledge of God, he did so in a way that was designed to please rather than persuade. He and others were not fit to change men's minds and take them away from vanity to true worship. Christianity, in contrast, has preached the truth about God 'to the peoples throughout the earth' and 'all over the inhabited world'. It is through the work of Christianity, not philosophy, that the sublime truths about God and immortality have become the property of ordinary people everywhere (Augustine 1943:226–7). The second charge against the pagan philosophers is that they themselves remained entrapped in idolatrous worship. A typical, and as it happens mistaken, version of this point is found when Athanasius contrasts Socrates' reputation as a noble philosopher with the fact that in *Republic* Book I he goes off to worship a man-made image of Artemis (Athanasius 1971:29–31). This accusation is repeated in Augustine's lengthy treatment of the inadequacies of platonism in Books VIII and IX of *The City of God*. To it are added the complaints that the platonists still believe that the world is divine, that there are many gods in addition to the supreme God, and that demons are needed as intermediaries between God and man. Platonism has failed to grasp fully that there is one and only one God to be worshipped and that he is not identical with the world or any part of it.

Point (3) lays stress on the role of sin as the cause of this perversion of the universally available knowledge of God. Athanasius expands on this Pauline answer to the question of why this knowledge should be of so little use in the salvation of mankind in his *Contra Gentes*. Before the fall man, being perfectly pure in heart, was able to contemplate God clearly and directly. After it he has become fixated upon bodily pleasures and thus enmeshed in sin. Swamped by desires and fantasies of the body, his knowledge of God has become perverted with the result that he deifies those things which desire is fixated upon, namely created things. Hence, the disorder of the soul through sin produces idolatry despite the knowledge of the true God that is available (Athanasius 1971:7–23). By these means peoples have turned away from the contemplation of the one true God and abandoned his true word. Paganism is the result of sin while also being an instance of it.

This emphasis upon human sinfulness helps to correct a misleading impression that might be drawn from the references made to Augustine's *Of True Religion* so far. For if Christ and his followers are praised above the philosophers as having made the truths of monotheism universally available where before they have been the uncertain possession of only a few, it may seem as if Christ were simply a more successful or dedicated religious teacher than Plato. Should Christ, however, be viewed only as a teacher of truths about God, then no matter how good he is in this regard, he cannot be at the centre of any worship of God. He may be hailed as a great messenger, but his person will not be part of the message; whereas emphasizing the connection between idolatry and sin allows for the possibility of a Christ-centred religion in which Christ remains central even after his message is delivered. As a reading of other parts of Augustine shows (such as *On the Spirit and the Letter* and Books XI-XIV of *The City of God*), the disorder represented by paganism is not for him something that philosophy, or the new preaching of the truths of monotheism and a spiritually centred morality could solve. What is needed is a mediator who, in atoning for man's sin, makes possible the restoration of human nature through grace. So though at least a portion of Christian truth has been universally available, it turns out that the way that truth has been rejected shows the need of something other than a further preaching of truths about God if men are to be saved. What is required is a historically located mediator and saviour.

We have yet to draw out the strands from Christian apologetics which indicate why human sinfulness can form part of a powerful reply to charges of divine injustice in relation to the uniqueness of Christianity. But we must turn first to Point (4) and the attempt to show how the appearance of a historically located saviour could be represented as part of a universal plan of salvation. Augustine states that Christianity is the 'universal way for the liberation of the soul . . . because it is granted to all nations by the divine compassion' (Augustine 1979:X,22). It is not the property of a particular nation or culture. The implausibility of such assertions is lessened in classic Christian apologetics by pointing to a number of ways in which the coming of Christ can be seen as part of a divine education of the whole race. Most of these points need only to be mentioned for our purposes. They include citing the natural knowledge of God discussed in the above as a preparation for Christ; stressing God's message to the patriarchs and prophets of Israel as further preparation; giving that message greater significance through the supposition that it was spread to other nations (perhaps through Egyptian sources; see Walker 1972:1 and 19–21); supposing that a knowledge of Christ-as-Logos was directly inscribed on the minds of non-Jewish peoples (Justin 1943:272). Finally, we should note the limited geographical conceptions indicated in the remarks of Augustine quoted above which allow him to claim that subsequent to Christ's ministry the truth has been preached throughout the earth and to the entire inhabited world.

We have now seen in broadest outline how traditional Christian aplogetics has an answer to the dilemma and problem created by Christianity's uniqueness in relation to the competing claims of natural religion. The necessity of a revealed knowledge of God can be defended and the superiority and justice of a geographically and temporally located dispensation established. These things may be accomplished where something other than the accumulation of truths about God is shown to be required for the achievement of man's destiny in salvation. This requirement may be strengthened and the justice of God defended, if it can be further shown that there have been some central truths about God universally available. However, the way these have been voluntarily rejected and perverted itself shows the need for something other than a further proclamation of truths about God if mankind's salvation is to be effected.

The elements of such an apologetics still leave room for doubts about the justice of God when faced with the possibility that there are many peoples on earth who have had no real chance to be aware of the essentials of salvation through Christ. Further exploration of the theme of man's sinfulness will suggest *one* way of giving a fuller answer to this doubt. The theme as set forth here is not meant to a universal element in all schemes of Christian doctrine, but it is important for our purposes. One reason why it is so is because it is paramount in the versions of Christian dogmatics that later exponents of natural religion were particularly concerned to combat. Moreover, treatment of it helps to bring out a number of useful general points. We shall see that questions about the justice of God cannot be raised in the abstract. They get their force from some conception of the nature of the divine-human relationship to which they are relative. They are relative to one of the determining factors in any conception of that relationship – a vision of the character of human nature. The question about the justice of God can only be pressed against the background of some accounts of human nature rather than others. A brief description of the account of human nature the deists wished to overthrow will enable their own account to stand out more clearly and bring out the nature of the humanism to which they were committed.

Many aspects of the necessity and justice of the dispensation preached by Christianity will be found implausible by writers in the modern period. Expanded views of human history and geography will make the claim that Christian truth has been universally available more questionable. A rediscovery and revaluation of pagan thought will make patristic criticisms of it seem dubious. But, above all else, differing views of human nature, and thus of man's end, will put the justice of the Christian God under scrutiny.

The elements of the vision of the divine-human relationship to which proponents of natural religion were particularly opposed can be traced in Augustine's *On the Spirit and the Letter*, which in turn provides much of the basis for Luther's *Lectures on Romans*. The essence of Augustine's argument is that man is powerless to fulfil the demands of the law unless he is supported by God's grace (Augustine 1925:54). Man is not saved by the works of righteousness he performs, because such works are the result of receiving· grace and do not exist without it (Augustine 1925:45–6). Man's knowledge of God's law, however acquired, is of no use by itself, and in fact makes matters worse. Through that knowledge man learns what is good and evil, but thereby becomes more inclined to do the evil. Because of man's disordered state the objects of his present desires become more attractive through being forbidden (Augustine 1925:39–40). It is significant therefore for Augustine that the pagans described in Romans 1:18–23 are not charged with ignorance of God, but with holding the truth of God in unrighteousness. The greatest minds of paganism had no solution to man's disorder, because it was not due to ignorance and was made worse by a knowledge of the truth (Augustine 1925:57–8). Idolatry is a disorder of the will.

It is an essential part of this scheme of ideas that God's grace must be free and unmerited. Prior to its gift no man is worthy to be saved, and thus God may freely decide who is to be called and who not. His gift and call create whatever merit brings worthiness to be saved.

In his further working-out of Augustine's account in the *Lectures on Romans* Luther draws out two consequences of importance for us. One is that the God-given righteousness which annuls our sin and justifies us before God is extraneous to us. It does not originate in ourselves but comes to us from without. It is a righteousness 'entirely external and foreign to us' (Luther 1961:4). It is a righteousness which stands in contrast to that normally described and dispensed by human beings under the names of 'merit', 'justice', or 'desert'. A further consequence of these reflections on sin and grace brought out by Luther is that human free will is at best diminished, at worst destroyed completely. For if man has no power to do that which is righteous in God's eyes, then he is not free in being unrighteous. Man is bound to keep God's commandments and yet is unable of himself to do so (Luther 1961:29–30). In *The Bondage of the Will* this vision of mankind bound to sin is expanded and related specifically to the need for something beyond natural knowledge and powers in the attainment of salvation:

> For if the power of free will is not wholly and damnably astray, but sees and wills what is good and upright and pertains to salvation, then it is in sound health, it does not need Christ the physician, nor did Christ redeem that part of man; for what need is there of light and life, where light and life exist already. And if that power is not redeemed then the best part of man is not redeemed by Christ, but is of itself just and sound. And then God is unjust if he damns any man, for he damns that in man which is very good and sound; that is, innocent.
>
> (Luther 1975:308)

What happens if, with this conception of man's sinfulness and need for redemption in mind, we now ask about God's justice in dispensing salvation through Christ when Christ is known only to some? I think we can see that the problem of the fairness of the Christian account of man's destiny which stems from the claims for Christianity's uniqueness disappears from view.

It does so in the first instance because our sight of it becomes obscured by other, more fundamental, apparent injustices. How can God seem just to us when he gives grace through Christ to some but not to others, even though no individual has, as such, any more merit than any other? How can God seem good when he destines some for damnation even though they have no power to do what is righteous in his eyes? If we inherit a radical corruption of the human will, how can any of our wrong choices be punished by God when all merely human efforts are bound to go astray? The uniqueness of Christianity is but one point in an entire scheme of salvation/redemption which Luther acknowledges is bound to seem unjust (Luther 1975:312 ff.).

These apparent injustices are to be accepted because the scheme of ideas which produces them, including the assertion of Christianity's uniqueness, is held to follow from a more certain truth – that Christ was absolutely necessary if mankind was to be saved (Luther 1961:29–30). If one identifies this simple message with the Gospel and stands by the Gospel's certainty then the paradoxes can be accepted. Indeed, the picture of man's sinfulness which produces these paradoxes generates from within itself further replies to the charge that God is made to appear arbitrary and unjust. Because of sin and radical evil God's righteousness is bound to seem incomprehensible if we rely on our standards of justice. But just because of our sinfulness we should not rely on those standards. As Luther puts it:

> Why do we not . . . say at this point: 'Our judgement is nothing compared with God's judgement?' Ask reason whether force of conviction does not compel her to acknowledge herself foolish and rash for not allowing God's judgement to be incomprehensible, when she confesses that all other things of God are incomprehensible.
>
> (Luther 1975:313)

We lack outside of the Gospel itself any reliable conceptions of what God's justice ought to be like. And if we still wish to complain, we can be met with Paul's:

> But who are you, a man, to answer back to God? Will what is
> moulded say to its moulder, 'Why have you made me thus?'
>
> (Romans 9:20)

Man is in no position to complain of God's seeming injustice to
him, not least because if God judged man strictly by the true merit
or desert he has, then all would be damned. Universal and radical
sinfulness entails that none of us *deserves* anything from God. God
cannot treat us unjustly. If we raise in our minds the questions
'Why has God chosen to give salvation only through Christ? Why
were his means so limited and so late?', the only proper thing to do
is to dismiss them:

> But wherever the knowledge of this way has already come, and
> wherever it will come in the future, no one has, or will have, the
> right to ask 'Why just now?' or 'Why so late?' for the design of
> him who offers it is inscrutable to the natural human
> understanding.
>
> (Augustine 1979:X,32)

We need to fasten on the kind of relationship between God and
man envisaged in a theological scheme which stresses man's
sinfulness and the futility of natural, human means to salvation. It
is a relationship in which man stands before an incomprehensible
judge, unsure of his own standards of what is right. He will be sure
only of his own depravity and the necessity of grace offered through
Christ. Since he would know of the need for human nature to be
annulled through grace, he could place no reliance on human
concepts in judging God's justice. He could not credit God with a
desire to bring about what normally counted as human good or
well-being. It is a vision of the divine-human relationship in which
it would be hard to conceive of what could count as God acting
arbitrarily toward man. The salvific worth of human religion and
morality would, needless to say, be nil.

An interest in human religion seems in an obvious way to be tied
to humanism. It will be hard to see the beliefs and practices of
religion in history as worthy objects of study and reflection if one
does not generally find value in human nature and the life that is
its expression. Deeper connections between the study of human
religion and humanism emerge once we consider the relationship

between Christianity and human religion. If an interest in the general religious life of mankind arises from within a Christian culture, it will be one that has to take into account Christianity's traditional claim to uniqueness. This claim typically involves a contrast and antithesis between Christianity and mankind's larger religious life. It can rest, as we have seen, upon a depreciation of things merely human and a preaching of the need for the annulment of human nature. Through the theology in which it is embedded, the claim that Christianity is unique may constitute a denial that there is worth to be found in human nature and its expressions. By the same token, a sufficiently high evaluation of human nature may call that claim into question. The particularity of Christianity will provoke the scandal of God's apparent injustice to mankind as a whole, and a high evaluation of human nature will enable thinkers to rest upon human conceptions of desert and justice in investigating the apparent arbitrariness of the Christian God. A re-valuing of human nature will bring with it a vision of what counts as a proper relationship between God and man in terms of which the Christian interpretation of history will present itself as the very model of an account of an unjust, partial deity.

2

HUMANISM AND RATIONALISM

LORD HERBERT OF CHERBURY AND RELIGIOUS HUMANISM

The choice of any one writer or group of writers to illustrate the rise of humanistic perspectives on religion must inevitably be arbitrary to some degree. If I fasten upon Edward Herbert, it is not because I wish to endorse John Leland's view of him as 'the most eminent of the deistical writers' (Leland 1757a:3). As recent students of Herbert's work have pointed out, the question of his relationship to and influence upon the standard authors of the eighteenth century rewarded with the title 'deist' is a complicated one (see Bedford 1979:239 ff.). His writings serve as an important illustration of the flow of ideas which led to the elevation of natural religion among religious thinkers of the Enlightenment, but it cannot be said of him that the high place he gives to universal forms of religious knowledge amounts to a total dismissal of revealed religion. Aspects of his account of the sources of experience and knowledge are at odds with a naturalistic perspective on religion and run counter to anything those more appropriately called 'deists' were prepared to accept. For a variety of reasons it would be misleading to describe Herbert as a rationalist thinker. Despite this he does illustrate how a growing humanism inevitably leads to an emphasis on timeless and universal ways of knowing and being reconciled to God. His writings exhibit an obvious embarrassment with claims for the uniqueness of Christianity. The sources of this embarrassment are much the same in outline, if not in detail, as the sources of later attacks upon Christianity's uniqueness. He can therefore be profitably used to examine the origins of the growing tendency to trace religion back to universal roots in human nature.

One thing of particular importance in Herbert is the revaluation of the divine-human relationship pointed to in the previous chapter. Moreover, an analysis of Herbert's grounds for this revaluation reveals a threefold basis, which in broad terms can be found repeated in writers up to Kant at the end of the eighteenth century. Two aspects of the basis of the revaluation are initially important. The first is a positive humanism which insists that the inherited depravity of man is a fiction and which creates an obligation on providence to save all. Nascent in Herbert is another correlative feature of humanism of great importance for later writers, namely the assertion of the unchangeableness of human nature. Humanism unites with a second thing to prompt the revaluation of the divine-human relationship when Herbert affirms God's immutable goodness: this emphasis upon the unwavering desire of God to act for man's benefit combines with humanism to produce the conclusion that the means to salvation must have been universally available, so that no single religion can be uniquely salvific. Here are two parts of the argument for the absolute necessity of a universally available way of understanding and following God. They join with the demand for some pointers to religious truth which arises from Herbert's preoccupation with the problem of religious certainty. With Europe irreversibly divided on points of doctrine and worship between a multiplicity of sects and churches, the question 'How can I be certain of anything in religion?' naturally now pressed harder. Herbert's answer to this question united with his reflections on man and God. Religious truth could be established on a firm foundation only if there were some universally available ways of comprehending and following God independent of any specific sects; otherwise we are lost in a sea of sectarianism.

We have, then, a triad of reflections which point to the same conclusion. From a certain kind of account of man and of God and of the demands of religious certainty, the non-uniqueness of Christianity (and the necessity of a universal religion underlying it and all other faiths) seem to follow. We shall see that in Herbert this does not in turn lead to the naturalism which we can find in those later writers still dominated by this threefold scheme.

Herbert produced two lengthy studies of the religious life of mankind in history: the *De Religione Gentilium* and *A Dialogue between a Pupil and his Tutor*.[1] At the beginning of both he confronts the assertion of Christianity's uniqueness in its strongest form – that outside the Church there is no salvation. His reply is simple: 'that this was altogether incompatible with the dignity of an universal providence' (Herbert 1705:2). In the *Dialogue* God's exercise of a universal providence or 'common fatherhood' over mankind is cited as his 'highest and truest attribute' (Herbert 1768:6–7). This attribute demands that the means to salvation should have been universally available to mankind from the beginning of time. No such universal, timeless means can be found in a Christ-centred religion. This last conclusion is not explicitly stated by Herbert, for obvious reasons, but we are left openly to draw it from his account of what divine providence has given by way of a universal path to salvation. The account makes no reference to the atoning sacrifice of Jesus. Now we have already seen Christian theologians accepting the conclusion that if Christianity describes the saving work of a good God then it must be a religion preserving a universal way to salvation. Herbert's unstated but evident disbelief that Christianity could be such a vehicle for a universal providence is in part connected with the extent of his temporal and geographical horizons. Religious history, he affirms in the *Dialogue*, can be taken to begin with the Egyptians. The chronology of their dynasties shows them to be the most ancient people we know of. It also points to the falsehood of the Old Testament chronology, and to the fact that the patriarchs of Israel, let alone Moses, are very late arrivals on the scene of history (Herbert 1768:14–15). It thus becomes incredible that Christianity as prefigured in the prophecy and teaching of the Old Testament is the religious educator of the whole world – a conclusion strengthened by references in both of Herbert's surveys of religion to the religious beliefs of the Indians and Chinese. Christianity evidently fails to have the marks of true antiquity and universality which distinguish a religion whose articles are necessary for the salvation of all mankind (Herbert 1768:10–11). Further reflection on Herbert's account of God and man will indicate more clearly why those truly necessary articles given by God, and traceable in the thinking of the best religious minds in history, should not allow reference to a Christ-centred path of salvation.

The nature of Herbert's account of God and man is indicated in the main reason he offers for rejecting the idea that salvation and damnation depend upon 'the good pleasure of God and the death of Christ':

> How could I believe that a just God could take pleasure in the eternal reprobation of those to whom he never afforded any means of salvation . . . and whom he foresaw must be damned of absolute necessity, without the least hopes of escaping it?
>
> (Herbert 1705:5)

The chief attributes of God are his unsurpassed greatness and goodness, but of these goodness is supreme: 'the goodness of God must necessarily be antecedent to his power'. God's attributes can to an extent be comprehended by us, and we can see that in being most good he must 'provide for all, in doing which he must be just, merciful and liberal' (Herbert 1705:258–9). The consequence of this seems to be that God's goodness contains an open and equal bounty to the whole human race. It entails a providence which intends to bring about the good for all men. Our conceptions of what is just and good are to a degree reliable in judging God. This is why those who preach the utter futility of works to salvation and thus the apparently arbitrary character of God's election 'destroy not merely human goodness but also the goodness of God' (Herbert 1936: 300).

We see that, for Herbert, God's being just and good is related to his seeking our good. There will be no eternal punishments for crimes merely temporal. Our natural desire for happiness will not be frustrated by God (Herbert 1768:26–7). The operations of providence have ensured that the means to human happiness have always been available, and on this ground we can actively expect God to grant an access to a life hereafter (Herbert 1768:56 and 90–1). Salvation is thus not the righteous annulment of human nature and its desires, but rather the beneficent completion of them. Herbert must therefore reject any notion of a human nature disordered at root through sin:

> I assert nothing here but that this principle of evil cannot be derived from Adam; for all of our sins and transgressions are our own mere voluntary acts; and no mortal was so necessarily

determined to do evil, but by the divine goodness, he could both
see and avoid it.

(Herbert 1705:266)

Given that Adam's 'innocent posterity' was not cast down by his sin
the question naturally arises why 'after so many ages nothing could
appease and reconcile God but more than human sacrifice' (Herbert
1705:266). Human nature seems to stand in no need of redemption
and therefore needs no redeemer. Herbert's positive humanism thus
plainly questions the need for a decisive redemptive act in history,
and, if such an act is not required, the uniqueness and
embarrassing particularity of the salvation-story offered by Christianity is seen as unacceptable. When Herbert affirms that 'the
world is under [God's] providence with absolute justice' (Herbert
1936:292) we can see why his revaluation of human nature should
give this statement a sense quite different from that which it might
have in the mouth of a Luther. The rewriting of the terms of man's
relationship to God entails, in the first place, that this justice
should be comprehensible by human standards; in the second, that
it should be concerned to foster human happiness; and in the third,
that God should deal equally with all according to their deserts.
We can demand fair treatment of God.

What God's absolute justice and universal providence require
is that, from the beginning of time and in all places, there should
have been available a true way of serving God. This way existed
through five key beliefs, universally known, and called by Herbert
'catholic articles' or 'common notions'. In *De Religione Gentilium*
they are given as follows: (1) that there is one supreme God; (2)
that he ought to be worshipped; (3) that virtue and piety are the
chief parts of divine worship; (4) that we ought to be sorry for our
sins and repent of them; (5) that divine goodness dispenses rewards
and punishments both in this life and after it (Herbert 1705:3–4;
similar lists can be found in Herbert 1768:6–7, 1936:291 f.,
1944:89).

These common notions are the key to understanding Herbert on
religion. Their universality and certainty depend on their having
been inscribed on the heart of man by God. It is through the
universal inscription of these notions that God has exercised his
providence and justice in religion. To this end, the five notions
prescribe a way to God which is within the compass of the human

understanding and will. While Herbert hesitates on some occasions, he seems committed to saying that they are sufficient for salvation (see Herbert 1768:8; cf. 1936:305–6). They form a 'perfect circle', and while it is not inconceivable that particular faiths could add to them, they provide the test of when such additions are warranted (Herbert 1936:306). They can be said to give the essence of 'true religion, or the worship of God in virtue' (Herbert 1768:253). In giving the essence of true religion, through defining the basis of a true worship and service of God, they also point to the universality of religion. The common notions engraved on the hearts of men can be found in all religions that truly serve the common father of mankind (Herbert 1768:6). All religions will therefore be strictly comparable by reference to the common notions, and Christianity will be but one instance of a universal phenomenon.

It is evidently difficult to maintain the positive evaluation of human nature in Herbert's writings and at the same time dismiss the whole of religious life outside of Christianity and Judaism as an unredeemed mass of superstition. In addition to this ground for attempting a revaluation of pagan religion Herbert has the demands of the consequences of his beliefs about God's goodness and justice. He has to make it plain that in matters of religion a universal providence *is* extended to all mankind (Herbert 1705:6). He must in particular vindicate the assertion that the five catholic articles are inscribed in the hearts of all. Thus the pagan religions of ancient Europe and the near East have to be shown to bear witness to the essence of a true service of God. He thinks indeed it is undeniable that the ancient heathens worshipped the same God as his Christian audience, had the same abhorrence of sin, and believed in rewards and punishments after this life. If, as some heathens undoubtedly did, they went on to live a good life, then they had the five catholic articles in their possession. The appropriate conclusion can only be that they were participants in a true religion, and 'partakers of the fullness of . . . divine grace' (Herbert 1705:7). Herbert leaves us to draw the conclusion that Christianity is not unique and Christ not a decisive point in the salvation of mankind.

What of the dismissal of paganism as mere idolatry by theologians? Herbert is of course aware that ancient heathenism departs in appearance from the common notions. Notions 1 and 2 seem to be abandoned by the belief in and worship of a pantheon of gods. Any knowledge of Articles 3 and 4 seems to be buried in the mass of extraneous and distracting forms of ceremony, ritual, and purgation that are part of pagan temple-worship. Herbert's response to these perceptions is presented in a lengthy, detailed, and repetitious commentary on the finer points of heathen belief and worship (see Herbert 1705 and 1768), but the outline of his answer is simple. Polytheism and the deification of nature do not get in the way of belief in and worship of a single and supreme God, provided they are kept in bounds. They are so kept by the best thinkers of antiquity, but the limits are cast aside through the bad offices of priests who invent the irrelevant and distracting forms of religion which get in the way of a perfect following of the articles. Paganism did become corrupt, but the corruption does not reflect on the whole of mankind or even the whole of paganism.

The clue to seeing how the pagan pantheon is compatible with an acknowledgment that there is one supreme God and that he is to be worshipped is contained in Herbert's affirmation that 'almost all ancient religion was symbolical' (Herbert 1705:31). The pagan peoples had the notion of a supreme God written in their hearts and possessed an inbuilt desire to discover and worship him. This longing was awakened by the contemplation of nature, through whose fabric God is manifested. Thus they come to worship God in and through the works of nature. But their veneration of aspects of the natural world is compatible with their acknowledgement and service of the one supreme God. Consistent testimony for belief in a supreme God in paganism is not hidden by veneration of Sun, stars, heavens, etc. while these things are worshipped as God's *representatives* or as bearing his image. And this is what polytheism and the veneration of nature amounts to in the best paganism. Herbert, for example, affirms that the Sun was worshipped as God's 'most noble and excellent representative . . . a kind of sensible representation of the supreme God' (Herbert 1705:32–3). The 'most wise' among the heathen knew very well that God himself could not be discerned in any one thing. Heathen polytheism is not idolatry and has much to recommend it, for it is right to give nature some 'honour and respect' as the image of God. Granting this honour is one way of worshipping the supreme God (Herbert 1768:57). Herbert allies himself with the natural theology of Varro (as described in Chapter 1) and at the same time denies the charge that, in worshipping the creature, the pagans necessarily turned their backs on the creator.

Varro's natural theology stood contrasted with mythical and civil. The spirit of this contrast is preserved by Herbert in his account of the corruptions of paganism. He distinguishes the truth in pagan natural theology from the errors in paganism as this came to be interpreted and fashioned by priestly power. The typical Protestant story about the corruption of simple Christianity by priestcraft is applied to the decline of paganism. Pagan priests spread the conviction that the subordinate parts of nature were gods in their own right, thus 'imposing their imaginary dreams on the people'. They did so because then there would be forms of religious service other than the piety and virtue demanded by God, which forms the 'crafty priests managed to their own advantage'. Through destroying in the minds of many the true symbolic understanding of polytheism, they succeeded in spreading the conviction 'that there was no other mediator betwixt the gods and men, but the priests' (Herbert 1705:16–17). The interminable details of this story (as set out in Herbert 1705 and 1768) need not concern us here, but we can note that there is more than a hint that Herbert wished to apply the general moral to the religion of his own day and to the manner in which it too has come to depart from the catholic articles. The opening page of *De Religione Gentilium* reminds us of how the priests of Herbert's time ('the divines of this last age') wish to confine salvation to the religion *they* define, condemning 'all those without their pale'. Here we have another respect in which Christianity is not unique, 'it having been the arcanum of the sacerdotal order in all times to teach men that no access could be made to God, but through their guidance and direction' (Herbert 1768:258).

After his survey of paganism, Herbert's conviction that we should be able to find the essence of true religion everywhere is vindicated. He does not deny that the pagan religion is guilty of error and superstition, nor that idolatry exists in some measure as a consequence of allowing inferior powers and deities independent of the supreme God (see Herbert 1705:368–9). But it is not part of Herbert's argument that the universally available common notions will be universally followed in practice. God's universal guidance is manifestly present in all religious history, even though some folk reject it.

In one respect Herbert's religious present is considerably worse than the pagan past: heathen times did not suffer from the degree of religious strife and controversy Herbert finds around him. The epistemological problem which this strife and controversy faces Herbert with is signalled in his complaint that every religion which proclaims a revelation is not good nor is every doctrine taught under its authority essential or valuable. Some doctrines allegedly revealed ought to be abandoned (Herbert 1936:289). But which? The pressing problem of religious certainty created by awareness of religious diversity (both within and without Christendom) is described in *De Religione Laici* in the following terms. What should the layman believe in religion, given that each of the great variety of professions in the world claims that it is divinely ordained and that there is no possibility of salvation outside its own pale (Herbert 1944:87)? The answer lies in the common notions:

> In this connection the teaching of the common notions is important, indeed without them it is impossible to establish any standard of discrimination in revelation or even in religion.
>
> (Herbert 1936:289)

They represent a solution because in the first instance they throw us back on religious beliefs that are capable of gaining universal assent and thus of providing an antidote to diversity and a basis for agreement. Moreover, they are common notions in that they reflect the providence of God who has engraved them on our hearts. They are thus a standard of truth in religion which has divine authority (Herbert 1936:291).

In asserting that the common notions are the right standard of certainty in religion, Herbert rejects other standards such as faith in the authority of the Church or of written or oral records of alleged revelations. A 'true catholic church' founded upon the common notions is bound to be superior to any founded on recorded revelation both in respect of clarity and universality. It cannot be supported on the 'inextricable confusion' of oral and written tradition to which men have given their allegiance; still less can it be comprised in one organization so as to embrace a restricted portion of the earth or its history (Herbert 1936:303). A standard of religious certainty that reflects divine providence will be available to all. Historical, reported revelation can equally be used to foster human error as divine truth and must pass a stringent set of tests if it is to be relied on at all. To be genuine, we would have to be sure that a revelation had been given to its original source, that it had come from God or one of his ministers, that it had been accurately reported by its source, and that it concerned other ages and persons so closely that it was a necessary article of faith (Herbert 1936:301–10). Credentials on all these points are necessary if reported revelation is to extend the religion of the common notions.

From the brief survey offered so far everything to produce the elevation of natural religion over revealed would appear to be present in Herbert's account of religion. In fact, this conclusion is unwarranted. Herbert's strictures on revealed religion are limited. His quarrel is with those who use the reported revelation of others as a foundation of belief. He does not deny, and indeed welcomes, the possibility of direct divine revelation to guide the searcher after truth. He speaks plainly of the possibility of receiving 'some truth by revelation which I think can occur in both the waking state and in sleep' (Herbert 1936:303). There are criteria to be applied to decide when an experience is revelation, but there is no doubt that 'Revealed truth exists; and it would be unjust to ignore it' (Herbert 1936:308). Revelation can be trusted when we employ prayers, vows, and the like to invoke God's providence. It must be given directly to some person, otherwise it is not revelation but tradition or history. It must command some action which is good and be accompanied by the immediate breath of the divine spirit. The tone and content of his description of divine revelation suggests it is a thing to be welcomed and fostered (see Herbert 1936:308–9). From his caution about using such experiences to teach new religious truths to other people, Herbert seems to have in mind by a true revelation a direct divine guidance in the affairs of one's own life (see Herbert 1936:303). The aim of *De Veritate* is stated in its opening to be that of reconciling general providence (nature) with special providence (grace). The passages on revelation indicate just how much special providence is to be cultivated. General providence in religion as represented by the common notions is in harmony with revelation, in that it provides one of the essential means whereby the genuineness of direct divine guidance is to be tested. The historically revealed, the local, temporally limited religious system is judged harshly, not only in the light of the universal gift of the catholic articles, but also in the light of the ever-present possibility of direct divine grace. We are far away from the kind of naturalism we anticipated finding in the radical proponents of natural religion.

Reflection shows further that even the religion of the common notions, unexpanded by direct revelation, is not quite natural religion in the important senses of that phrase distinguished in Chapter 1. Much of the force of the phrase comes from a contrast between what is generated naturally by the human intellect and what is the result of direct divine gift. But this contrast in turn depends on having an appropriately naturalistic conception of the operations of the mind, one which portrays its normal functioning as proceeding without continuing divine aid. But Herbert's conception of the mind lacks this important naturalistic perspective. In Herbert's system the discovery of universal religious truths is given to faculties of the human mind which may be distinguished from reason as such, and these faculties operate under a continual divine inspiration.

To understand Herbert's conception of the mind, we must turn briefly to the general teaching of *De Veritate*, a work which sets his account of religious knowledge within a larger picture of the origins and nature of certainty. Being in part an answer to the revival of Classical scepticism by authors such as Montaigne, *De Veritate* is concerned to show that truth does exist among things human beings claim to know. Truth is defined after the fashion of correspondence theories as the conformity between the faculties of the mind and their appropriate objects (Herbert 1936:105). The detection of such conformity between intellect and reality depends on a generalized use of the theory of the common notions. The mind needs assured rules for deciding upon when its subjective faculties are in accordance with the facts. These rules rest upon those intellectual truths which 'are the common notions found in all normal men' (Herbert 1936:105). In all areas of thought, and not only in religion, certain truths or notions find universal assent and provide criteria for what else may be affirmed with certainty in those areas (Herbert 1936:117). So the common notions of religion are but instances of a larger class.

Baldly stated, Herbert's account of the foundations of knowledge seems no reply to scepticism at all. Contemporary critics were quick to point out that even where universal consent could be found on basic notions, it could not guarantee their truth. It could just as well signify common agreement on errors (Popkin

1979:160–1). There is, however, more to Herbert's account than such criticism supposes. For he does not regard universal consent on fundamental truths as of itself making them true; rather, such consent is the sign of God's providence, and it is through his wisdom that we can be sure truth is present: 'this universal consent is the teaching of Natural Instinct and is essentially due to Divine Providence' (Herbert 1936:117). The common notions, outside as well as within religion, are directly placed in the mind by God. They form the content of a faculty – natural instinct – which supervises the work of the three others that contribute to human knowledge: internal apprehension, external apprehension, and discursive reason (Herbert 1936:115). Herbert's non-naturalism with regard to the sources of knowledge (including religious knowledge) appears not merely in the fact that the content of natural instinct is directly given by providence but also in the relationship with the divine that follows from this. The fact that the truths and notions possessed by natural instinct are imprinted upon the soul does indeed show that they are not the discoveries or products of reason itself. Reason is, by contrast, the process of applying these truths or notions (Herbert 1936:120). Herbert has no time for the theory that the mind comes to experience at birth as a clean sheet. Without the divinely implanted intellectual rules which are the common notions, it would have no means of acquiring experience for it would lack any grounds for distinguishing true from false experience (Herbert 1936:132).

We can see that the human mind is not autonomous in relation to God in its discovery of truth, relying on a directly given deposit of truths from God before it can discover anything for itself. The link between the mind and God is strengthened through the thought that the existence and content of natural instinct makes us partakers of God's nature:

> [the common notions] form that part of knowledge with which we are endowed in the primeval plan of Nature. When freed from the contact of confused theories and arranged in systematic order, they shine forth as . . . an image of the divine wisdom.
>
> (Herbert 1936:121)

Herbert affirms of the human mind in general that it is an image of divinity, but of natural instinct in particular that it is the first reflection of God's imparting of his image to us. This is because those things which are implanted in natural instinct are the very principles of the divine wisdom by which nature is fashioned and governed. So, as Herbert affirms, if it is a common notion that we should do unto others as we would be done by, 'we should conclude that the universe itself is governed according to this maxim' (Herbert 1936:133). The theory of the divine origin of the common notions is vital to his view of the nature of man, entailing not only that man is created in the divine image but also that man has a share in the divine universal providence (Herbert 1936:150). Mind and natural instinct come to reflect the very principles by which reality is constructed. This is why we can be sure of truth through the common notions – they mirror the nature of reality, or the 'divine eternal counsel of the universe' (Herbert 1936:207). If the mind has a grasp of truth this is only because of an analogy between its constitution and the reality of things outside it. The existence of that analogy is only secured because of another analogy – that between the content of the mind and God. He it is who not only creates both mind and reality but directly attunes them to one another. The human mind and knowledge are thus directly and continually dependent on the divine. Moreover, it is impossible to understand human nature without understanding its relationship to God, since no account can be given of how the mind functions as a cognitive organ unless mention is made of the common notions directly given by God.

One of the important consequences of this vision of the nature of knowledge is that reason is given a much less central place in Herbert's account than in those of later writers who, unlike him, are clear proponents of natural religion. Indeed, the importance of the role of reason in natural religion can best be appreciated when we contrast reason's later elevation with its downgrading in Herbert.

In *De Veritate* Herbert writes of reason as a discursive faculty whose essential task is to draw inferences from the knowledge provided by internal and external modes of experience. As it does so it is guided by, and at the same time applies, the common notions furnished by natural instinct. Within Herbert's fourfold scheme of faculties it emerges as the lowest. Its work presupposes the deliverances of the other three, and it is less certain than they. Indeed it is 'superfluous when a Common Notion is at hand or when inner and outer forms of experience are the judges of events'

(Herbert 1936:232). Not only does discursive reason fail to add to the certainty of truths given directly by natural instinct and inner and outer sense, it frequently leads to error (Herbert 1936:23–4). Its only defence against its innate waywardness is the guidance it receives from the common notions implanted in the mind by God. It does have a valid use in drawing inferences from and connecting together the various common notions, but it cannot discover truth on its own, because it 'does not of its own right have access to the analogy which exists between us and the first cause or which exists between us and objects' (Herbert 1936:235).

We see the extent to which, for Herbert, the mind is a divinely guided instrument. Without a directly given, divine deposit of notions and principles, our power of drawing inferences is as much likely to yield error as it would truth and can give us no certain knowledge. We can also see just how great a limitation the restriction of the sources of knowledge to inner sense, outer perception, and reason could seem in Herbert's age. This more restricted theory of knowledge, which we find in Locke, must at the same time be a more naturalistic one. Without a faculty corresponding to Herbert's natural instinct and directly stocked by God, the knowing human subject of later thought has the entire and immediate responsibility for the discovery of truth and construction of knowledge itself. God can only enter the process in a secondary way at best.

Herbert's humanism anticipates part of what is encountered in the elevation of natural religion. It does entail that we can expect certain things of God and his providence towards us. It implies that God must be viewed as just and benevolent and thus as someone who will deal with all peoples justly. God's essential fairness is further demanded by the uniformity Herbert finds in human nature. His comment that man is 'the same or very little differing in all ages and countries' (Herbert 1768:56) will be found repeated in the later proponents of natural religion. Yet his reason for asserting this reminds us of the distinctive character of his humanism: the same faculties and common notions 'have been imprinted on the soul of every normal person in all ages' (Herbert 1936:78–9). Both the positive value in and the uniformity of human nature depend on the operations of God's providence and the image of God which that providence has placed in all. Since the image is undestroyed, a redemption in history is unnecessary.

Given that the universal condition of man remains similar to the character it enjoyed before the fall, as described by some theologians (cf. Athanasius 1971:7), with everyone able to enjoy an easy, unmediated awareness of God, a knowledge of God through the dubious means of historical revelation is unnecessary. The problem of religious certainty created through the different construals by sects and churches of alleged historical revelation is solved by the account of the direct knowledge we have of God through inscription. God's nature, the worth of human beings, the problem of religious knowledge – all are tackled by a religious humanism. Herbert's 'catholic religion' of the common notions is thus not quite that natural religion which we saw could be derived from natural theology with the addition of morality. It is not the product of human reason's reflection on nature, though such reflection may stimulate or awaken it (see Herbert 1705:11). It is essentially a religion which has a divine source (inscription) as well as a divine focus. A different kind of naturalism is involved in the elevation of natural religion.

One further point in Herbert needs to be brought out. I have said that for a variety of reasons it would be odd to take the study of human religion seriously if one did not think that human life and nature were worthy of respect and attention. Equally, if one did not think human religion was important as an expression of human life and human nature, one could not see it as a central component part of the study of human nature. It seems that among other things the study of religion must presuppose a view of religion as important in human life as a whole. Such a view may be found in Herbert and will be displayed, in different versions, in other writers important in the development of the concept of religion. The presence of this kind of perspective on religion in the authors treated in this study is linked to the fourth sense of 'natural religion' described in Chapter 1.

We have seen why Herbert should think it worthwhile to survey the course of religious history in antiquity: to do so is to trace the universal providence of God through all the ages. An extra reason for being interested in religious life is provided by the argument in *De Veritate* for the conclusion that religion is the defining feature of being human. So, commenting on the weakness of scholastic attempts to distinguish man as a species by reference to reason, Herbert affirms: 'upon closer examination there emerges as the unique and ultimate differences of man, religion and faith' (Herbert 1936:256). Added to his strictures on reason, Herbert has as positive grounds for his definition the fact that human nature is distinguished by bearing the divine image. Religion is the means whereby we are aware of our relationship to God, and it is that which constitutes the possession of the likeness of God within us. Neither God nor the brutes possess religion. The religion grounded upon the common notions shows *all* mankind to share a common status, poised between creator and creation. Despite the possibilities of corruption described in *De Religione Gentilium* everyone in possession of their senses has some reverence for God in some guise (Herbert 1936: 257 and 291). Religion, therefore, defines humanity because in some measure it unites all men, combining 'the past and the future' (Herbert 1936:257).

What Herbert has done is take over from Christian theology the notions that man is constituted by being the bearer of the image of God and that this image consists in the capacity for relationship to God. The nature of this image has been defined in the particular fashion of the providential inscription of the common notions, and it has been asserted to be displayed in the actual religious life of man in history (barring lapses and corruption). No stronger reason than this could be given for making that life an object of serious attention.

JOHN LOCKE ON THE NATURE AND NECESSITY OF REVELATION

Anyone who reads Locke's *Essay concerning Human Understanding* Book 1, chapter 3 will be puzzled as to how both he and Herbert might be used to illustrate the same current of religious ideas. For in sections 15 ff. of that chapter Locke forcibly attacks Herbert's belief in common notions in religion produced by divine inscription. Locke contends that such notions do not in any meaningful sense receive universal consent among mankind, and that even if they did the consent would not prove their innateness. His attack is of course part of a larger case in Book 1 of the *Essay* to the effect that theories of innate ideas cannot be squared with the actual state of opinion in any of the major branches of human thought, and are in any case internally inconsistent. Such theories lack any consistent account of what it is for an idea to be both in the mind and yet to exist as such prior to conscious reflection upon it (Locke 1823a:I,4,22). The only internally coherent account of human thought, which at the same time explains the actual state of human thinking, is one that grants human beings faculties and capacities by nature but regards all knowledge and opinion as produced by experience, both inner and outer, stimulating these faculties in the ordinary course of human nurture and development.

It follows at once from Locke's arguments that he cannot have quite the same view of God's providence toward man that we found in Herbert. Hence, his account of the origins and nature of religion is bound to be different in some respects. These differences will be seen to be wide-ranging and important. Yet, at the same time, we shall find significant similarities and common emphases, which enable us to present the thought of both authors as illustrators of themes connected with the emergence of the notion of natural religion. Locke will be found to agree with Herbert in rejecting the belief in the total depravity and corruption of human nature. They are alike, too, in some of the consequences they draw from this rejection. Locke shares the emphasis upon God's justice as comprehensible and entailing a universal fairness to humanity. For Locke, then, Christianity's alleged uniqueness presents itself as a major problem. His solution is very different, and much of his disagreement with Herbert on how to treat this problem can be traced back to that divergence over the nature of reason and knowledge already noted. But even here there is some common ground in the proposition that the existence and nature of God and his demands upon humanity must be universally knowable, and in relation to epistemology there is common acceptance of the centrality of the problem of religious certainty as we have described it.

Later writers, who demonstrate the elevation of natural religion more clearly than either Herbert or Locke, could accept the Lockean account of knowledge, while in effect agreeing with Herbert's answers to questions concerning the uniqueness of Christianity and the universality of religion. This is because, though they thought that human reason was as Locke described it, they were more optimistic about the progress of reason so described. With this shift of emphasis, a more naturalistic account of man and knowledge could lead to the same conclusions on the universality and unchangeableness of true religion Herbert draws from slightly different premisses.

That Locke's account of knowledge is at the same time a decisive move towards naturalism is something that needs to be brought out at the beginning of our discussion.[2] Locke's account of the faculties that produce human knowledge parallels in outline aspects of Herbert's scheme. Herbert's quartet of faculties is replaced by the trio of reflection, sensation, and reason. Reflection is a mode of awareness of the mind's own inner states and operations; 'sensation' is the general term for awareness of the outer objects through the five senses (Locke 1823a:II,1). Locke's 'reason' is defined much in the manner of Herbert's 'discursive reason': 'reason being taken to mean the discursive faculty of the mind, which advances from things known to things unknown and argues from one thing to another in a definite and fixed order of propositions' (Locke 1954:149). As enlarged upon in the *Essay concerning Human Understanding* Bk 4, ch. 17, Locke's account of reason is linked to his definition of knowledge as the perception of the agreement and disagreement of ideas, it being reason's job to search out and perceive the connections between ideas. The one faculty missing from Locke's list is, of course, Herbert's natural instinct with its stock of notions and truths inscribed by God. This means that in Locke's scheme the store of ideas on which reason has to work is not the product of direct divine agency but of wholly mundane transactions between the faculties of sense and inner and outer events. Locke's scheme also entails that the manner in which reason conducts inferences from one idea to another is wholly natural and without divine guidance. Thus the grounds for giving assent to propositions, even in religion, are immediately produced by natural means alone. (This last point will be found to survive Locke's admission of faith and revelation as well.)

Locke himself signals the naturalism entailed by his theory of the mind when he affirms that, in denying innate ideas, he hopes to show how men can attain to all the knowledge they have 'barely by the use of their natural faculties' (Locke 1823a:I,2,1). His account of how we acquire knowledge of the natural law will rest upon 'the use and due application of our natural faculties' (Locke 1823a:I,3,16). He dismisses the Herbertian argument that God's providential goodness entails the necessity of a direct divine inscription of the idea of God in men's minds in the following way:

I doubt but to show that a man by the right use of his natural abilities may, without any innate principles, attain the knowledge of a God, and other things that concern him. God having endued man with those faculties of knowing which he hath, was no more obliged by his goodness to plant those innate notions in his mind, than that, having given him reason, hands, and materials, he should build him bridges or houses.

(Locke 1823a,I,4,12)

Human knowledge, even of God himself, is as much a product of natural human powers as the towns man lives in. Or, as Locke later puts it, the knowledge of God is 'the most natural discovery of human reason' (Locke 1823a:I,4,17).

That Locke's rejection of innate ideas and his account of the origin of belief and knowledge in sensation, reflection, and reason lead to a more thoroughgoing naturalism was evident to his contemporaries (as will be clear when we examine some of the deists below). Locke himself illustrates the critical possibilities offered by his epistemological naturalism in his account of how much that passes for innate, God-given truth comes to be accepted as such. He describes a human process whereby through upbringing and prejudice people come to the mistaken belief that the foundations of their religion and morality have been given them by God (Locke 1823a:I,3,22). This leads to what might seem a paradox in Locke's account of the nature and universality of religion. Having given a more naturalistic portrayal of the foundations of belief and having placed God's providence at one remove from human nature, Locke is much less sanguine than Herbert over the success of mankind in universally attaining for itself that which is sufficient for salvation. He is led on this ground to argue for the necessity of revelation in history. Locke accepts the uniqueness of Christianity and the insufficiency of natural religion.

Locke's argument for the special place Christianity must occupy within religion may be divided into two parts. He contends that the knowledge of God and of the demands required for a right relationship to God has been insufficiently and imperfectly spread throughout human history (if we leave Christian revelation out of account). In addition, the requirements on human behaviour those demands lay down cannot be properly met in the course of ordinary human conduct.

The first part of this argument is related to Locke's denial of an immediate inscription of the principles of religion and morality upon the minds of men. This denial implies that it is only through effort and activity on the part of the human mind that we will be able to discover

God. Locke endorses St Paul's statement in Romans 1:19–20 that a knowledge of God's nature has been available from the beginning of creation through the manifestation of God in his works. He adds the significant gloss:

> The invisible things of God lie within reach and discovery of men's understanding, but yet they must exercise their faculties and employ their minds about them.
>
> (Locke 1823*f*:258)

Locke expands on the point in the *Essays on the Law of Nature*. From the evidence provided by sense we can infer the being of God and can use this inference to guide us in discovering the universal laws governing our lives which are evident in the works of nature. But 'granted our mental faculties can lead us to a knowledge of this law, nevertheless it does not follow all men make proper use of these faculties' (Locke 1954:133). For

> Careful reflection, thought, and attention by the mind is needed, in order that by argument and reasoning one may find a way from perceptible and obvious things into their hidden nature.
>
> (Locke 1954:135)

In his discussion of the pitfalls which face unaided human reason in this task, Locke agrees with Aquinas' conclusion that it is only the 'more rational and perceptive' among mankind who will be able successfully to carry through the work of inference (Locke 1954:115). A knowledge of God and the principles of morality not being thus given but set as a task, Locke becomes aware of the extent to which laziness and corruption of the mind will prevent the task being undertaken by most, and also of the extent to which men will simply be content to accept whatever passes for religious and moral knowledge in their own country. Custom rather than reason will be the guide that many follow, and thus peoples will be found who lack any satisfactory notion concerning God and right (Locke 1823*a*:I,4,12).

We now can state one part of Locke's case for the necessity of an historical revelation in *The Reasonableness of Christianity*:

> Though the works of nature, in every part of them, sufficiently evidence a Deity; yet the world made so little use of their reason, that they saw him not, where, even by the impressions of

himself, he was easy to be found.

(Locke 1823e:135)

Sense, lust, careless inadvertancy, fearful apprehensions: these things, singly or in combination, blinded men to God. They gave themselves up to priests who in turn filled people's heads with false notions of the deity and introduced foolish rites:

> In this state of darkness and ignorance of the true God, vice and superstition held the world. Nor could any help be had from reason; which could not be heard, and was judged to have nothing to do in the case; the priests everywhere, to secure their empire, having excluded reason from having anything to do in religion. And in the crowd of wrong notions and invented rites, the world had almost lost sight of the only true God.

(Locke 1823e:135)

This ignorance carried over into the principles of natural moral law. For while Locke acknowledges that it is possible in principle to establish morality on firm foundations by unassisted reason, in practice the task seems to be beyond even the best minds. Even the best pagan philosophers before the proclamation of moral truth in the Gospel produced systems very far short of 'the perfection of a true and complete morality' (Locke 1823e:139). Locke concludes that the knowledge of morality by unaided human reason 'makes but a slow progress, and little advance in the world' (Locke 1823e:140).

Two consequences immediately follow from this half of Locke's case for the necessity of an historical revelation, and both point to his distance from Herbert on the universality of religion. From the idea of God being an achievement of reason, Locke is quite happy to accept the conclusion that there may be 'whole nations ... among whom there was to be found no notion of a God, no religion' (Locke 1823a:I,4,8). Locke has thus no prior reason for supposing that there is anything more in ancient heathenism than the polytheism and superstition that meets the eye. His conclusion in *The Reasonableness of Christianity* that, before Christ, a knowledge of the true God was all but lost to mankind, is tempered by only two exceptions – the national religion of the Israelites and the pagan philosophers, referred to as the 'rational and thinking part of mankind' (Locke 1823e:135). Locke, however, is keen to point out that the philosophers' knowledge of the true God had no influence upon pagan religion in general, repeating the complaint made by earlier Christian writers that they kept this knowledge to themselves and were afraid to publish it widely. Lacking Herbert's assumptions about the necessary universality of knowledge of God and the neoplatonist inclination to see something worthwhile in the veneration of sun, stars, and heavens, Locke sees paganism as unredeemed folly. Of the pagans in general he says: 'What are these people, pray, but disguised atheists?' (Locke 1954:175). A further, connected, consequence of Locke's pessimism on reason is that Christian revelation becomes the vehicle for God's universal providence toward mankind, thus completing the reversal of Herbert's thought. Locke assigns to Scripture the function of the 'instruction of the illiterate bulk of mankind, in the way to salvation' (Locke 1823e:5). In this purpose it has been successful, for Christ has 'made the invisible true God known to the world' (Locke 1823e:137). Since Christ's mission 'the belief of one God has prevailed and spread itself over the face of the earth' (Locke 1823e:137). Even in Islamic countries, where one God is professed by the bulk of the people, it is Christ's revelation that is at work, according to Locke, for Islam has borrowed its knowledge of monotheism from Christianity.

This part of Locke's argument for the necessity of an historical revelation is obviously not sufficient to establish the uniqueness of Christianity. For, as we have noted already, to make Christianity necessary only as the restorer of the knowledge of a pure ethical monotheism is not to defend the need for a religion which preaches Christ. Locke accordingly argues that it would be wrong to make Jesus Christ 'nothing but the restorer of and preacher of pure natural religion' (Locke 1823e:5). To counter this mistaken version of Christianity's role and message we must insist on the need for a redemption even after the truths of natural religion are made known. In this need lies the second part of Locke's argument for the special place of Christianity. Even if someone had, by whatever means, a knowledge of the true God and of morality he would still be unable fully to satisfy the demands for salvation God lays down unless he had faith in Christ. While Locke agrees that the picture of mankind bound in sin through Adam's fall is inconsistent with the justice or goodness of God, it is wrong, he argues, to reach the conclusion that redemption beyond natural religion is unnecessary.

As the case in *The Reasonableness of Christianity* has it, this additional redemption is required because the complete bliss of immortality offered by God to man depends upon the condition that man be perfectly obedient to God's law. Since Adam mankind has not in fact been able to supply this complete obedience (Locke: 1823*e*:7), and God has therefore justly denied the reward of immortality, for he has judged subsequent generations in the light of the demand to obey his law fully and perfectly. His graciousness towards man shows in introducing, via Christ, an alternative means of achieving salvation and perfect bliss in the form of repentance, and faith in God's promises. This repentance and faith are made possible through Christ (Locke 1823e:14–15). If Christians sincerely repent and have a true faith in God's promises, this will be counted as equivalent to a complete obedience and righteousness. The specific form which the faith necessary for us to gain the reward of eternal life takes 'in the Gospel' is the acknowledgement of Jesus as the Messiah (Locke 1823*e*:17). The content of this acknowledgement is obscure in Locke. We are told that to believe that Jesus is the Messiah is one and the same thing as believing him to be the Son of God (Locke 1823*e*:21–2), but while this is connected with believing in Christ as a source of miracles, little else is said. We know in fact from Locke's private correspondence that he was sympathetic to unitarian views and was reluctant to give Jesus the status of membership of the Godhead (Montouri 1983:124 ff.). Since a saving faith is defined earlier on in the argument as a credence in, and faithful reliance on, God's promises, the faith in Jesus-as-Messiah that saves can safely be identified with a faith and reliance upon Jesus as a bearer of God's promises and as a representative of God's demands.[3] This entails a belief that Jesus rose from the dead (Locke 1823*e*:20) because it is by this most central miracle that Jesus is confirmed as God's representative. So, as I interpret Locke, it is through Jesus that the generality of mankind can become aware of the nature of God's promises and have the means of gaining the faith in those promises which will enable them to achieve ultimate bliss.

Locke's account of man's relationship to God can now be seen to exhibit the paradoxical union of a naturalistic account of human nature and knowledge with a downgrading of natural and an elevation of revealed religion. Locke can still describe the awareness of true religion as the result of a divine gift of grace

(Locke 1823e:102–3). This is because the various elements in this religion – the status of Christ as Messiah, the possibility of salvation through faith in him, and so forth – are truths 'above reason' as Locke defines this category in the *Essay* (1823c:IV,17,23). Unaided reason would never have reached them by inference from ideas derived from sensation and reflection alone. There had to be a revelation of these truths by a divine granting of the revealed ideas to those who were to publish the essential truths of saving religion. Many thinkers after Locke were to query how the union of naturalism and appeal to revelation in his work could be anything other than a contradiction. In exploring the basis in Locke's account for this accusation of incoherence we may focus on two things in particular: how far the demands of the humanism behind Locke's thought are compatible with reliance upon a divine granting of truths above reason as necessary to salvation; and how far Locke's circumscribed, naturalistic account of the operations of reason allows for certainty in revelation.

Locke's humanism is shown forcibly in his rejection of the Lutheran account of a mankind enslaved by sin through Adam's fall. In describing this picture of fallen man he endorses the opinion of those who reject it as 'so little consistent with the justice or goodness of the great and infinite God' (Locke 1823e:4). Locke comments on the conditions for salvation this picture lays down:

> Could a worthy man be supposed to put such terms upon the obedience of his subjects? Much less can the righteous God be supposed, as a punishment of one sin, wherewith he is displeased, to put a man under the necessity of sinning continually, and so multiplying the provocation.
>
> (Locke 1823e:6)

Not only is the depressing picture of fallen man rejected, but the rejection rests upon affirming the applicability of human conceptions of justice to God. The worth of human nature and human conceptions is thus doubly affirmed. Locke, as a direct consequence of this humanism, is loath to accept that God offers terms for salvation to some portions of the human race, while withholding them from other portions. He outlines clearly the objection that, if Jesus is *the* Messiah, God has dealt unjustly with those who through no fault of their own have never heard of him. Locke responds:

> To this I answer, that God will require of every man 'according to what a man hath, and not according to what he hath not'. He will not expect the improvement of ten talents, where he gave but one; nor require any one should believe a promise of which he has never heard.
>
> (Locke 1823e:132)

This seems extremely clear and seems to imply that those who have not heard of Christ will not be required to believe in the Messiah to be saved. Locke continues by describing how God will judge all by the use of the gifts he has given them, and in the case of those who are strangers to Christ it will be by reference to how they have made use of their natural reason. The undeniable consequence of saving God's justice in human eyes after this fashion is that Christ is not the unique path to salvation for mankind. Locke then is faced with the objection that this consequence cannot be squared with the plain Scriptural pronouncement (upon which Locke himself has relied) that Jesus is *the* Messiah. The reply is a collapse into mystery:

> It is enough to justify the fairness of anything to be done, by resolving it into the 'wisdom of God', who has done it; though our short views, and narrow understandings, may utterly incapacitate us to see that wisdom, and to judge rightly of it.
>
> (Locke 1823e:134)

Others were to judge this appeal to mystery to be out of place. It fits in ill with the surrounding dogmatic claims that salvation is through Christ as Messiah, that salvation is a work of justice, that the terms of salvation are fair to all. Locke's claim is that the Christian dispensation, once expounded properly by reference to the true meaning of Scripture, will be seen to be reasonable. An appeal to mystery is, however, a way of saying it cannot be so expounded.

Dissatisfaction with Locke's account of the justice of God in relation to man may be sharpened by considering his differences with Herbert. We may note how Herbert includes among the 'catholic articles' of religion (4), the need for a sincere repentance before God of our sins. This article is present because of the realization that human beings will not serve God perfectly through virtue in all their actions. All will fall short of complete obedience,

46

hence the need for repentance. One wonders why such simple means of reconciling God's demands with human performance should not have been adopted by Locke. Of course, if such a means of reconciliation is available the need for a mediator, and hence for Christ, vanishes, but we have seen that the role of a mediator creates difficulties for the kind of humanism Locke in part espouses. Locke's commitment to this humanism remains in the end partial. In Book I of the *Essay* he denies that there is a universal awareness of the common notions in religion (ch.3, §§155 ff.). And we have seen that in both the *Essays on the Law of Nature* and *The Reasonableness of Christianity* he casts doubt on the ability of the majority of mankind to attain a clear knowledge of the naturally given moral law, and without that knowledge the possibility of seeing the need of repentance is obviously limited. If Locke were true to his promise these defects in human nature would have their remedy in the proclamation of Christ as recorded in Scripture. Yet we have seen that Locke makes no pretence of supposing that this proclamation is universally known. He does not, in addition, maintain that the more specific revelations given to the Jewish patriarchs and prophets somehow spread abroad to other lands and peoples (Locke 1823e:137–8). His rejection of inscription as a source of knowledge of God and moral law forecloses other traditional means of providing a knowledge of Christ among all nations. It is hard, therefore, to avoid the conclusion that Locke has simply failed to show how God has offered terms of salvation to the 'illiterate bulk of mankind'. He does not have an account of how a divine, universal scheme of salvation is affected.

If Locke's reliance on truths above reason were compatible with a humanistic emphasis on God's justice to man, then it would not only show how revelation was a universal path but also how it was a sure means of discovering God's will. God's fairness would be in question if, in addition to showing partiality to some peoples, he had also surrounded his disclosure in too much doubt and uncertainty. Locke's account of the grounds on which revelation rests suggests precisely that there will be too much doubt and uncertainty surrounding it. Revelation will not solve the problem of religious certainty described in the preceding section if Locke's account of revelation is followed. The failure of Locke's description of revelation in this regard redounds on the justice of Locke's God.

The uncertainty which surrounds revelation and its correlative attitude, faith, may be displayed by reference to Locke's definition of the two:

> Faith . . . is the assent to any proposition, not . . . made out by the deductions of reason; but upon the credit of the proposer, as coming from God, in some extraordinary way of communication. This way of discovering truths to men we call revelation.
>
> (Locke 1823c:IV,18,2)

Though a proposition which is revealed in this way is absolutely certain (for it comes from God, who cannot do other than deliver truth), it is a matter for judgement, checked by reason, that a proposition has been revealed. Our assurance in revelation can in fact 'be no greater than our knowledge is, that is a revelation' (Locke 1823c:IV,18,5). While reason cannot independently discover the truths given in revelation, it can, and must, be able to decide that something has come from God 'in an extraordinary way of communication'. Even one who believes he is in receipt of an original revelation from God must check its credentials as revelation. So though Locke can speak of faith/revelation as a distinct ground of assent in Bk 4 of the *Essay*, his ultimate conclusion is that reason must be 'our last judge and guide in every thing' (Locke 1823c:IV,19,14). This statement is made in the light of conflicting claims to revelation and the ever-present possibility of delusion and error among those who think they have revelation. Locke confronts the same problem of religious certainty we met in Herbert and in general outline tackles it in the same way – by positing grounds of religious certainty independent of competing sectarian claims. But he is less sanguine than Herbert about the certainty of immediate revelation (as the discussion of Enthusiasm in Bk 4, ch. 19 of the *Essay* testifies) and is without the apparatus of common notions to provide a ready answer.

Surveying the material on attesting revelation in the *Essay concerning Human Understanding*, *The Reasonableness of Christianity*, *Discourse of Miracles*, and *Third Letter for Toleration*, we may say Locke points to a variety of negative and positive criteria, which we can briefly summarize as follows. Attested revelation must in the first instance be consistent with the clear judgements of reason as to what is true or highly probable. It may not contradict what is plainly in accordance with reason. This in turn means that we must rely on whatever knowledge of natural religion we have to judge how far would-be revelation is in accordance with it. On this ground we can dismiss the claims of the religions of the Far East to be containers of genuine revelation (Locke 1823*g*:258). They fail to teach the monotheism that in natural religion is demonstrated to be true. This reliance on natural religion as a negative test merges into the positive criterion of looking in an attested revelation for truths 'relating to the glory of God, and some great concern to men' (Locke 1823*g*:262). They must, in other words, be truths which deepen and extend the perceptions we have through natural religion in important ways. When these factors are present, we may finally look to see in a genuine divine revelation marks of supernatural power and agency surrounding him who vouches it. These marks will be the performance of miracles (though the fulfilment of prophecy may also figure). On these complex grounds we may be sure that in the Old and New Testaments and in them alone there is a series of truths above reason, genuinely revealed and therefore indirectly attested by reason.

Locke's procedures for attesting revelation have their parallels in earlier attempts to show that faith rests on rational preambles and external credentials, and in his hands the procedures do produce the orthodox conclusion described. Yet there is something distinctive about Locke's use of them which makes the certainty of revelation questionable on his account. Followers of Locke's Way of Ideas (as his epistemology was described) could find plenty of ammunition in his narrow conception of reason and in his frank discussion of the problems surrounding the attestation of revelation if they wanted to dismiss the certainty of revealed truth.

They could note his denial that innate/inscribed truths could serve as a starting-point in establishing what is revelation. They would mark his insistence that everyone (even those who think they have revelation directly given to them) is bound to follow his own conception of what is probable and improbable in assenting or not to revelation. There can be no route to an acceptance of revelation that by-passes a conscientious judgement that it is more probably attested than not (so there will be no reliance on implicit faith or on the judgement of others or tradition). One must believe as one's own reason directs (Locke 1823*c*:IV,6,4, and IV,17,24). So far from tradition being a source of assurance in accepting a report of revelation, the longer the tradition behind a claim to revelation, the weaker it appears that claim will be. For, according to Locke, testimony tends to lose its force the further it is removed from its original source. A 'traditional truth' (one known only from the hearsay report of what some original witness said) is weaker than an 'original truth' and loses strength according to the number of removes it is from the original source (Locke 1823c:IV,16,10). This appears to entail that the revelation in the Old and New Testaments is not backed by miracles but by the reports of miracles, which must have less weight and force than the original miracles.[4] The critic of Locke could also note his arguments to the effect that when relying on others' testimony for a knowledge of an event, the likelihood of the event itself must be taken into account along with the reliability of the witness. In the case of events very unlikely from our own experience, we can have good ground for dismissing the strongest testimony (Locke 1823c:IV,15,5). Here is further reason to doubt whether, in the report of miracles, reason has firm enough grounds to attest historical revelation.

To these difficulties which the Way of Ideas has in establishing with certainty what claims, if any, are the product of revelation, a critic could add the problems Locke advertises over the important question of how we could interpret and understand claims to revelation. Locke again insists that in relation to such judgements the individual is bound to consult his own reason and may not take them from any authority. 'If I believe for myself, it is unavoidable that I must understand for myself' (Locke 1823f:22). The judgement as to what the text of revelation means does not wait on any spiritual illumination but on the discovery through reason of the ideas and thoughts of him who set it down (Locke 1823f:21). To understand the 'mind of him that writ it' (Locke 1823f:14) seems inevitably to involve another exercise of historical reason relying on judgements of probability. The judgements as to what ideas were in the minds of the scriptural writers seem uncertain in the light of points raised by Locke himself in the *Essay concerning Human Understanding* Bk 3, ch. 9. The language of the writers belongs to remote ages and countries: 'And in discourses of religion, law and morality, as they are matters of the highest concernment, so there will be the greatest difficulty' in recovering the precise ideas involved (1823b:III,9,22). So major do the problems of interpretation seem to Locke that he momentarily lapses into despair and into offering a verdict on revelation contrary to his own sense of its centrality in religious truth. Having noted the many disagreements between Biblical commentators, Locke concludes:

> Since the precepts of natural religion are plain, and very intelligible to all mankind and seldom come to be controverted; and other revealed truths, which are conveyed to us by books and languages, are liable to the common and natural obscurities and difficulties incident to words, methinks it would become us to be more careful and diligent in observing the former, and less magisterial, positive, and imperious in imposing our own sense and interpretations of the latter.
>
> (Locke 1823b:III,9,23)

A complete survey of Locke on revelation and reason could not ignore his attempts to deal with the doubts concerning revelation we have just surveyed. Any such survey would want to mark in particular the material in the *Essay concerning Human Understanding* Bk 4, ch. 16, § 13 and in the *Discourse of Miracles* which endeavours to give positive ground for establishing the probability of miracles in history. It would also be proper to note the optimism displayed in the *Paraphrase and Notes on the Epistles of St Paul* and in *The Reasonableness of Christianity* on establishing the plain and literal sense of Scripture. We have done enough, however, to indicate how one sympathetic to Locke's conclusions on knowledge could be encouraged to see revelation as less than certain from Locke's own account of its foundation in reason.

We have seen a number of characteristics in Locke's approach to the availability of religious truth: humanism, naturalism, rationalism, and a marked individualism. There are serious difficulties apparent in his writings in reconciling such intellectual tendencies with a continued belief in the necessity and centrality of revealed religion. A more optimistic conception of the ability of man to use reason as Locke described it produces a simple solution to these difficulties – the dismissal of revealed and the complete elevation of natural religion. This will inevitably seem better suited to the conceptions of God and man and to the problems of religious certainty as these are present in Locke himself. Above all, Locke's clear commitment to the sovereignty and autonomy of reason seems to fit ill with any essential reliance upon revealed truth.

3

DEISM AND THE CASE FOR NATURAL RELIGION

INTRODUCTION

In the previous two chapters the progress of the concept of natural religion in modern religious thought has been declared to be of interest in the development of our concept of religion. This is because the emergence into prominence of the concept of natural religion brings with it types of reflection typical of modern thought about religion in general. These types of reflection encourage a belief in the universality of religion. From that follows a willingness to regard Christianity as strictly comparable to traditions and institutions found elsewhere. These reflections also tend to see all religious traditions as naturalistically explicable and thus as fully parts of human history.

Steps toward the elevation of a concept of natural religion have been found in Herbert and Locke. For different reasons the process is incomplete in both thinkers. The full elevation of natural religion in radical religious thought needs still to be illustrated. This will be done through discussion of some representative English deists. They will be found to argue for natural religion by combining a humanism similar to Herbert's with a naturalistic conception of knowledge similar to Locke's (though with a narrower conception of what reason can license in religion). In this and the next chapter we can see how their approach to religion produces the kind of reflections on religion we are particularly concerned to track down. In this chapter I begin with the positive affirmations of deism and try to disentangle and discuss the arguments offered in my selected writers for the elevation of natural religion. For convenience discussion is organized around the three concerns found in Herbert's attempt to discover a universal religion: the doctrine of God, the doctrine of man, and the problem of religious certainty.

The conclusions of deism may strike us as naive in many respects. Its importance lies in the way in which it opens up vital issues in the history of religion. It is concerned, among other things with the universality, comparability, and naturalness of religion and, through these things, with profound questions about the nature of history. To affirm the universality, comparability, and naturalness of religion is to place an obvious question-mark against the kind of traditional account of the place of Christianity in history discussed in Chapter 1. What is under debate in radical religious rationalism is the extent to which human destiny and salvation are centred upon a special period of history, as traditional theological accounts affirm, and ultimately whether salvation is offered through an historical process at all. In denying that one period of religious history is the focus for all else, deism is affirming the comparability of all periods of history. Likewise, the universality of religion rests upon the uniformity of history. One obvious legacy of deism that makes it of enduring interest is the clear way in which it raises questions about the nature of history and about the role of religion in history.

THE DOCTRINE OF GOD

The doctrine of God found in religious rationalism provides a primary ground for denying that man's destiny or salvation are tied to a particular period of history. To be noted first is the common repetition of the argument found in Herbert's insistence on God's providence. The case in Charles Blount's *Oracles of Reason* is typical. It begins with the premiss that God, being infinitely good, 'provides for all his creatures the means of attaining that happiness, whereof their natures are capable'. This leads to the irrelevance of any religion tied to a particular segment of history when supported by the following simple argument:

that rule which is necessary for our future happiness, ought to be generally made known to all men. But no rule of revealed religion was, or ever could be made known to all men. Therefore

53

no revealed religion is necessary to future happiness.

(Blount 1695a:198–9)

Blount summarizes here the main elements of this oft-repeated argument from God's providence. The assertion that no revealed religion was, or ever could be, known to all men is in part a reflection of the widened geographical horizons noted in Chapter 2 and also a pointer to Blount's perception of the problem of religious certainty to be discussed below. Of particular importance is the automatic link Blount makes between God's perfect goodness and his uniform and unwavering concern to make human beings happy. As William Wollaston puts it: 'God cannot be unjust or unreasonable in any one instance' (Wollaston 1724:205). The demands of justice and reason upon God will entail for Wollaston that God aims to see the completion of human happiness for all (Wollaston 1724:199–200). God's justice and reasonableness seem obvious deductions from his perfection. That these in turn should be seen to entail a uniform and universal benevolence represents a shift in attitude, apparent when one considers how a Luther would have viewed the operations of God's justice. Divine justice might seem liable to be quite other than benevolent in its effects when directed against man's sinfulness. Some of the change in understanding the consequences of government by a perfect providence is therefore to be explained by the humanistic downgrading of human sinfulness marked already. Yet Blount and other deists were not unaware that even human beings free of the inherited stain of the fall could still do wrong on occasions. Despite this, they insisted upon a God whose primary concern was the securing of his creatures' happiness.

Part of the explanation for the disappearance of the wrath of God and the unquestioned equation of his perfect justice with a perfect benevolence lies in a simple conception of what could count as a reason for divine action. While debate raged among eighteenth-century moralists as to how far a man could be moved by the unselfish prospect of other people's happiness, the matter could be easily settled in case of God on the side of perfect disinterestedness. It is so settled by Matthew Tindal in chapters 2 and 3 of *Christianity as Old as the Creation*. Tindal there shows how, if God is absolutely perfect, he must be 'infinitely happy in himself' (Tindal 1730:14). His perfection and happiness will in fact consist solely in following the dictates of right and of reason (Tindal 1730:22–3). Now, a being perfectly and infinitely happy cannot act so as to secure or augment its own happiness, for that happiness needs no securing or augmenting. Therefore, following the dictates of right and reason for such a being must entail acting uniformly for the sake of others' happiness (Tindal 1730:14–15).

The righteous God of St Paul and Luther has thus become an agent of universal benevolence who is disinterested in being literally without any interests of his own. His justice has become a mode of his benevolence, and retribution has been taken from it. Since the divine law includes everything that tends to promote the happiness of mankind, we can say that, for Tindal, God's retributive justice has been taken over completely by his distributive. In thinking of God as the source of justice we are no longer contemplating a being who is the scourge and punisher of sin, but rather one who ensures an equal and reasonable distribution of the sum of happiness. Tindal's God will punish sin, but punishments will be strictly proportional to the nature of the offences God judges, and therefore not eternal. Moreover, the purpose of punishment, as of the laws which it is designed to enforce, is strictly to secure our own good. Punishment is meted out just so far as is sufficient to preserve the beneficent ends of the general system of God's laws and to benefit the wrongdoer (Tindal 1730:41–2). This is why it may be said that Tindal's God deals only in distributive rather than retributive justice. He cannot act out of a motive of retribution distinct from a desire to secure his creatures' happiness. Blount has an exactly similar thought in relation to God and punishment (Blount 1695a:90).

We can see, again in contrast to Luther, that the justice of this God must be perfectly comprehensible to us and in no way foreign to what *we* recognize in mundane dealings as right – as Tindal points out (Tindal 1730:26). This is because it is evident to us what makes the difference between happiness and misery and what is thus reasonable or not. God's justice merely follows this standard, embodying as it does a perfect fairness in the distribution of happiness. The strong link between God's justice and human happiness and fairness explains why it is evident to the deists that God's justice is contradicted by the thought that he may have given even a small part of essential saving knowledge to mankind by means of a historically located revelation known only to some.

Perfect divine justice must on the contrary entail that all saving knowledge in any way essential has been available to the unaided human reason at all times and places. The justice of God, so interpreted, can only be expressed through a natural religion.[1]

This mode of thinking seems to be a clear example of that influence of humanism upon the doctrine of God we found in Herbert. Both in its detailed points and its overall conclusion we see an account of the divine nature based upon the idea that God must be made in the image of man. He must be judged according to the standards expected of a good and just human being and is finally transformed into an agent for the securing of human happiness. At no point is there room for the thought that there might be a justice or goodness different in nature from the human and in relation to which the human can be rejected or judged imperfect.

We are now able to see clearly why Blount in 'A Summary Account of the Deists' Religion' so firmly rejects the need for a mediator as the means whereby man could become reconciled to God (Blount 1695a:88–9). Blount affirms that a mediator 'derogates from the infinite mercy of God'. Once the need or appropriateness of a mediator has been rejected a further reason has been found to separate the true religion from a particular path or period in history and God need not be thought of as manifesting himself more directly in his creation at one time or location than another. The mediator must be abandoned if God's retributive justice has been all but rejected in the manner we have noted. In traditional theology a mediator is needed so as to prevent the absolute abhorrence of sin, which comes from God's justice, falling without mercy upon mankind. Yet there is no need in the radically humanist theology we are describing for anything to stand between God's justice and human failings, since that justice is but an aspect of a disinterested concern to distribute happiness among human beings (cf. Tindal 1730:40).

The deists we are considering were aware of the Lockean objection that, though natural religion may in principle be sufficient for becoming reconciled to God, in reality men fail to discover completely its laws or to live up to them, so that for practical purposes an additional and revealed means of being reconciled to God is required. In Blount this objection is met with a reply which reflects at once a negative judgement on the availability of specific revelation in history and the peculiar conception of God's justice we have been describing: 'then there is no visible means for the greater part of mankind to be happy' (Blount 1695a:199). It was simple to maintain that natural religion did contain a *generally* known means of coping with the gap between the demands of God's law and our imperfect performance in matching up to those demands: 'viz. penitence, and resolution of amendment' (Blount 1695a:199–200). Granted that less radical writers like Locke accepted the possibility of a general knowledge of the content of natural religion (here, essentially, the existence of God and the moral law), it would be hard to argue that this could not include an awareness that repentance was due for failures to live up to the injunctions of natural religion. Given the concept of divine justice held by the deists, it is equally hard to see why their God would require anything other than repentance to be reconciled to even the greatest sinner. So benevolent and reasonable a deity as this would not have needed a third party to carry the repentance over or make it acceptable. Such mediation could only seem an unnecessary and unhelpful complication.[2]

The arguments for the sufficiency of natural religion considered so far may be strengthened by a simple line of reflection to be found in Tindal and which he employs to lay the foundations of his entire case for the conclusion that what is true in Christianity (or any religion) must be as 'old as the creation'. Tindal sees a short cut in arguing from the simple belief that God is perfect to the claim that natural religion is complete and perfect. Granted that from creation God wished to give mankind some rule by which it could live rightly towards him, then his original rule must have been perfectly and completely matched to its end just in being the dispensation of a perfect being. If by 'a religion' we mean no more than such a rule for human conduct by which we can be acceptable to God, it follows that there must have been an original and perfect religion incapable of later addition or alteration,

> since no religion can come from a being of infinite wisdom or perfection, but what is absolutely perfect. Can, therefore, a religion absolutely perfect admit of any alteration or be capable of addition, or diminution and not be as immutable as the author of it? Can revelation add anything to a religion thus

absolutely perfect, universal and immutable?

(Tindal 1730:3–4)

We now seem to have completed the case in radical religious thought of the early Enlightenment for the character of God being such that he cannot be followed through a religion tied to any specific part of history. For we have seen how from his justice, reasonableness, and perfection it may be inferred that he relates to man in laws which are the presuppositions or foundations of history rather than being revealed within it. But the picture of an a-historical God must be further filled out by reference to discussions of the necessity of God and of his relationship to nature.

We find in these discussions the working-out of a tendency in rationalistic theology to deny any personal dimension to God's will and make it identical with the fixed order inherent in creation. The picture of God's immutability and impersonality this tendency promotes enforces a final and complete separation of God from history. This tendency is evident in Latitudinarian theologians, such as Clarke, who are rationalistic in temper. His *Discourse* on natural religion is one of the important sources for the idea that the difference between right and wrong is founded upon reasons derived from 'the nature of things'. The difference between right and wrong conduct is said to be founded upon 'the same necessary and eternal different relations that different things bear one to another; and the same consequent fitness or unfitness of the application of different relations one to another' (Clarke 1738:608). The notion that good conduct is defined by its fitness to relations between the nature of things likens the moral law to the scientific or mathematical, so much so that in Wollaston right action is equated with following the truth and wrong with denying it (Wollaston 1724:25). These ideas are not incompatible with the belief that all conduct pursues happiness. Wollaston, for example, argues that while the pursuit of happiness is a duty upon all intelligent beings, it will be successfully undertaken only if we follow the nature of things (see Wollaston 1724:38 and Tindal 1730:26). From the link between rightness and 'the nature of things' Clarke can go on to identify the moral law ('the eternal rule of equity and right reason') with the law of nature, arguing that the moral law must be universal and absolutely unchangeable because it is written into the constitution of nature (Clarke 1738:624–6). In addition, God must follow this moral law. His perfections, Clarke contends, make it necessary for him to follow it (Clarke 1738:627 and 638). Since he is perfectly rational he can do no other than follow the standard of right reason, which in turn means following the moral laws in nature.

Clarke's system allows God to have exercised creative will in the original fashioning of those things the relations between which then determine independently of his further volition what is right and wrong for both man and God (Clarke 1738:640). The thought, however, of a God of necessity bound to follow the rule of reason in the nature of things seems to leave little room for a personal and thus mutable involvement with the lives of creatures. It is in addition hard to resist the mutual identification of God's will and the law of nature which Clarke's Stoic and rationalist language at more than one point suggests. In more radical writers the one idea which might throw doubt on the identification of divine and natural law – that of a fallen and corrupted world – is absent. Wollaston can, for example, identify without qualms pursuing happiness, acting in conformity with the nature of things, and following the will of God (Wollaston 1724:38–9.)

The ready identification of the will of God with the reason inherent in nature has important implications for the manner and certainty with which God's will may be known. These implications will be explored below. For the present it is crucial to note the strong sense of the immutability of God these conceptions produce and the consequent impersonal and a-historical account of his nature they lead to. These points are nowhere more clearly expressed than in Tindal's treatment of the theme in *Christianity as Old as the Creation*. Following a Clarke-like account of the difference between good and evil, Tindal contends that the difference must be fixed and immovable. So, therefore, must be God's will since it must conform to the fixed and immovable natures of things (Tindal 1730:26). Any departure from the unchanging rule of good and evil would entail that God is an arbitrary being (Tindal 1730:30). Since God cannot be arbitrary it follows that the divine precepts cannot vary and the voice of God is fixed through all the circumstances of life (Tindal 1730:31). The inferences just recorded are possible both because of Tindal's identification of the divine will with nature and because of his vision of nature as essentially static. Here we have one side of his many-sided attack upon the idea that there might be some things in an alleged revealed dispensation which are truly from God and yet different in substance from the decrees of an unchanging natural religion. In chapters 10 and 11 Tindal uses the principle of God's necessary obedience to the unchanging, eternal 'reason of things' as a key premiss in rejecting the idea that God may give decrees to one people at one time but different ones to others at other times. Given his account of the source of reasons for divine conduct, he can equate such varying decrees with the arbitrary and the indifferent (Tindal 1730:116–17). They could not be founded upon any reason or be of any substance. He can equate that in religion which does not flow from any inherent reason, and is thus merely positive, with that which departs from what was immutable from the beginning of creation. Alleged laws which can be known only through revelation because they are beyond the law of nature must be merely positive in being commanded for the sake of commanding. They cannot really then be commanded by the perfect God at all.

So close is the identification of God's will with a fixed order in creation that it is hard to see how Tindal's thought leaves any room for a personal relation to God at all. Yet it would be too simple to identify the affirmation of the link between God and nature just described with what passed for deism in the nineteenth century, namely the belief that the universe has a first cause which has since left it alone to go its own way. That belief is essentially an expression of scepticism about the providential (moral) ordering of the universe, whereas in the religious rationalism we are surveying the moral character of the world we live in is central.

We can achieve a final clarification of these points by briefly considering Wollaston on the nature of providence. Wollaston argues from the constitution, economy, and design in nature to the existence of God (Wollaston 1724:79). The providence of God shows initially in his creating an ordered and law-like structure to the universe which will serve the ends of his creatures. This general providence will, in the case of mankind, be a moral providence because, as we have seen, there is a general connection in Wollaston's thought between following nature and being rewarded with happiness (Wollaston 1724:38–40). Providence and moral government are thus exercised in a general way, independent of history. Wollaston goes on to argue that even special providence in the affairs of man – that is, providence directed toward the specific ends of particular people – is most probably the result of the operation of general laws (Wollaston 1724:99–104).

I hope to have shown how the conception of God in rationalist thought makes incredible the kind of involvement of God in history that Christian theology posits. This refusal to credit the Christian conception of God relates to his disinterestedness, justice, perfection, immutability, and immanence in nature. In respect of all these things religious rationalists of the early Enlightenment found no case for supposing God could have followed a particular path of salvation in history or shown himself in a specific historical revelation. It is to the deists' conception of human nature that we must now turn.

THE DOCTRINE OF MAN

We have noted how for a writer like William Wollaston in *The Religion of Nature Delineated* the moral law, which determines right conduct for human beings, may be expected in the normal course of events to produce happiness if followed conscientiously. The natural coincidence of right and happiness stands out as a testimony both to the elevation of human nature in rationalist thought and to the denial of the fall. Tindal argues that the story of the fall and inherited corruption is theologically incredible (Tindal 1730:389–91). His arguments perfectly reflect those of Herbert and Locke in rejecting the dogma of the fall as incompatible with God's goodness and perfection. He also finds the details of the Genesis account of the historical fall absurd.

The belief that right conduct and human happiness are naturally connected produces two important consequences: one, a seductively easy argument for the immortality of the human person; the other, a simple account of the nature of salvation and human destiny. Both consequences can be traced in Wollaston's work and ultimately lead us to see exactly why the content of natural religion for such a writer becomes identical with morality.

The argument for immortality in Wollaston takes the following form (Wollaston 1724:199–200; and for an exactly similar argument see Blount 1695a:126–7). Though Wollaston believes that the virtuous life is the happiest in this present state of existence, he notes certain 'perturbations in human affairs' which

61

mean that some who are virtuous but unfortunate are without that happiness which is their due. It would be a defect in God's providence and scheme of justice to allow such an imbalance to exist. Moreover it would be unreasonable in God to have implanted a natural desire for immortality within us and not to satisfy it. Because God cannot be unreasonable in any degree and because his providential order must be perfect, so there must be a life after this in which undeveloped talents will have the scope to flourish freely and in which all will achieve that happiness their conduct entitles them to. This argument controverts that of Locke in *The Reasonableness of Christianity* which held that we cannot rightfully demand immortality and future bliss of God. The difference of opinion is down to the peculiar interpretation of God's justice, reasonableness, and providence we have noted in the deists. What Wollaston has done is to establish a presumption, through the arguments from natural theology he employs, that the world is under moral government. This government must be a benevolent one, given the belief about the relationship between morality and happiness Wollaston holds. He then notes facts which seem to count against the extent of this moral and benevolent government, only to conclude from his presumption that the scheme of government is completed and perfected in a future state. It is essential to the outlook Wollaston defends that the world must be under a perfect moral government. This is not just optimism, but a commitment to the essential rationality of things, which thus reflect the rationality which is the chief mark of the human person. Man and reality must be matched and in harmony.

It is central to Wollaston's argument that the future bliss we may expect (at least if we are virtuous) be a continuation of that happiness we enjoy in our present state. It is equally essential that the rules of mundane morality provide a complete guide to the achievement of salvation, or what passes for it. At a number of points his argument requires that a knowledge and following of ordinary morality be sufficient to achieve our highest good. This presents an immediate contrast to Aquinas, who (as we have seen in Chapter 1) does not regard natural morality as the whole of saving doctrine, since salvation consists in a destiny – blessedness – which is above that well-being achieved through following natural law.

The difference between Aquinas and Wollaston points to the

distinctive change in the concept of religion achieved by religious rationalism. Having followed Wollaston's argument to this point it comes as no shock to read this odd definition of 'religion':

> If there be moral good and evil . . . there is religion; and such as may be styled 'natural'. By 'religion' I mean nothing else but an obligation to do . . . what ought not to be omitted and to forbear what ought not to be done.
>
> (Wollaston 1724:25)

Having thus identified religion with morality, he can go on to define 'natural religion' as 'The pursuit of happiness by reason and truth' (Wollaston 1724:52). Religion so defined is natural in three respects: its doctrines and practices follow the nature of things; it has happiness as its end; and it follows human reason (Wollaston 1724:40–52). These particular consequences follow from the identification of religion with morality and the account of morality we have already discussed. Morality so described can be plausibly identified with religion because we have seen that it contains a sufficient knowledge of our salvation, and also of our immortality. Moreover, the natural moral law contains a knowledge of God's will, so to follow it is to serve the will of God.

In contrast to the identification of religion and morality, traditional Christian theology had taught that religion is a mode of worship and service of God not wholly absorbed in the simple practice of virtue. Aquinas adopts Cicero's definition of it as 'offering service and ceremonial rites to the superior nature that men call divine' (Aquinas 1974:2*ae*,81,1). Religion is a special virtue, being a distinct part of justice. It is offering what is distinctly due to God. Though natural reason can discover that service is owed to God, the determinate forms this worship must take are hidden to it (Aquinas 1974:2*a*2*ae*,81,2). The fact that religion is a mode of service distinct from the general practice of virtue suggests that it cannot be expected automatically to be universal. Aquinas indeed implies what must be the case if religion is a distinct kind of relationship to the divine, namely that it can only be present where the right kind of notions about God are held. It will be absent, for example, in its true form where faith in more than one god is professed or where the full ontological distinction between God and his creatures is not grasped (Aquinas 1974:2*a*2*ae*, 81,1 and 3). So that the presence or absence of the right kind of theology is necessary for religion to exist.

If religion is simply identified with morality such restrictions on the universality of religion vanish. There is thus a train of ideas which commences with the elevation of a religion of reason, leads to its identification with morality or virtue in general, and ends up by finding a new basis for the universality and comparability of religion. The identity of religion with morality becomes a commonplace in rationalist religious thought. Morgan defines religion as 'purely an internal thing, and consists in moral truth and righteousness, considered as an inward character, temper, disposition, or habit in the mind' (Morgan 1738:416). Tindal defines true religion as consisting in a constant disposition to do all the good we can (Tindal 1730:21; cf. Blount 1695a:135). Rationalism has a basis for the comparability of religion, and thus for seeing Christianity as but one instance of a general phenomenon, in the presence or absence of the pursuit of virtue in a culture. With the limitation of some acknowledgement of the existence of a supreme God, the scope of religion in human society and beyond Christendom becomes as wide as knowledge of the moral law. This not only provides a basis for that extensive comparability we noted in the modern concept of religion, but also for the naturalistic perspective it contains. The pursuit of true virtue is a naturally generated and naturally describable aspect of a whole range of human cultures. Moreover, fastening upon morality as the essence of religion provides one source for detachment from and criticism of the West's own dominant religious tradition. The measure of the pursuit of virtue can be used to criticize Christian history in the light of an independent norm of true religion.

We return yet again to the rejection in deism of the idea that Christianity rests upon a portion of human history which is distinct from all others and the means of making sense of the whole. The respect for the pursuit of virtue which flows from deistic humanism can be used in principle to dignify all ages. And those, like many epochs in Christian history, which apparently subordinate the pursuit of virtue to the practice of special, religious forms of devotion or conduct can be accordingly castigated. We have here a timeless means of evaluating religious history which knows no favourites. The philosophers of antiquity who attacked contemporary superstitions in the name of the pursuit of virtue can be celebrated as heroes in the history of religion and as wanting nothing that later Christians had. Socrates, for example, is given first place by Collins in a long list of free-thinkers on account of his scepticism of contemporary religious mysteries and his reflection of the virtues (Collins 1713:1225–6). Tindal affirms that the heathen philosophers must be allowed to have the truth about religion and human nature, if anyone had it (Tindal 1730:383–4). What distinguishes the Christian centuries for Tindal and many deists is not the unique presence of true religion, but unsocial zeal and persecution – that is, the very opposite of true religion (cf. Tindal 1730:406; Bolingbroke 1776:106–7).

The humanism that aids the identification of religion with human morality also supports as a consequence the belief that the truths of religion can be discovered through the unaided use of natural reason. While thus encouraging in an obvious way the elevation of natural religion, this humanism will not lead straight away to one conclusion present in the elevation of natural religion, namely the belief that true religion is in point of doctrine the same in all times and places. We have seen this latter belief to be connected with thoughts about the immutability of God and about the unchanging character of his will as displayed in the workings of nature. Belief in the sameness of a naturally known religion for all is of obvious importance in rationalist thought in relation to the universality of religion, to the search for common foundations for all faiths, and to the desire for a single standard of religious criticism. The unchangeableness and uniformity of natural religion will not gain support from its identification with morality unless it is also contended that human nature, which is the ground of morality through happiness and the relations between things, is itself unchanging and uniform. Preaching that true religion must answer to human nature and that human nature is uniform and unchanging in its essence puts another nail into the coffin of belief in periods of history unique and different in kind from others. It is also a direct way of denying the doctrine of the fall. It connects with the notable belief that human nature is characterized by reason, through the supposition that man's rational nature does not vary. A natural religion will be one which, on these grounds, is uniform, independent of relevation, and more-or-less identical with morality, because it is an expression of a uniform human nature which is rational and fulfilled through the pursuit of happiness by virtue.

Blount sums up belief in the uniformity of human nature in a statement which is typical of many others:

Mankind have ever lived and died after one and the same method in all ages, being governed by the same interests and the same passions at this time as they were many thousands of years before us and will be many thousands of years after us.

(Blount 1695a:93)

It would have been common to articulate the uniformity of human nature in the terms Wollaston employs, whereby the distinctive, supreme and ruling faculty in the human person is reason, and reason is engaged in a never-ending battle to subjugate the passions (Wollaston 1724:169–70).

The clearest and most penetrating use of the belief in the uniformity of human nature in the definition of natural religion is provided by Tindal in *Christianity as Old as the Creation* where it is combined with the conception of God's unchanging nature already discussed. In the context of arguing for a close link between religion and morality, Tindal in chapter 2 defines natural religion as consisting in those duties founded upon reason and the nature of things (Tindal 1730:13 ff.). Such duties, he argues, must always be the same since God cannot be both perfect and inconstant. It would prove an inconstancy in his nature if the duties he laid down in reason and the nature of things ever varied:

What unerring wisdom has once instituted, can have no defects; and as God is entirely free from all partiality, his laws must alike extend to all times and places.

(Tindal 1730:20)

Tindal continues:

From these premises, I think we may boldly draw the conclusion that, if religion consists in the practice of those duties that result from the relation we stand in to God and man, our religion must always be the same. If God is unchangeable, our duty to him must be so too; if human nature continues the same and men at all times stand in the same relation to one another, the duties that result from thence too, must always be the same; and consequently our duty to both God and man must, from the beginning of the world to the end, remain unalterable; be always alike plain and perspicuous; neither changed in whole or in part: which demonstrates that no person, if he comes from God, can teach us any other religion, or give us any precepts, but what are founded on these relations.

(Tindal 1730:20)

It would be easy to ridicule the belief in the uniformity of man expressed in this passage and in Blount. Tindal and other deists are not unaware of changes in custom and opinion across history and the globe, as their criticism of actual religions illustrates.[3] But such criticism is based on the idea that man's essence does not change. If religion reflects what is essential in man's relations to God and nature it equally will not change. This is one reason why they are so ready to put departures from natural religion down to the machinations of priests, a process extrinsic to the expression of the human essence. The underlying desire to see in religion something more than the mere sum of man's changing fashions and fancies is surely wholly commendable in the philosophy and history of religion. The working-out of this desire through the identification of 'essential to human nature' and 'unchanging' has important and far-reaching consequences, of which four need particular mention.

The first consequence relates to the positivity of religion. While Tindal initially employs the deduction of the unchangeableness of natural religion to criticize the idea that Christianity might offer a new dispensation, not available before or elsewhere, he is in effect rejecting all beliefs or customs in religion that vary with time and place. The point is contained within the quotation given above. His attack on the positivity of religions in history thus becomes not merely a rejection of beliefs and practices which have to be accepted on trust without independent reason for them being given, but a more general refusal to accept that what is valid in religion could in any way vary with time and place. A local, time-bound system of religion must be arbitrary, because it cannot follow reason and the nature of things when these refer back to the unchanging essence of man, God and nature. In attacking the uniqueness of Christianity deism substitutes in effect its own, unique, single system of belief. True religion is still a unity, but its locus has shifted from Christian revelation to natural religion, with the important difference that this unitary system can in principle be found at all times and places. Systems of religion and morality in non-Christian times and places can be appreciated by the deist not because he has discovered a love of the local and time-bound, but because he can see in such systems the presence of something not confined to any locality or time and standing above all particularity.

In so far as religion reflects what is essential in man and God's dealings with him it will be uniform, universal, and unchanging. The second important consequence of this belief is that, in a fashion, true religion will not be a part of culture and history. This is because religion is the product of a relationship between two terms (man's essence and God's nature), and these terms are not materially affected by the divergences of culture or by historical change. If we follow the logic of this conception of religion to its conclusion, we reach the odd result that true religion has no history. Kant (as we shall note in Chapter 5) was able to see this implication of rationalist thought about religion. Man's fashions and inventions are parts of culture and history, and there is only a story to be told of how these have come to enmesh and surround the universal truths of natural religion, though even this story becomes a repetitive tale of the corruption of the moral and simple (natural religion) by the self-interested and complicated (traditional religion).

The association of true religion with man's unchanging essence produces a third important consequence. The capacity for religion becomes for the deists, as for Herbert, one of the important distinguishing marks of mankind. When properly expressed in the acceptance of natural religion, it is a distinguishing mark uniform through the human race. It is easy to see that if reason is that which initially sets man apart, and if to follow reason is to know and serve the will of God through natural religion, then religion must also distinguish man from other creatures (see for example Wollaston 1724:169–70). Again, man may be distinguished from other creatures as a moral being, yet to be such is to be capable of pursuing happiness through reason, which is at the same time to follow natural religion. This consequence means that great importance has to be attached to religion in the study of human nature in rationalist thought. For the errors of religion are not peripheral. Departures from natural religion alienate man from his true self. To expose them is to reopen the paths to human fulfilment.

The link between religion and the unchanging essence of human nature produces a fourth and final consequence in the commitment it brings to a natural human religiousness. 'Religion' has a reference not merely to 'a system of divine faith and worship' (see Chapter 1), but also to a permanent, universal facet of human nature. This element to human nature exists and is expressed regardless of the circumstances human beings find themselves in. Natural religion is natural not merely in being not revealed, founded on reflection on nature, and produced by human causes, but also in being the immediate expression of a primary element in human nature. Traditional, priestly religions are natural in being the product of human causes, but they do not answer to human nature (in so far as they do not preserve the truths of natural religion), only to its corruptions. They are the product of secondary influences which take man away from what is fundamental in his nature. We shall see in the next chapter a tendency to articulate this particular distinction between natural and traditional religion through a simple idea, which contrasts that which is original to man and that which arose later through the influence of society upon primal human nature.

In tracing how key beliefs about human nature were important in contributing to the elevation of natural religion, we have detected resultant ideas about the nature of religion which are both helpful and limiting to its study. The elevation of natural religion leads to the assertion of religion's universality. It is also linked to a conception of religion's centrality and importance in human nature. But the universality of religion posited is limited to noting the presence of natural religion and of its corruption through priestly superstition throughout culture. What are given centrality and importance are not the local and changing forms of traditional faith which folk actually live by. The negative appraisal of change in religion – the lack of any notion of religion as a developing phenomenon – is evidently a grave limitation in the philosophy and history of religion. At this point in the survey of the legacy of deism we can see it as posing a major problem to later thinkers – that of preserving a conception of religion's universality and importance in human nature – while producing a more positive appreciation of variety and change in religious history.

RELIGIOUS CERTAINTY

We have seen that a group of mutually supporting ideas in early rationalist thought about religion leads to the inevitable elevation of natural above revealed religion. The aim of this section is to show how this goal can be reached by a distinctively epistemological route. The natural religion reached through reflection upon the nature of God and man consists of tenets wholly deducible from present facts by natural powers which all can in principle exercise. On this ground natural religion may be seen as the providential answer to the problem of religious certainty described in our discussion of Herbert. Epistemology, as well as reflection on God and man, leads to the rejection of revealed religion. No claims about revelation in history can be established with certainty, and no distinction can be drawn in practice between genuine claims to revelation in history and mere human imposture. History is once again of great importance in relation to the elevation of natural religion. Concentration upon the problem of religious certainty suggests to some writers that the past cannot be considered as normative for present belief. Beliefs to be followed in the present must be based on evidence available in the present; no such evidence establishes an alleged past revelation with certainty.

Through what it implies about the use of history as a rule for belief, the epistemological side of the deist case also highlights again the comparability and naturalness of religion. No parts of the human past stand out as epistemologically privileged. No periods of history provide norms for present belief or for the present search for human happiness. All are thus objects for present study in equal degree. Since from the standpoint of the present no distinction can be drawn with certainty between genuine revelation and human imposture, all past religious developments can be explained naturalistically. Epistemology suggests a strategy for the uniform treatment of the past, as much as any other source of deism. With that uniformity will inevitably go comparability and naturalism.

I shall now illustrate the chain of ideas that has just been described in general terms. It will be seen that the distinctive force of appealing to reason as a basis for religious certainty consists in affirming that religion must rest upon a faculty that is independent of, and indeed opposed to, reliance upon any authorities or traditions. It is an individualistic faculty and one that is concerned with evidence now available to the believer. Finally, it will be seen to be a faculty wholly natural in the manner of its operation.

The properties of reason, on which true religion rests, are in large measure derived from Locke's account of the workings of reason. A particularly clear statement of the essential characteristics of reason in religion can be found in a work commonly regarded as heavily influenced by Locke – John Toland's *Christianity not Mysterious*. Toland's title echoes Locke's *Reasonableness of Christianity* and his argument is an extension of points in that work and in Book 4 of Locke's *Essay*. It is Toland's case that there is nothing in true Christianity (i.e. Christianity faithful to the real meaning of the Gospel) which is either contrary to or above reason. So nothing in true Christianity can be a mystery – a proposition or notion impenetrable to ordinary, human intellectual capacities (Toland 1696:71–3). The presence or absence of truths and notions above reason becomes for Toland in effect the means of distinguishing what is superstitious from what is acceptable in true religion. Mystery introduces a blank cheque to superstition and falsity, for, once it is allowed, we have no means of directly checking for ourselves what is true or false in religion (Toland 1696:26).

Since Toland allows for weaker senses of 'religious mystery' and 'propositions above reason' in which they are acceptable, he leaves the door open to some assistance of natural reason by revelation. His customary classification as a deist by historians thus demonstrates the elasticity of this term. However, in his insistence that religious truth must be open to everyone and in the consequences he draws from this, he provides ample support for the full elevation of natural religion. If religious truth is so open, then everyone must be capable of judging the truth of religious claims themselves. This means relying upon the reason which they possess. Toland holds

> that reason is the only foundation of all certitude, and that nothing revealed, whether as to its nature or existence, is more exempted from its disquisitions than the ordinary phenomena of nature.
>
> (Toland 1696:6)

Relying upon reason as the foundation of religious certainty means, for Toland, relying upon evidence, and particularly that evidence provided by our mind's ideas, as our guide (Toland 1696:18–19); so that even faith, if it is worthwhile, must be 'a most firm persuasion built upon substantial reasons' (Toland 1696:138). This way of defending the availability of religious certainty enables Toland to be clear about the grounds for religious assent in a way that Locke is not. Despite the presence of arguments in the *Essay* to the contrary, Locke's avowed opinion is that faith and revelation are distinct principles of assent (Locke 1823c:IV,16,4). Toland takes the arguments to the contrary seriously and contends that, if all assent is rightly based in the end upon ideas present to my mind, then revelation and faith are not distinct grounds of assent. 'Faith' is but another name for reason, and revelation but an additional source of information at best. Revelation may contain some religious truths which, prior to my acquaintance with revelation, I was unaware of. But this is the only sense in which genuine religious truths may be 'above reason'. Once such truths come to my notice through revelation, I must be capable of inspecting and understanding them and comparing them with evidence now available to me. Without this openness to individual judgement religious truth, as opposed to second-hand opinions, would not be available to all. This in turn explains why there cannot be any genuine mysteries in true religion. Doctrines 'inconceivable in themselves' (Toland 1696:73) would remain opaque to individual assessment and judgement even after revelation. So they would have to be accepted *because* they were allegedly revealed.

Toland has asserted the sovereignty of reason in religion by denying that revelation can be a ground, as distinct from a source, of proper belief (Toland 1696:37–8) and by equating true faith with a judgement based on evidence. The limitation of revelation he proposes does not wholly deny the relevance of the past to the religious present, but it does subordinate the past to the present. The past has ceased to be a norm of belief, because that norm has been located in ideas clearly available to the mind in the present. Truths that come from history are to be accepted because they are open to present inspection and are warranted by evidence now available. The ultimate reason why this is so is perhaps best expressed by Toland thus:

To say that what we believe is the word of God will be to no end, except we prove it to be so by reason; and I need not add, that if we may not examine and understand our faith, every man will be obliged implicitly to continue of that religion wherein he is first educated.

(Toland 1696:141–2)

If the tradition that something is revealed is the *ground* of a proper assent, all religions will be based on 'firm' ground. There is no answer to the problem of religious certainty in such a reliance on the past for a norm of belief. As Anthony Collins points out in his *Discourse of Free-Thinking*, unless the ground of religious assent is our own free use of reason then we will be right in religion by chance (Collins 1713:33; cf. Locke 1823*c*:IV,17,24). Moreover we will have no means of sorting out the different and incompatible claims the past makes upon us. It is largely because the past, after years of schism, speaks with so many voices that the deists agree with Herbert and Locke that there must in the present be some means of distinguishing true from false in religion. The appeal to tradition and authority has become hollow on this ground, and so the deists are happy to embrace the anti-authoritarian and individualistic connotations of Locke's account of reason. What is essential in embracing religious truths turns out to be what Collins defines as free-thinking:

The use of the understanding in endeavouring to find out the meaning of any proposition whatsoever, in considering the nature of the evidence for or against it, and in judging of it in accordance to the seeming force or weakness of the evidence.

(Collins 1713:5)

Toland's reflections on how the use of reason answers the problem of religious certainty allow for the possibility that some religious truths are known only because some revelation in the past has prompted our reflection, so that without the help of revelation, though in principle knowable by the human mind, they would in practice have been lost to us. More radical questioners of revealed religion cannot allow even this limited role to the past. One principal argument offered against the circumscribed but essential use of historical revelation in the discovery of religious truth appeals to the familiar theme of God's justice. The means of becoming aware of religious truth must be commensurate with that justice and so cannot employ any specific doings in history, for specific historical truths, no matter how faithfully recorded by tradition, can never be universally known. A just God would not only give all peoples the capacities for judging of religious truth, but also make readily available any evidence needed for that capacity to function. Revelation cannot be evidence for religious truths if it speaks 'to all mankind from corners' (Collins 1713:38).

The above arguments point to the conclusion that if some truth is an essential part of saving faith it must: (1) be within the capacity of any normal human being to comprehend and reason through; and (2) be supported by evidence available in principle at any time and place. Point (1) suggests that it cannot be a truth above reason, in Toland's pejorative use of that phrase. Point (2) suggests that it cannot be a truth relying upon specific past events. We are close to concluding that it must be discoverable by use of the unaided human reason reflecting upon universal and plain facts of nature. We can get closer if we further suppose that if God is just (that is impartially and perfectly benevolent), then (3) the evidence available for an essential saving truth will be absolutely plain and make it perfectly certain. Conclusion (3) is presented by Tindal as yet another deduction from the perfections of God (see Tindal 1730:106). Only the simple, moral truths of natural religion can be essential to salvation and also have these three characteristics of being within the normal capacities of all, supported by universally available evidence, and perfectly clear and certain to the human reason (Tindal 1730:106).

The search for an answer to religious strife and perplexity has become a search for some religious truths of which the individual reason can be certain while relying only on the evidence directly available to it. This latter quest in turn demands that these truths be few in number, simple in content, and dependent on contemporary evidence. Morality, with the addition of a minimal theism and belief in immortality, provides such a simple set of tenets. Its truths are plainly available to mankind through all generations. They are to be contrasted not only with the claims opaque to the human understanding which Toland complains of, but also any truths deriving their evidence from the past. Claims resting on the past are excluded for a Tindal not only because they could be known only to a limited number, but because in resting upon evidence that comes from the past, they must be less certain than truths which deal only in the present. The tenets of true religion must be evident, and truths that depend on the past are not even evident to those acquainted with the tradition that preserves their source. Tindal's entire discussion of the comparative certainty of natural religion and traditionary religion (that is, one founded upon a past, alleged revelation preserved by a tradition) clearly anticipates Lessing's famous distinction between the accidental truths of history and necessary truths of reason. And like Lessing he concludes that only truths discoverable by reason and dependent on present, because universally discernible, relations can have sufficient certainty in religion.[4]

But why should a truth whose evidence lies in the past be for that reason uncertain? One could argue, as is done in Blount's *Oracles of Reason*, that the fact that there is no universal agreement on the truth of any revealed religion shows that none is evident, for of each we can say 'those marks of truth in it were not visible which are necessary to draw a universal consent' (Blount 1695a:221). This is, however, a weak argument, equating as it does the evident with what all will be found readily to accept. A deeper line of thought is uncovered by Tindal. The discrimination against revealed, traditionary religion it makes is in accord with much deistic criticism of the certainty of traditionary religion. A religion based essentially on some past source of revelation must, argues Tindal, be one which lacks sufficient internal marks of truth to be able to abandon reliance on its past evidence. So a knowledge of its truth now depends upon our relying in turn on the tradition which passes it on to us. This is itself an immediate ground for judging it to be less certain than a religion based wholly on present facts and relations. For the traditionary religion must be accepted through trusting fallible human judgements and not through first-hand acquaintance with facts. In addition, the tradition that preserves its alleged, past source will be an interested and therefore biased one. So, as Annet notes, the tradition which proves the claim that Jesus rose from the dead is solely *Christian* and amounts to no more than 'the bare testimony of partial evidence' (Annet 1743:89). No wonder such traditions decry one another and face us with a depressing scene of hopeless disagreement and histories of hopeless corruption (cf. Tindal 1730:222–3). An independent examination of the truth of such traditions now faces many difficulties and is bound to discover less certainty in traditionary religion than in the religion of nature.

Much of the force behind rejection of Christian tradition as a ground of certainty will only become apparent when we turn in the next chapter to the historical criticism of Christian belief inspired by deism. The sense of the difference in certainty between past, alleged revelation and the present truths of natural religion for a writer like Tindal depends on his rejection of fidelity to a tradition as a starting-point for religious, moral, or philosophical judgement. Judgement in these areas must be exercised independently of allegiance to any historical traditions. That a proposition or event is testified to by a tradition of thought simply becomes another fact about the proposition or event and provides no privileged access to truth. The testimony of tradition is just another piece of indirect evidence for the claim of a revealed religion to be weighed alongside any other piece of present evidence for those claims. In the case of claims stemming from a past revelation in some essential way, *all* the evidence now available is indirect. The externalization of tradition thus leads inevitably to the contrast we have noted between the uncertain past and the certain present. To be added to the externalization of tradition is the thought of its 'humanization' – for we see in Tindal's remarks the picture of a religious tradition as something compounded merely out of a number of *human* acts of witness, rather than containing the assurance of, say, the continuing witness of the Spirit (cf. Bolingbroke 1754:374). The way is thus clear to oppose a series of fallible, human acts of witness, which provide at best indirect evidence for a locally known truth, to the ever-present natural and moral relations which are the 'perman-ent voice of mankind' (Tindal 1730:31) or the 'testimony of God himself' (Middleton 1749:x) and which speak directly for the truth of natural religion.

The thoroughgoing naturalism of the view of religious traditions implied here will again only be fully revealed when we turn to critical work on the Christian tradition in the following chapter. A wholly naturalistic view of the sources of knowledge and error is indeed implied in the deists' consistent borrowing of Locke's account of knowledge and belief. Toland and Tindal, for example, both follow the Way of Ideas closely in their accounts of reason and knowledge (Toland 1696:9–13; Tindal 1730:180–3). Locke himself provides the apparent refutation of divine inscription as a separate source of knowledge. And the kind of direct, personal revelation beloved by Herbert fares no better in Locke's discussion of Enthusiasm in Book 4, chapter 19 of the *Essay*. In relation to both these contemporaneous divine helps to human reason a common argument is to hand showing them to be of no importance in adding to the certainty of religion based on human reason alone. For (as Locke demonstrated) in both divine inscription and direct revelation there are conflicting claims which cannot all possibly be true. Some of these claims must be the result of early prejudice, in the case of inscription, or imposture or delusion, in the case of direct revelation. There can, therefore, be no automatic inference from 'it seems to be inscribed/revealed' to 'it is inscribed/revealed'. The rationalists influenced by Locke see the need for a criterion to check such inference and the only certain one they find is provided by what is independently discovered to be true in religion by a direct application of reason. Inspiration, no matter how immediate, is not automatically to be credited. Men are

> to bring the doctrines themselves to the test of reason and sound judgement and consider their nature and tendency, thereby to know whether they come from the spirit of truth and righteousness, or of error and delusion . . . And therefore the doctrines themselves must be judged by the same test and rule as if they had come to us in the most common or natural way.
>
> (Morgan 1739:80–1)

But if we rely upon such knowledge from reason, then these other, more questionable sources of knowledge seem to become irrelevant. A knowledge of rationally discovered natural religion must be necessary if non-naturally produced forms of knowledge are to work. The entire set of ideas described in this chapter seemed to allow of only one answer to the question 'If natural religion is thus necessary as a criterion of truth, why is it not sufficient?' (cf. Tindal 1730:220).

Such naturalism in knowledge is ultimately derived from the fundamental belief that to judge of truth in religion by placing trust or reliance in anything other than our perception of the evidence available to us is a sin against reason, and in consequence against religion (see Toland 1696:19 and 145). Influenced no doubt by the Stoic sources of his theology and ethics, a writer like Tindal can occasionally wander into writing about natural religion being implanted in us by God (Tindal 1730:59). This does not disturb Tindal's otherwise clear commitment to a Lockean theory of knowledge, provided 'natural religion' refers only to the human capacity for religion. Tindal does affirm that there is no divine inner light (as Quakers maintain) and that the 'light of nature' does not deliver religious truths to us independently of reason's deductions from the mind's ideas (Tindal 1730:182–3 and 376). There is no need for an implanting or revelation of truth separate from the work of reason. This is because the truths concerning God's will we are required to know are clearly 'inscribed' or 'revealed' in nature itself, which in turn is the source of our ideas, and due to the beneficence of God our minds are well adapted to discovering these truths (Tindal 1730:106). The perspicuity and harmony of mind and nature and God's will stand out as fundamental underpinnings of the early eighteenth-century account of natural religion we have been examining. This underlying assumption of perspicuity and harmony in the sources of natural religion enables the epistemological difficulties in revealed and historical faith to count as reasons for the rejection of these forms of faith.

4

DEISM AND THE CRITICISM OF RELIGION

INTRODUCTION

If any one thing unites the thinkers now called 'deists', it is their readiness to question aspects of traditional, revealed religion. The volume of deistic criticism of orthodox Christianity is accordingly enormous. It has been comprehensively and excellently surveyed in works such as those by Redwood, Burns, and Stephen (see 'Works cited' below). I do not, in a single chapter, wish to compete with such studies. The aim pursued here will be the more modest one of analysing, again by reference to a limited number of examples, what must follow for the criticism of religion from, in particular, questioning the uniqueness of Christianity and affirming the humanity of religious traditions.

In expounding the trust of deistic criticism of revealed religion the second and third of the important contrasts implied in the notion of natural religion (as described in Chapter 1) will be important. The deists take up the challenge implied in the distinction between Christianity as a supernatural religion and all the rest as natural (that is, human) and attempt to demonstrate that Christianity may be considered as much a human artifact as other departures from the religion of reason. Their description of the human causes behind distinctive Christian doctrines, rites, and institutions makes reference to the kinds of mythical and civil theology Varro distinguishes. The distinction between the religion of the philosophers and the religion of priests re-emerges, with that of the latter being set down to worldly and political interests. In rationalist criticism of religion many aspects of traditional faith are

79

explained through the myth-making powers of human beings, especially as these are corrupted by designing and interested priestcraft. The general form of such explanations was not new. They had been applied to 'paganism' and aspects of Christianity before. The novelty lay in attempting to use them so as to explain away all that was distinctive in historical Christianity. Crude though rationalist criticism is on many occasions, it is a major step towards a comparative stance embracing all of man's religions that also sees them as humanly explicable phenomena.

We have noted the tendency in rationalist thought to locate the essence of religion in the preaching and practice of morality. It would not be difficult to come to believe that most of what belongs to traditional religions in their various forms is alien and distracting to this rational bedrock, since such systems of belief and practice end up by laying new injunctions on their devotees, distinct from and competing with the plain duties that pertain to self and neighbour. Those parts of traditional religion which are distinct from natural religion inevitably come to be thought of as hostile to it because they are corruptive of moral thought. The defender of natural religion is therefore inclined to be critical of traditional religion and to see its origins in something evil, if he sees traditional religion as hostile to virtue. A reappraisal and adoption of heathen philosophy's attitude to religion is one of the results of these critical attitudes. The history of religion comes to be fitted into an ever-repeated pattern whereby philosophic virtue is swamped by the corruptions of civic superstition to the detriment of human happiness and liberty. Christianity is no exception to this pattern. This history of religions is uniform, if uniformly depressing:

> Natural religion was easy first and plain,
> Tales made it mystery, offerings made it gain;
> Sacrifices and shows were at length prepared,
> The priests ate roast meat and the people starved.

(Toland 1704:130)

Through the readiness to apply the critical ideas described above without favour, the deists made some attempt, however crude, to set Christianity in a larger context of the history of religion and to show how an anthropocentric, naturalistic history of it might be possible. Certain of the elements of the resulting picture of

Christianity were already widely accepted. It would be common ground among thinkers of varied persuasions that for many centuries aspects of the Christian Church fitted the picture implied in Toland's verses. Medieval and modern Catholicism, it would be agreed, were akin to the corrupt, immoral, and tyrannical parts of paganism. They were indeed a departure, engineered by priest-craft, from something morally pure and simple, but for the more conservative the departure was from an original *Christianity* – a mode of belief and worship beyond natural religion but still praiseworthy. Locke in arguing for the reasonableness of Christianity evidently thinks that a rational and morally pure system of belief can be found in the Gospels and the Pauline Epistles. Going forward from the Apostolic Church he acknowledges that miracles persisted right up into the fourth century (Locke 1823d:449–52). Going back from Jesus, he argues that the religion of Moses confirms that of Jesus and can be considered as part of one divine religion (Locke 1823g:258). Clarke likewise contends that there is a pure and early core to Christianity which sceptical and naturalistic criticism cannot touch. Those who are inclined to doubt the merit of Christianity can only do so, he says,

> by confounding the inventions of men, the superstitious practices of particular persons, or the corrupt additions of certain particular Churches or societies of Christians, with the pure and simple precepts of the Gospel of Christ.
>
> (Clarke 1738:674)

Clarke can contrast the divinely assisted Church of primitive times with the 'later corruptions introduced among Christians' (Clarke 1738:678). Locke and Clarke thus testify to the idea of an original, pure revelation that was divinely sanctioned, and to the corollary of a pure, primitive Church to act as the custodian of this divine and reasonable dispensation. The divine warrant of this original revelation, and of the Church that received and propagated it, is shown by a combination of internal and external marks (as set out in the discussion of Locke in Chapter 2).

The attempt to separate out a pure and divine kernel from the surrounding impure and all-too-human history of Christianity in subsequent centuries could be defeated if both internal and external criteria could be shown not to be satisfied by even the most primitive manifestation of the religion. Hence the keenness and ferocity of the discussion which raged over the character of the Fathers, and of the Old and New Testaments. The deists tend to argue that, so far as the content of Christianity is concerned, no matter how far back one goes into the tradition one can find a mixture of reasonable and unreasonable doctrine, and pure and impure precepts and moral examples. In relation to the alleged probative external circumstances and facts, they contend that there are no convincing miracles and prophecies attending Christianity or Hebrew religion at any time. They way is then open to borrow the terms used by liberal Protestantism to attack medieval and modern Catholicism and apply them to the very roots and beginnings of Christianity. The clue to this opening-up of religious criticism lies in the human character allegedly found in even the primitive essence of Christianity. The documents and institutions of primitive Christianity are seen, just like later Catholicism, as human creations. They are not divinely inspired in any sense. They have, therefore, no special authority among human books or institutions. Their departures from natural religion are evidence of human error, not divine sanction.

A GENERAL PICTURE OF THE HISTORY OF RELIGION

The general scheme of the history of religion favoured by deism has already been indicated above. This scheme is remarkable, not merely in presenting the history of religion as a simple battle between moral purity and priestly corruption, but also in its commitment to an actual period when moral, rational religion was followed without its later surrounding superstitions. As one writer puts it, deism is the true, original religion of reason and nature (Anon ?Annet 1746:5). How could anyone believe that religion once did exist in its 'native simplicity' and that all of its outward trappings are later corruptions introduced by priests (see Tindal 1730:311)?

We have already seen the spell which these ideas cast upon Herbert (in Chapter 2 above). At the beginning of the eighteenth century they still contained a great attraction, as these words of Blount indicate:

Before religion, that is to say, sacrifices, rites, ceremonies, pretended revelation, and the like were invented amongst the

heathens there was no worship of God but in a rational way.
(Blount 1695*b*:3; cf. Toland 1704:7 and Morgan 1738:230)

Blount's use of 'religion' is most interesting in revealing that most
of what is distinctive in belief and behaviour in the history of
religion goes beyond, and is opposed to, natural religion. This
increases the oddity of the supposition that these beliefs and
practices should be explained as extraneous to the true core of
religion.

The fact that this naïve picture of the origins of religion
employed a pattern already familiar from the interpretation of
Christianity's history provided it with some initial plausibility. Its
prior use in that context offered one immediate response to the
difficulty of supposing that mankind, once in possession of the
rational truth, should later abandon it in favour of something
inferior. It was already acccepted that 'the plain institution of Jesus
Christ could degenerate into the most absurd doctrines, unintel-
ligible jargon, ridiculous practices and inexplicable mysteries'
(Toland 1704:129). A further explanation of how this general
picture of the history of religion could appeal despite its many
implausibilities can only be revealed when we delve into some of its
details.

Morgan, Toland, and Blount agree that the history of religions
began in Egypt. The apparent antiquity of Egyptian civilizations,
the witness of Classical historians, and the influence of writers
like Herbert all prompt this opinion (see for example Toland
1704:34 ff.). To explain the corruption of natural religion into
the various systems of 'sacrifices, rites, ceremonies, pretended
revelation and the like' a variety of factors was called upon. All
point to a complex and developed society as a necessary background for this process. The mode of explanation is testimony
to the belief that the corruption of reason displayed in actual
religion is possible in social circumstances absent at the very
beginnings of human society. This in turn suggests that the
corruption of reason cannot have been an original fact about
human life and hence that natural religion might indeed have once
been lived. The corruption of reason is a political process. No one,
says Toland, would voluntarily give up the use of his reason,
so the first corrupters of it in religion must have been identical
with those who first practised upon human liberty (Toland

1704:12). The belief in a natural religion that was once lived becomes one with belief in an original, free society unburdened by political institutions and out of which tyranny is a later corruption. Both beliefs seem to be necessary to ground the philosopher's optimism that a free, rational public life will be possible in the future.

Blount supposes that the corruption of natural religion into idolatry was engineered by the civil power in ancient society: superstition 'received its birth from princes, at whose charge it was after educated, by ecclesiastics' (Blount 1695*b*:7). For political purposes a cult of the Prince when alive is introduced. It is extended to the dead Prince by priests who see in this a means of keeping to themselves a cult in which they are privileged and successful intermediaries. While most lose from this oppressive institution, the 'crafty and covetous, sacerdotal order' (Blount 1695*b*:2) gains because it alone manages the sacrifices which are the means of finding favour with the pantheon that eventually results. The religions of ancient heathenism become in fact merely varieties of sacrifice according to the custom of time and place (Blount 1695*b*:36). Once instituted, the state finds that further civic purposes can be promoted through the practice of sacrifices and its associated beliefs. Priest and ruler continue in their mutually beneficial conspiracy against religion, reason, and liberty (Blount 1695*b*:42 ff.). Toland agrees in seeing the corruption of religion in a politically motivated introduction of veneration of the dead, encouraged by priests after profit (Toland 1704:72–3). The concentration on ancestor-worship as the source of idolatry is of course by no means new (see Augustine 1979:VII,19). Throughout the history of religions the progress of superstition is, according to Toland, linked to the loss of political liberty. So that when, for example, Rome was a 'free republic' the 'impious humour of God making' was not to be found in it (Toland 1704:98). Toland seems prepared to allow some original proneness to unreasonableness to explain the growth of the political and religious conspiracy against natural religion. So he can write, in a manner which points forward to Hume, of the 'incredulity of the simple' and the 'fluctuation of men's minds between hope and fear' as predisposing factors in the corruption of religious reason (Toland 1704:73 and 78). Morgan writes in a similar vein that the fall of man into paganism 'came about by the power of priestcraft working upon ignorance, guilt

and fear' (Morgan 1738:237). This at least points to some primal
tendency to myth-making upon which 'civil theology' could set to
work.

In deism we see a point of view which describes ancient
heathenism by adapting elements of both Christian theology's
polemic against it and classical philosophy's apology for it. The
civil and mythical theologies behind heathenism are described and
explained in the debunking, worldly terms of an Augustine. But the
theology of the pagan philosophers is allowed in its best
representatives as an instance of true religion in want of no
correction. Heathenism is a corruption of the 'Light of Reason' but
that light does indeed give perfectly sound notions (Toland
1704:116). The philosophers of antiquity did teach a pure rational
religion, which the people followed for a while until seduced by
priests (Blount 1695*b*:3). Philosophy remained an island of reason
amidst the sea of corruption. Those who think all in heathen times
were heathen are therefore mistaken and 'show their ignorance of
what is meant by the words, or that they perceive not the
distinction between the law of nature and all positive institutions'
(Toland 1704:119).

The political developments and growth of wealth which lie
behind the philosophers' lost battle with superstition indicate why
an early, primitive state of simple society was thinkable. Yet the
main reason for the acceptance of the simple history of religion
illustrated by Toland, Blount, and others is that it is an evident
deduction from the *a priori* account of human nature to be found
behind so much deistic thought. This account rests upon a
steadfast belief in man's basic goodness and reasonableness, and is
matched by a corresponding account of the obviousness of true
religion. It was inevitable to seek to found such optimism on the
idea that this reasonableness was once exemplified in an original
state of natural religion that is the historical starting-point of all
religions. We have noted in the preceding chapters how this belief
in the fundamental soundness of human nature and reason is
formed by a denial of the doctrine of the fall, and in that doctrine
there is a model for equating what is basic and foundational with
what came first in the order of history. The corruption of reason
and liberty comes to occupy in Enlightenment rationalism the
same place as the fall of Adam and Eve in Christian theology. As
in Adam's fall, an agent and circumstances extrinsic to the basic

condition of man are required to account for the corruption – so as to avoid contradicting the assumption of primal goodness (hence, the recourse to a special group separate from the great mass of humanity and the appeal to the influence of institutions). Railing aginst priestcraft and political power is not a cheaply polemical, extraneous part of rationalism. Without some such group as priests, and some circumstances such as political society allegedly external to human nature, the particular problem facing deism of reconciling the imperfect scene presented by observation with the perfection demanded by theory would be insoluble even on the surface.

We would all recognize that the general history of religions offered by deism does not in fact succeed in reconciling philosophical theory with religious fact, if only because the history is totally implausible when measured against the actual religious facts discovered by nineteenth- and twentieth-century scholarship. The notion that a philosophically pure and simple religion was actually lived at the dawn of history was the subject of devastating criticisms even in the eighteenth century (some will be discussed in the next chapter). Should we suppose, however, that, as Tindal hints, superstition and idolatry are 'mischiefs mankind have at all times practised' (Tindal 1730:88), it does not follow automatically that the idea of a natural religion that is also morally pure and rationally simple is of no use in providing the framework for the history of religion. One might still see natural religion as primary in human nature and still seek to represent the history of religion as the outcome of a constant battle between two ever-present forces: pure natural religion and priestly superstition. This might still recommend itself as a means of seeking coherence and unity within and between the histories of various religions. As well as providing less ground for optimism about the eventual triumph of true religion, such a scheme is open to two major objections. First, it can be seen to adopt the odd principle of trying to explain most of what is distinctive in the history of religion as secondary to the primary features which generate true religion. It was this oddity which convinced many later writers opposed to rationalism that one could not begin the history or description of *religion* from the standpoint of so simple an opposition. Second, one can object, in the manner foreshadowed by Locke in his criticism of similar ideas in Herbert that, if the scheme matched reality, one should expect to see much greater evidence of the presence of pure natural religion in the religions of history than was actually found.

An answer of sorts to such objections to the explanatory use of the idea of a pure, rational, natural religion is provided in Blount's *Oracles of Reason*. The outward ceremonies of each religion follow the custom of the country concerned, and these established forms of religion, Blount argues, naturally draw the 'vulgar'. These forms are so many 'superstructures', but the true enquirer will seek the 'foundations' of religion and not labour in what 'are only the modes and circumstances of religion' (Blount 1695a:202–3). In the hands of Kant this kind of distinction between foundation and superstructure could be employed in harness with the ideal of a religion of reason to great effect, as we shall see in the next chapter. We may note now how Blount is in effect arguing that any philosophically valuable history of religion will seek a unifying core to religion beneath its outward, nationally determined customs, because it will want to show religion to be the expression of something essential and important in human nature. This underlying core will, in the first instance, be the natural human religiousness denoted by 'natural religion' in its fourth sense, and secondarily it will be natural religion as the pure rational religion which is the immediate expression of our natural religiousness. Hence, no philosophical history of religion can rest content with the outside of religion or accept refutation at the hands of facts about its mere modes and circumstances. All such histories will be in the position, then, of postulating something beneath the apparently disparate and aimless external facts of religion. They will all want to show how 'the vast variety of religions which have prevailed in the world, are derived ultimately from a few general principles, common to all men because they arise from the common fund of human nature' (Bolingbroke 1776:192–3).

Many will think the general picture of religion's history in deism a crude offshoot of a one-sided polemic against established faith. I hope discussion in this and surrounding chapters indicates a greater depth to this admittedly simple picture than that. The general picture does at least try to describe religion as part of the political and civil life of mankind. It further seeks a genuinely humanist history of religion. By this I mean not merely a history which seeks the causes and developments of religion in things human, but also a history which attempts through religion to demonstrate important conclusions about human nature and to offer moral instruction to humanity. The means used to achieve these ends may be crude, but the ends cannot be dismissed. They constitute a fundamental challenge to the philosophy and history of religions which was rightly seen as such by later writers. Some of those who took up the challenge will be discussed in subsequent chapters.

THE CHURCH

The general picture of the history of religion favoured by deism is such that all departures from the pure natural religion preserved in philosophy are on a par. Christianity can be no exception to the pattern of description and explanation which philosophical history discovers.

Rationalism's approach to the Church involves a significant redrawing of the distinctions between pagan and non-pagan, and between true religion and idolatry. In European thought hitherto these distinctions had been drawn by taking Christianity itself as the point of judgement. The uniqueness of Christianity in respect of salvation entailed its uniqueness as a system of belief and worship different in character from all others. The point of classification is now switched to natural religion, and from this standpoint the lines separating pagan–non-pagan or true religion–idolatry have to be redrawn. The redrawing leaves the Christian Church as comparable to other religious institutions and as itself an instance of paganism, superstition, and idolatry. Consider one example of how this redrawing and reclassification can proceed. In so far as the Church is distinctive as an institution it is because it rests, among other things, upon certain distinctive rites and ceremonies allegedly necessary for the service of God. But to hold that God requires us to perform rites and ceremonies, over and above the pursuit of virtue, in order to placate or to please him is to suppose that God has special interests that need satisfying or that he is in some way to be feared. Both of these beliefs are false to the nature of God and therefore superstitious. Therefore the Church is founded upon superstition (cf. Collins 1713:37–8,132–3).

The way is now open to secure the comparability of Christianity with other religions in the most striking manner by explaining it as simply the continuation of paganism into modern Europe. This judgement is not so odd as it sounds when we recall the new basis offered for marking the presence of paganism, and the accepted belief that much of the Church had indeed been captured by Babylon. Paganism and the Church, which had previously seemed essentially different, could from the new standpoint be seen as similar. The redrawing of the boundaries could be done so as to leave the person of Jesus untouched by taint. For, as Locke notes, some could make Jesus 'nothing but the restorer and preacher of pure natural religion' (Locke 1823e:5). With this step the figure of Christ became divorced from *any* later Church founded in his name, since the point of his entire mission came to be represented as to preach the pure moral service of God and to decry rites, ceremonies, and functionaries in religion.

A striking illustration of this judgement about the place of the Church in relation to paganism occurs in Toland's *Christianity not Mysterious*. Toland argues that the great advance of Christianity that came with its acceptance as the official religion of the Roman Empire was in fact no more than the adoption by paganism of a Christian exterior, completing a process whereby Christ's simple religion became a thing of rites and ceremonies – all this, of course, in the interests of priests and zealously furthered by their guile (see Toland 1696:162).[1]

Using the positive mark of natural religion much could be found in the present state of the Church that could count as pagan. Thus Toland argues that almost every point of superstitious heathenism has been revived in modern Christianity. In respect of such practices, ancient and modern heathenism, Western Christianity and 'all the Oriental sects' are on a par (Toland 1704:127). The impression of the continuity of religious history and of the failure of the Christian Church to offer any decisive exception to this continuity comes over strongly in such criticism.[2] The rationalist critic viewing the present state of religion is observing the same battle between superstition and reason as the philosophers of antiquity. The religious scene is unaffected by the Church's official condemnation of idolatry and superstition: 'for notwithstanding the nice distinctions of supreme and absolute, of inferior and relative worship, all the common people are gross idolators' (Toland 1704:123). The continuity between paganism and Christianity is equally displayed in the forces really responsible for the shape of Christianity. These forces include the desire for 'riches, influence and power' on the part of ecclesiastics (Tindal 1730:311), and fear and excessive veneration of the dead on the part of ordinary Christians (Toland 1704:123). Blount's generalization about the human causes of change in religion is specifically intended to include the foundation of the Christian Church:

> all revolutions whatever, both in Church and state, as well as in matters of faith, be they never so pious and sacred or never so beneficial and useful to mankind ... yet they still must be seconded by some private temporal interest and have some human prop to support them, or else all will not do.
>
> (Blount 1695a:128)

In the history of religion, ecclesiastical Christianity turns out to be a particularly zealous and cruel form of superstitious wrangling, distinguished only by the intolerance which has accompanied it. It marks a *degeneration* of religion because in ancient times 'Men generally agreed in that mild and peaceable principle of allowing one another to think freely and to have different opinions' (Collins 1713:102). The cause of liberty, virtue, and reason go hand in hand. Christianity has turned out to be more destructive of each of these than the religions it decries as 'heathen', given its liking for persecuting those it disagrees with. Even contemporary Islam fares better in point of peace and tolerance. Thus Collins quotes and endorses the opinion that 'ecclesiatical history consists of nothing but the wickedness of the governing clergy' (Collins 1713:102; see also Tindal 1730:406).

As we have seen, many liberal theologians of Collins's day agreed with such strictures upon the Church, provided they applied only to a later corruption of something originally pure. Yet there was a considerable body of argument within deism for the belief that these criticisms could be taken right back to the early Church. We have met an inkling of this point in Toland, and a number of writers could be used to illustrate it further. I shall concentrate upon the argument of Conyers Middleton's *Free Enquiry into the Miraculous Powers* because of its clarity and completeness in demonstrating this point and its concern to show the similarity between the early Church and its pagan surroundings.

The specific aim of Middleton's work is to show that the Christian Church has never had any credible powers of performing miracles. Just as Protestants claim to be incredulous of miracles in the present Church of Rome, so they should be incredulous of the miraculous powers claimed by the Church throughout its entire history. Middleton offers a general reason for being sceptical of miracle-stories no matter when and by whom reported. This I shall ignore for the present, for it is of greater importance in relation to the discussion of the historicity of the Bible in the next section. In addition, he alleges many specific grounds for disputing the miracle-stories offered by even the Greek and Latin Fathers. What emerges from the exploration of these specific grounds is a picture of the early Church (the Church before Constantine) which makes it out to be no different in point of veracity and purity from the heathenism contemporaneous with it or the contemporary Roman Catholicism Middleton decries as pagan in his *Letter from Rome*. Middleton's significance then is that he takes the characterization of the Church turned superstitious and heathen which has been drawn to fit the despised Church of Rome and endeavours to show that it also fits perfectly the early Church – that is that Church in which distinctive Christian rites and doctrine took final shape. The general case against the credibility of miracles is important in this condemnation, because it establishes the point that the presence of miracle-stories is a sign in itself that the source which contains them, far from having a special divine authority, is fabulous and untrustworthy. This is how Protestant theologians react to Catholic miracle-stories and it is how, in consistency, they should respond to those from the early Church. The Church of the first century (that is 'immediately after the days of the Apostles') is exempted from these criticisms, because it is said not to have claimed miracles (Middleton 1749:9). Middleton makes at least a show of preserving a primitive Christianity that is not superstitious, but only, like Toland, at the cost of assimilating it to rational religion. Even such a concession to a pure primitive Christianity is left doubtful by the text.

In his specific criticisms of the credibility of early Church miracles, Middleton is concerned to show that the judgement and veracity of the Fathers is not to be trusted, no matter what kind of event they relate. This verdict is based on evidence to the effect that they were credulous, superstitious, prejudiced, enthusiastic (in the eighteenth-century sense of that term), unscrupulous men who would stop at nothing to gain their ends (Middleton 1749:xxvi). They were men divided about what the Apostolic tradition taught

(Middleton 1749:60). They believed in demons and they forged books (Middleton 1749:70 and 67). In short they were no better and no more trustworthy than 'our modern fanatics' (Middleton 1749:197). In the kind of miraculous gifts they claimed they were no different from the pagans of their day. In the case of healing miracles, for example, 'the same cures were performed also by knaves and imposters of all sects' (Middleton 1749:80). The credit and evidence behind the Fathers' miracles were no stronger than that behind the miracles ascribed to the Roman emperors, or to Catholic wonder-workers like the Abbé de Paris. In the history of such characters we distinguish the fabulous and the credible, ascribing the former to superstition and prejudice. From the standpoint of historical judgement, we must put the miracles of the Fathers down to the same cause (Middleton 1749:176 and 226).

Christianity appears to be tainted with superstition and falsehood down to its very core. We are left only with the Church in the generation following the Apostles, in which miracles were absent, and the Church of the New Testament itself. Jesus and the Apostles performed miracles, and Middleton is prepared to exempt them from the charge of superstition and fanaticism:

> The history of the Gospel I hope may be true, though the history of the Church be fabulous.
>
> (Middleton 1749:162)

The discrimination is a tentative one and its ground uncertain, given Middleton's conviction that by the very nature of the case a miracle-story is more likely to be the product of superstition than not. And if the Fathers are so corrupt how can we trust the Scriptures which have passed down to us from them? Middleton offers the thought that the New Testament enjoyed too wide a transmission in its early life for the Fathers to corrupt it subsequently. Yet he later suggests facts which tell against this defence (Middleton 1749:190–3 and 197). We may justly suspect Middleton of hiding his real conclusion behind these evasions. The point was stated more frankly and clearly by Thomas Chubb. It is impossible, he contends, to acknowledge that the miracle-stories of the second-century Fathers are utterly fantastic while also maintaining that the stories of earlier Christian ages transmitted through those Fathers are of undiminished credibility (Chubb 1748:225). Because of how we know about the beginnings of

Christianity, the distinction between its pure origins and its impure later growth has been placed in jeopardy:

> we know nothing of the first century but by, and through the second; and therefore, if what was wrote in the second century of and concerning the second century may justly be suspected, then what was wrote in the second century of and concerning the first, and what was transmitted to the world by the second as relative to the first, must needs be more so.
>
> (Chubb 1748:225–6)

If no distinction between a corrupt Church and a pure initial founding of Christianity can be made, then the boundary separating true religion and superstition will have been redrawn so radically as to cut through the text of the Bible and the teaching of Jesus. What is beyond natural religion in these will then be fit subjects for rational criticism and explanation. The last ground for giving Christianity a uniqueness and authority in religion will apparently have gone.

THE BIBLE

The deistic criticism of the claims for Christianity's uniqueness and authority naturally focuses on the character of the Biblical witness, for it was on the Biblical witness that eighteenth-century theology rested these claims. To question the status of Christianity as a uniquely divine dispensation was to question the status of the Scriptures as divinely inspired writings recording events supernatural in character. In the deistic onslaught on the Bible, discussion of the alleged miraculous, supernatural character of the events it relates and of the divine status of its words are inextricably connected. The common apologetic argument in Locke and others linking inspiration to the warrant provided by miracles was enough to ensure this.

The matter of the Bible's authority naturally concentrated upon whatever proof it provided for religious truths and practices that went beyond natural religion. The deistic denial that it contains such a proof at the same time sets the Christian Scriptures in a strictly comparative context. The Bible becomes like any other religious text which goes beyond natural religion. The Bible is either a work of human reason, in so far as it is a re-publication of the religion of nature, or a work of human un-reason, in so far as it departs from natural religion. All religions thus become alike parts of human history in their origins. The criticism of Christian Scriptures and origins is at once an attack on their alleged uniqueness and an assertion of their natural and historical character. They become episodes in a general history of religions which is conceived independently of them and which is naturalistic in the terms of explanation it employs.

It cannot be affirmed that the deists were the inventors of the historical-critical approach to Scripture and Christian origins. This accolade, if such it be, could be given with greater justice to French writers of the seventeenth century and to Spinoza (see Popkin 1979 chs 11 and 12, also Craig 1985:101–23). Nonetheless the importance of the deists as developers and publicists of the ideals and methods of historical criticism is immense. They explore and extend the idea of an historical investigation of the Bible and Christian origins which must be both governed by assumptions independent of allegiance to the Bible and Christianity, and also naturalistic in its terms of description and explanation. A great deal, therefore, of what we understand by the 'historical approach' to Scripture and Christian origins can be traced back to the deists.

The importance of the concept of natural religion in the development of historical criticism can be seen if we remind ourselves of what it is to treat a text historically. Something like the following five points give the essence of an historical approach to texts. To treat a text historically is: (1) to see it as the product of a human author (or authors) living at a particular time and place; (2) to see its content and form as dependent upon, and intelligible only against the background of, that author's intentions, beliefs, conceptions, and so forth; (3) to see the author's intentions, beliefs, etc., and therefore the text, as conditioned by the context of ideas of the society of which he is a part, and as a consequence to see both the author's ideas and text as intelligible only against the background provided by that context; (4) to be ready to accept the fallible nature of the text, from the fact of its human authorship and from the context in which that authorship is enacted; (5) to accept that the degree to which the text is comprehensible to us, and applicable by us to our circumstances, is relative to the distance in time and cultural space that separates us from it. Since this way of regarding texts is inevitably problematic and critical in its implications, it is possible to have more than one opinion about its worth and about the value of deism in anticipating it. It is problematic in implying that a text from the distant past will be for that very reason more difficult to comprehend and apply in the present than any contemporary document. We shall have to strive for a context for understanding such texts, and the older they are, the greater will be the struggle involved in even approaching a full understanding of them. The critical implications of the historical approach are apparent when we realize that to uncover the human authorship and social context of a text involves a readiness to see it as limited and fallible in the way all human writings are. Deism and historical criticism are in natural alliance. The elevation of natural religion leads to a naturalistic, historical approach to texts like the Bible, while the methods of historical criticism entail a degree of critical detachment from the text which fosters the search for independent norms of belief. The problematic and critical implications of historical method secure an important end for deism by calling into question how a particular historical product could be normative for present belief and practice. We may investigate the text from the standpoint of the present and may hope to learn much about it, but the terms we use to judge it must be justified by reference to the present and cannot without examination be derived from the past.

The target of the naturalism implicit in an historical approach to religious texts is hard to define, since there is room for an almost unlimited variability in the ideas that Scripture is divinely inspired and Christianity divinely instituted. A significant contrast between naturalistic and non-naturalistic approaches can only be maintained if we think of the rationalists' opponents as holding that God, in some manner, inspires the words of Scripture, and that in the foundation of Christianity events occurred which are without sufficient natural explanation. Such beliefs may still, of course, allow some role for human authorship in the production of the Bible and allow also for the founding events behind Christianity to enmesh in some degree with an enduring natural order. The form of the supernatural, divine character of the Bible in dispute between deism and orthodoxy is indicated in Thomas Chubb's key question (answered by him in the negative) of 'whether the minds of the writers were under such a divine direction as that almighty God immediately revealed to and impressed upon them the subject matter therein contained' (Chubb 1734:3) In other deistic works their opponents are also spoken of as maintaining that the 'deity immediately dictated to, and impressed upon, the mind of each writer, the subject matter contained therein' (Anon (?Annet) 1746:26).

Because of the nature of orthodox apologetics, much of the debate over the divine or natural character of the Bible boils down to the credibility of the miracles recorded in the New Testament. Accordingly, the prosecution of an historical perspective upon Scripture by the deists concentrates to a large extent upon attacking the credit of these miracles. This attack rests upon one, very important, matter of principle and a whole host of specific points supporting and clarifying it.[3]

The argument of principle for dismissing miracle-stories as incredible is the one frankly set out by Locke in the *Essay concerning Human Understanding* Bk 4, ch. 15, § 2 which we have encountered already. Locke's discussion makes it clear that when we are appraising the truth of the relation of an event we are making a judgement of probability dependent on the interplay of two factors: the bearing of the evidential value of the testimony for the event, and the bearing of our background-knowledge concerning the likelihood of that kind of event in general. So important is this latter ground of appraisal that should the event be *a priori*, very unlikely because contrary to our uniform experience, 'the untainted credit of a witness will scarce be able to find belief'. Quite properly we place, in these extreme cases, a greater reliance upon our general experience of nature than upon specific reports of witnesses. This presentation of the matter could be taken over by deism, because it so obviously coheres with the idea presented in the previous chapter that our present knowledge of nature will always be a more certain guide in judging of religious truth than any reports that come from the past.

If the knowledge of nature now available provides a fundamental starting point for judging the probability of reports, then miracle-stories must be dismissed as more likely to be false than true. They will be thus incapable of lending credence to anything else. Locke himself avoids this conclusion by suggesting that judging the probability of reports of unusual events claimed to be miracles involves an exception to this apparently rigid rule:

Yet there is one case, wherein the strangeness of the fact lessens not the assent of a fair testimony given of it. For where such supernatural events are aimed at by him, who has the power to change the course of Nature, there, under such circumstances, they be the fitter to procure belief, by how much more they are beyond or contrary to ordinary observation. This is the proper case of miracles, which well attested, do not only find credit themselves, but give it also to other truths, which need such confirmation.

(Locke 1823c:IV,16,13)

The rule for judging the report of a purported miracle must be different from that applied to an event not claimed to be a miracle, because the evidence of testimony must be weighed in the light of different background beliefs. We must consider the event not as one that took place in the course of nature but as one that could have been brought about by God. So, if we add a well-grounded belief that there is a God willing and able to intervene in the course of history and consider what sorts of ends he might have in so intervening, then an event of the right character may be judged *a priori* probable against these background beliefs. The whole report may then be credited when the quality of the testimony behind it is considered. Locke uses miracles to vouch for the divine status of Christianity and its Scriptures as part of a cumulative, holistic argument (see Burns 1981 chs 3 and 5 for a full exploration of this point). I have touched upon elements of this complex case in Chapter 2 above. Using knowledge of God's existence and character that comes from reason, Locke searches for a religion in history that shows marks of flowing from God and of serving God's ends. Testimony of miracles in this religion, if it is sufficiently strong, confirms the divine status of the religion by adding extra evidence for its being an instrument of supernatural providence. The parts of this cumulative argument are mutually supporting. Testimony for miracles is essential as sealing the presumption that the religion's spokesmen have a message which is more than human in origin, since such testimony tends to show a super-natural power and thus authority behind these messengers. On the other hand the supporting context of the messengers' doctrines and proclamation shows that the miracles reported are fit to be considered as miracles and not merely as blank, improbable exceptions to the course of nature (see Clarke 1738:696ff and Leland 1757a:297 and 1757b:90–1 for other versions of this cumulative miracles-apologetic).

Religious rationalism is able to call into question this entire apologetic for the special status of scriptural revelation, and the elevation of natural religion provides the means of doing this. The elevation of natural religion stresses goodness and virtue as the decisive marks of divine ends or actions. So if any relations of God's actions in history were true, this would show in those actions 'being subservient to virtue and goodness, and consequently to the happiness of mankind' (Chubb 1741:37). But no actions performed so as to attest a revelation given to a particular people at a particular time and place could display conformity to the ends of God, because such a revelation would not justly serve the general happiness of mankind (at best it would unjustly serve the happiness of a portion of mankind). The taint of *a priori* improbability can be removed from miracles only if alleged miracles can be shown to be likely candidates for intervention by the divine in history. No likely candidates can be produced, if they are linked to the attestation of a revelation so limited in scope as that of Christianity. Thomas Chubb neatly puts the point thus:

> But if such a revelation should be given to one nation or people only, when the rest of mankind stand alike in need of it, then it may be urged, that such partial conduct makes it probable that it was not God . . . who wrought those miracles in favour of that revelation.
>
> (Chubb 1741:42–3)

The counter to the cumulative miracles apologetic from Chubb moves from some seemingly obvious objections about God's justice to reinstate Locke's original, naturalistic criterion of probability. So miracles are reduced to the general run of alleged events which are contrary to the course of nature. The relevant background beliefs which might make scriptural miracles exceptions are judged to be inadmissible. The deistic rejection of the background beliefs employed by Locke, Clarke, Leland, and others to make the miracles-apologetic appear plausible should not be regarded as mere dogmatism. For the considerations relating to God's justice presented in Chapter 3 amount to the charge that the kind of cumulative apologetic favoured by defenders of revealed religion is incoherent. It may not consistently start with a rational doctrine of God and end by supposing that God has ends which are best served by intervention in history (see especially Tindal's criticisms of Clarke described in Chapter 3 above). It is hard to avoid the conclusion that the miracles-apologetic is indeed broken-backed for this reason, and requires radical reconstruction. As a further problem, we may note a point that emerges from the general pattern of Middleton's argument in his *Free Enquiry*. For the Protestant theologians whom the deists opposed, the relevant background-belief about God being willing and able to intervene in history and the natural order could not be supported by the present experience or witness of the Church. Present experience and witness were all to the contrary effect, and intervention was regarded as a thing of the past. Claims to miracle in the present were indeed signs of the invasion of religion by superstition and enthusiasm. This means that belief in God as a personal, intervening agent must either rest entirely upon a general proof from natural theology, or upon the data of history. The former seems difficult to accomplish given the kind of conception of God which *a priori* reasoning encourages, and the latter seems hopelessly circular because what is in question is precisely the legitimacy of concluding from the data of history that the divine has been at work in it. (This dilemma will be discussed again in Chapter 8.) Middleton's question to his contemporaries extends back from their attitude to the history of the Church to the very foundation of Christianity: 'How can you accept miracles as likely in the past, while dismissing them as unlikely in the present?'

As against the apologists for the uniqueness and special authority of Christianity, the deists claim that a consistent doctrine of God will either have him working miracles throughout history or not needing miracles at all. If God's purposes required him to work miracles once, those same immutable purposes will require him to work miracles now (see Annet 1743:96 and Chubb 1748:229–30). If human nature once needed the aid of miracles, that unvarying nature will require the aid of miracles now (Annet 1743:96–7). 'The belief *of past miracles* is destructive to the moral character of the deity' (Annet 1743:98, my italics) and to the coherence of any theology which tries to defend that character.

We have seen how the argument of principle against the credibility of miracle-stories gains renewed vigour in deism, because deism attacks the doctrinal and apologetic assumptions which allow miracles to escape the general rule of probability Locke lays down. The first rule of probability becomes, in Wollaston's words:

> That may be reckoned probable which, in the estimation of reason, appears to be more agreeable to the constitution of nature.
>
> (Wollaston 1724:56)

The lack of credit attaching to miracles recorded in ancient religious texts is then an instance of a conclusion explained in discussing religious certainty in Chapter 3: no past reports have any power to overturn beliefs which are certain and confirmed by present evidence. Before the incredibility of the facts recorded in Scripture, the credibility of the witnesses to those 'facts' must give way (see Middleton 1749:ix-x). From the nature of things we must be suspicious of events that depart from the normal. They require a much stronger degree of testimony than usual. Far from alleged miracles being exceptions to this rule of historical enquiry, it is essential to historical enquiry that we discriminate against miracle:

> to submit our belief implicitly and indifferently to the mere force of authority in all cases, whether miraculous or natural, without any rule of discerning the credible from the incredible, might indeed support the faith, as it is called, but would certainly destroy the use of all history. . . . But to distinguish between things totally different from each other, between miracle and nature; the extraordinary acts of God and the ordinary transactions of man, to suspend our belief of the one, while on the same testimony we grant it freely to the other; and to require a different degree of evidence for each, in proportion to the different degrees of their credibility, is so far from hurting the credit of history . . . that it is the only way to purge history from its dross and render it beneficial to us.
>
> (Middleton 1749:230–1)

So it is in the nature of historiography to be naturalistic and, because of that, critical of all that claims to report the miraculous. Miracles, far from being additions to the authority of Scripture, are reasons for withholding credit from it. They are not indications of divine warrant but of human error, superstition, and enthusiasm.

Locke's judgement on the Biblical narrative is reversed in the deistic critique in the interests of what is claimed to be a greater consistency.

The *a priori* judgement that there must be error, superstition and enthusiasm behind miracle-stories is confirmed for the deists by their detailed examination of the Biblical narratives, in which we find much that anticipates later Biblical criticism. The number of points made in this examination is legion. I shall pick out three types of detailed point, to be illustrated from the works of Thomas Chubb and Thomas Woolston.

We have seen that for Chubb the chief mark of any true intervention by God into the affairs of men will be that it serves the ends of goodness and wisdom. Such intervention will have to be transparently benevolent in its intention and outcome. But many of the reported miracles of Jesus do not meet this requirement. Of his alleged miraculous powers which are benevolent in intention, such as healing the sick, it can be asked why they were not exercised more widely. Why does he cure some but 'let great multitudes of the blind, and otherwise distempered people go by him'? (Woolston 1729*d*:5). Other actions show plainly that he is not a miracle-working agent for the God of justice and reason. Favourite examples are the exorcism of the devils into the Gaderine swine and the cursing of the fig tree, which Chubb describes as an 'unworthy application of a miraculous power' (Chubb 1748:190) and Woolston roundly condemns as absurd, foolish, malicious, and ill-natured (Woolston 1729*c*:4). Considering the ends served by the alleged miracles of Jesus, the stories, if taken as literally true, liken him more to 'a conjuror, a sorcerer, and a wizard' rather than the agent of 'the most high God' (Woolston 1729*a*:15).

The first detailed ground of suspicion against the truth of the miracle-narratives combines with a search for incoherences in the narratives themselves. For not only do the deists offer the theoretical assertion that we must be critical of miracle narratives, but they act upon this assertion by offering detailed expositions of oddities in the narratives apparent when considered as literal record of facts. Such treatment is in the spirit of Woolston's judgement on the narratives of the resurrection: they do not make 'an intelligible, consistent and sensible story' (Woolston 1729*f*:29). One of the many examples Woolston examines is the miraculous healing of the paralysed man lowered through the house where

Jesus preached. He offers it as a paradigm of a 'romantic tale of improbable and surprising circumstances' (Woolston 1729d:52). Such examples illustrate Woolston's dictum that 'the literal history of many of the miracles of Jesus, as recorded by the Evangelists does imply absurdities, improbabilities and incredibilities' (Woolston 1729a:4) and Chubb's statement that we are dealing with 'fictitious history' at certain points in the Gospels (Chubb 1748:187).

Such internal oddities are not surprising if one accepts the third ground of criticism we shall mention, which rests upon the proposition that the Gospels are not plain, eye-witness records of Christ's life at all. Chubb argues that the Gospels are an obvious mixture of factual record and of the Evangelists' interpretation and comment on those facts (Chubb 1734:18–19). Moreover, the Evangelists endeavour to relate facts 'which took place many years before those histories [the Gospels] were written, things they could have no personal knowledge of' (Chubb 1748:192). This points to the conclusion Woolston reaches in his *Discourses* – that the Gospel accounts of Jesus as a miracle-worker have to be considered as theological statements. Theologians should not try to reconstruct them as literal history, as if the Evangelists 'could not write an intelligible and coherent piece of biography without your help at this distance of time' (Woolston 1729a:66). They should see them as allegorical, symbolical statements employing the form of narrative history. For each miracle-story that seems part of 'an absurd and incredible romance' (Woolston 1729a:66) when taken literally, we can find a true allegorical interpretation that makes theological sense. Place the Gospels in the right literary genre (not that of attempted biography), and they become intelligible, their miracle-stories being then 'parabolical narratives' (Woolston 1729b:3).[4] Such a recourse to a theological, symbolical intent behind the miracle narratives is the only way to avoid Woolston's conclusion on their literal sense, which he expresses thus:

> there is not one so well-circumstanced as to merit a considerate man's belief, that it was the work of an omnipotent, all-wise, just and good agent. Some of them are absurd tales, others foolish facts, others unjust acts, others ludicrous pranks, others juggling tricks, others magical enchantments.
>
> (Woolston 1729d:29)

Just as the judgement of the apologetic worth of miracle-narratives is reversed by deistic criticism, so a similar reversal of judgement is encountered in relation to prophecy.

Whereas defenders of the special status of revelation can cite the fulfilment of prophecies made in one part of the Bible by events recorded in another as evidence of the divine character of the Biblical witness, rationalism sees in these connections further evidence of religious enthusiasm among the Bible's human authors. Collins, in his *Discourse of the Grounds and Reasons of the Christian Religion*, is famous for his advocacy of this point, and his argument is particularly important for exhibiting an awareness of the larger historical claims which must lie behind any defence of the supernatural character of the religion of the New Testament.

Collins is concerned to show that the argument from prophecy cannot merely be one piece of apologetics among others. This is because it is absolutely essential to Christianity to affirm that Jesus fulfils the religious expectations and history recorded in the Old Testament. Collins has two kinds of argument for this contention. One is the specific point that the authority of Jesus is claimed in the New Testament to rest on his fulfilling the prophecies and expectations of the Old. The Gospel writers and Paul, according to Collins, allege this link to be the chief ground on which the apparently new religion centring around Jesus rests (Collins 1724:4–13). Collins's second argument is more general and echoes points made by Christian apologists centuries before (see Chapter 1 above). No new religion, argues Collins, can present itself as entirely new. New alleged revelations are always grafted onto old, because their status as revelation would be in grave doubt if not presented as part of a larger scheme. All religions must claim to be parts of an eternal revelation, even though they come and go (Collins 1724:21). Christianity must present itself as the culmination of a larger scheme, and the divine status of Scripture accordingly depends upon it being seen as recording a coherent stretch of salvation-history in which the one God can be seen to be at work at all times. Collins concludes 'that the truth of Christianity depends, as it ought, on ancient revelations which are contained in the Old Testament' (Colins 1724:25–6). The two halves of the Bible must fit together, and the fulfilment by Jesus of the Messianic prophecies is the most central way in which this

103

could be done and a coherent scheme of salvation-history established.

In the course of surveying the connections between the prophecies and their alleged fulfilment Collins outlines a simple procedure for judging whether they match. In establishing what the prophecy exactly foretells, he takes it that we must be guided by its literal sense, which is determined by considering the prophecy in its Old Testament context and in the light of what its author could have had in mind. To see whether it then foretells, say, Jesus' actions as recorded in the Gospels, we must ask 'Could we have predicted those actions on the basis of the prophecy prior to their occurrence?' (see Collins 1724:253). The result of these tests is disturbing in Collins's eyes. When we consider the alleged Old Testament prophecies of the Messiah we find all interpreters 'have judged them to be applied in a secondary, or typical, or mystical, or enigmatical sense', that is, in a sense different from the obvious or literal sense, which they bear in the Old Testament (Collins 1724:40). Upon examination the prophecies are found to have a literal reference to something else and only an allegorical, obscure reference to Jesus. Collins implicitly condemns allegorical interpretation and reasoning in his lengthy descriptions of the absurdities to which they lead. The main point to emerge about them is they are no more than a form of 'cooking the books' since one can only establish an allegorical link between a prophecy and Jesus after the belief that Jesus fulfils the prophecy is already given. Thus allegorical reasoning is no true reasoning at all, since there are no limits to its employment. It cannot remove or lessen the fact that the literal sense of the Old and New Testaments are 'in an irreconcilable state' (Collins 1724:48), but is merely a bad way of disguising this fact through falsifying the text.

Collins, in his tounge-in-cheek description of the fantastic lengths to which the search for spiritual senses has been taken, has done more than merely pour scorn on one of the 'external signs' of the Bible's authority used in apologetics. He has registered and defended the opinion that Christianity was, upon its founding, a new religion. A different category for explaining its rise has been invoked, one which rejects the idea of a special divine stretch of history. The naturalism and comparative perspective with which this enables Collins to view the origins of Christianity is evident in the remarks he makes introducing his long list of new religions which have been claimed to be mere continuations of everlasting revelations:

> This grafting on old stocks, we see by experience to be the case of all the sects, which alike and according to the natural course of things, rise up in the several great and domineering religions of the world. Nor is it less true of the domineering religions themselves; some of which we know to have been originally but such sects themselves.
>
> (Collins 1724:21–2)

The implication of Collins's entire argument is that Christianity fits this pattern: a new sect arising out of an old religion becomes in time a new religion, while inevitably claiming to be but a continuation of the old. In fact it is only the interpretative zeal of the founders of the sect that establishes this continuity, a zeal common to the human religious imagination wherever and whenever we find it. It is in this that the continuity between old and new lies and not in the unfolding of a divine plan in history.

The various parts of the deistic critique of Scripture point to a common concern to establish the humanity of the text which leads in turn to anticipations of the elements of historical method. We can bring the various parts of the critique together, showing their link to the concept of natural religion and the humanism it inspires, by considering Tindal's comprehensive discussion in *Christianity as Old as the Creation* (largely contained in ch. 13 of that work). Tindal's advocacy of natural religion entails that, in so far as the Gospel is true at all, it is no more than a *Republication of the Religion of Nature* (Tindal's subtitle). This gives him a motive for making discriminating judgements with regard to Scripture and a standpoint, independent of allegiance to it, from which to make these judgements. Tindal is conscious of the fact that the words of the Bible contain much that is not a republication of the religion of nature. His aim, therefore, is to show in discussion of Scripture that we cannot be bound by its words. The verbal content of a religious scripture cannot be authoritative for a rational individual. He asserts that he is in favour of 'men's being governed by things, rather than words' (Tindal 1730:318). 'Things' here refers to the nature of man and God as delineated in the eternal, and therefore contemporary, truths of natural religion. The clarity of these 'things' is a good reason for Tindal to suspect any attempt to found religion upon words handed down from 1700 years ago. In his discussions of the Bible Tindal highlights the humanity of these words as an additional and important reason for questioning the place of ancient writings in a rational religious life. The negative critique of Scripture's certainty becomes a positive demonstration of its humanity. Tindal's method in enforcing these points shows that he is largely without new facts to present in his discussion. He proceeds rather by showing that his conclusions are already implicit in the theology of his day. Locke and the latitudinarian theologians supply his facts and principles. We have seen how in the general stream of eighteenth-century thought there is much rationalistic and naturalistic comment on the history of religions, including Christianity. Tindal is at one with others in using the standpoint of natural religion to publicize the extension of existing ideas to the Bible and Christian origins and to sharpen already extant modes of historical criticism.

Tindal's attack on the authority of the words of the Bible can be divided into a body of external and internal criticisms. The former make no essential reference to the content of Scripture; the latter do.

In beginning with his external criticisms we may note first his frequent reference to the corruptions and great variability discovered in the manuscript tradition of the Bible. This leads to the desired conclusion that we cannot place absolute confidence in its words. Here we have an indication of the historical unreliability of the Bible that comes from its place as part of a human tradition:

> supposing prophets and apostles impeccable as well as infallible, yet what certainty can people have, that those things which were taught by them have been faithfully conveyed down many generations together by men, who were far from being infallible or impeccable.
>
> (Tindal 1730:245–6)

Religion cannot be trapped in books because all are fallible and all ancient books are dependent on human traditions for their transmision (Tindal 1730:292–3).

The citing of 'external evidences' in support of the assertion that the original authors of the Bible were inspired and therefore spoke with authority is another object of Tindal's criticism. Tindal combats the argument from miracles to authority by asking why the reported performance of marvels should guarantee the infallibility of the author of a religion. Apparent marvels can be performed by evil men, and in any case a number of figures in the Bible can be seen to be inspired in the relevant sense (for example, some of Christ's disciples) but still capable of moral fault, even of lying (Tindal 1730:254). The apparent failure of these external evidences to establish the more-than-human authority of the text is confirmed in Tindal's eyes by placing the Bible and the claims for its status in the context of other religions and their scriptures. Other traditional religions claim, in fact, just as much as Christianity. He points to uncontested miracles as one of the external marks all the faiths claim for themselves (Tindal 1730:234). He can be seen here as taking up Locke's assertions about other faiths when Locke dismisses their miracle-stories as obviously fabulous (see Locke 1823g:257). Tindal asserts that this merely reflects the way people of one faith are taught to think about the faith of others (Tindal 1730:234). Locke would no doubt reply that the external signs of other religions can be dismissed if we judge their weight in the light of the fabulous and superstitious internal content of those religions. Tindal's interlocutor is allowed to contrast the books which 'contain the traditional religions of other nations' and the Bible on the ground that the former contain 'fables and monstrous tales' whereas the latter 'must needs be free from all errors of consequence' (Tindal 1730:326). In outlining what Tindal has to say about the content of the Bible, we shall see he thinks that this contrast cannot be maintained. Tindal has at least raised a fundamental question for the student of religion: should we approach all religious texts with the same expectations and modes of explanation? We shall return to this question in Chapter 8.

The theory of meaning Tindal brings to Scripture provides another source of external criticism of its alleged extra-human authority. Throughout he relies upon Locke's Way of Ideas for an account of what it is to understand a text. The sense of its words depends upon the ideas immediately signified by them in the minds of its authors. Recovery of sense depends on recapturing these ideas. Tindal draws out the full sceptical consequences of this notion of understanding. In passages reminiscent of Locke on the 'imperfection of words' (see Chapter 2 above), he concludes naturally enough that it is well-nigh impossible to recover the original meaning of the Biblical text (see for example Tindal

1730:287–90). From this theory of meaning Tindal draws the obvious inference that we can only recover the sense of the words of the Bible, if we can discover the context of ideas in which its authors moved: 'it will be likewise necessary to have an accurate knowledge of their manners, customs, traditions, philosophy, religious notions, sects, civil and ecclesiastical polity' (Tindal 1730:290). Though undeveloped, this is a clear plea for an historical understanding of the Biblical books. It connects with a point Tindal makes in discussing their linguistic difficulty – that understanding the Bible is a matter for experts (Tindal 1730: 236–7). Tindal, of course, uses such contentions to establish a contrast with natural religion and as reasons against regarding the words of ancient texts as important vehicles for any communication from God to man.

Tindal's employment of Locke's Way of Ideas extends to his rejection of the age of the Christian tradition as any kind of authority for the Bible. His interlocutor is allowed to say that the authority of the Christian revelation increases through its being taught in so many past ages. Tindal simply quotes Locke's *Essay* on the distinction between traditional and original truths by way of reply (see Chapter 2 above) and goes on to welcome natural religion as founded upon relations among things discernible in the present (Tindal 1730:294).

As we should expect Tindal casts a jaundiced eye over the internal content of the Bible. The criteria he uses to assess it are explicitly derived from Locke's discussion in his *Discourse of Miracles* and closely parallel those outlined by Clarke. (These criteria have been discussed in Chapter 2 above.) The result of applying these criteria is very different from that found in Locke or Clarke. Scripture is judged to contain many things that dishonour God, such as recording him as a deceiver, an oath-breaker, and punisher of the innocent (Tindal 1730:256–7 and 265–6). The Bible includes many examples of human immorality, even, as we have seen, in the case of 'inspired figures'. The Old Testament heroes are approved of in the New, but this only shows how deep the moral corruption in the Bible runs (Tindal 1730:263). Even Jesus is imperfect as a moral guide. Not only does Confucius have the truth of 'Do not seek vengeance on your enemies', he avoids the moral silliness of asking us to love them (Tindal 1730:341–2).

The internal sense of the Bible thus leaves a great deal to be desired and certainly does not set it upon some pedestal. Tindal notes further many instances of contradiction in the teachings of the Bible. These are nowhere more apparent than between Old and New Testaments. After a long list of contradictions on points of doctrine and ethical teaching between the two halves of Scripture, Tindal asks rhetorically 'Are there any thus so absurd, as to endeavour to reconcile Old and New Testaments?' (Tindal 1730:269). Like Collins he presents the Old Testament as the expression of a distinct religious consciousness.

Additional confirmation of the human character of the Bible comes with Tindal's happy discovery that both Testaments contain many assertions that with later knowledge can be seen to be plainly false. Among the most important of these false beliefs is that held by the New Testament writers in the imminent end of the world. Tindal finds this belief in Jesus himself and uses this discovery of error as a further ground for questioning whether the words of the Bible can be relied upon, even when they come from 'inspired writers' (see Tindal 1730:262).

Finally, we should note the frequent places where Tindal laments the inherent obscurity of Scripture (see for example the remarks on the Trinity, Tindal 1730:322–3). For him, this is yet another mark that it does not come from God as natural religion describes God to us. It is useless as religious authority.

Tindal is aware that the force of these strictures upon the content of the Bible can be mitigated or escaped altogether, if one is allowed to argue that in the offending passages the literal sense of the text is subordinate to a spiritual sense free of defect. Our apparent perception of things contrary to the honour of God, of immoralities and so on, can then just be taken to be evidence that we had not grasped the true spiritual sense behind the imperfect literal message of the words. Tindal accordingly attacks the readiness to allegorize the text of the Bible, agreeing with Collins that there are no rational constraints on allegorical reasoning. Its use will result in our being unable to rely on anything said in Scripture (Tindal 1730:226). Once we indulge in allegory, we do away with the idea that the text has any certain sense at all.

Our brief review of Tindal on the Bible demonstrates how the advocacy of natural religion leads to an approach to the Biblical writings which incorporates the five important aspects of an historical understanding that have been distinguished. Tindal's anticipation of an historical approach is not employed to give any detailed, positive interpretation of Scripture. The most, for example, that we learn about the Jesus of the Gospels is that, apart from having an expectation of an imminent end to the world, he did not aim to teach new moral principles but merely to induce sinners to repent of breaches of already known duties (Tindal 1730:48–9). But the nature and significance of this mission is not clear from Tindal's text, for he says in the same place that each of us has sufficient knowledge to be his own physician in removing the sickness of sin. Since the Bible cannot teach new, distinctive doctrines and at the same time be correct, and since even Jesus was deceived on some material matters, the impression given by Tindal is that the Gospel is redundant and at best a very imperfect republication of the religion of nature.[5] Tindal's historicism is, then, developed in the service of his negative aim of showing that the words of the Bible are not to be compared as a ground for judging religious truth with the material facts that are the basis of natural religion. Yet we have also seen a positive end intertwined with his critique, and with deistic criticism of the Bible in general. Tindal has claimed the text for human authorship.

5

THE PROGRESS OF THE CONCEPT OF NATURAL RELIGION

INTRODUCTION

Examination of the deists' positive and critical ideas about the nature of religion has revealed the extent to which their conception of religion approaches what I have called our modern perspective on religion.

Their notion of religion has been seen to have an important universal element and thrust. All religions become comparable. Any one religion becomes an instance of a general category of phenomena to be found in principle at all times and places. There is a universal and uniform human awareness of the moral law, which just as universally gets overlain by the superstitions and corruptions of popular religion. Each faith is then seen as an instance of a general class, and all can be used to illustrate and add to our understanding of how the the general class ('religion') arises and develops.

They also have a strong sense of the humanity of religion, religion for them resting on human causes, whether good or bad. If one regards the modern assumption of the humanity of religious phenomena as an achievement, one will be inclined in this regard to consider the deists' critique of the concept of revelation, and with it the concept of a 'divine' religion, as a major advance in thought. For the deists present with great clarity the historically vital idea that, for all that religion focuses on a divine object, its character can be explained by reference to the principles of human nature. This naturally leads to an historical perspective on religions. For now even the founding of the allegedly divine religion, Christianity, becomes the subject of independent historical enquiry. We have the idea of an independent historical investigation of religious change and development which will illustrate the universal principles of human nature. With this has come a new perspective on scriptural documents. They are no longer to be seen as offering unique insights into salvation or divine history, but instead are parts of history, namely the history of a particular people at a particular time and place.

If we are content with the way religion is viewed in the modern study of religion we might see the elements in the legacy of deism just listed as major advances, but would have at the same time to acknowledge much that was imperfect in the deistic anticipation of our modern perspective. All these imperfections stem from the identification of the original and natural religion of mankind with the philosopher's religion of reason. This identification produces a distorting influence on the deists' conception of religion's universality, of its humanity, and of its historical character.

The notion of religion's universality is distorted through the continued belief that religion is a unity. Deism does not in the last resort abandon the older theological idea that there is a single unique religion; it merely replaces the belief that this religion resides in Christianity with the belief that it is to be found in the religion of reason. Little room is left for the possibility that *different* sets of beliefs and practices could equally be manifestations of religion. Rather, each of the world's faiths must be ransacked for the presence of a single set of beliefs if they are to be judged true examples of religion. That in which they differ – their peculiar customs, institutions, and theologies – is also that which detracts from their character as examples of religion, since the differences among faiths are evidence of the corruptions of religion by local superstition etc. The humanity of religion suffers through the identification of the religion of reason with the natural religion of mankind because of the manner in which it encourages so limited an account of the human causes of religion. These causes boil down to reason and its corruptions. Indeed, much that is part of what we want to call religion turns out to flow not from humanity as such but from the corruption of humanity, from processes which are extraneous to the human essence. They are evidence of our ability in history to depart from that which makes us human. All this connects with the distorted conception of the historical character of religion which the same identification leads to. As noted in the discussion of Matthew Tindal above, the centrality given to the timeless religion of reason yields a static view of religion as a whole, to the extent that, in so far as religion is subject to change at all it ceases to reflect anything humanly important. One can give an identical account of the origins and development of faiths wherever and whenever one finds them.

These various deficiencies have clear implications for the type of description and investigation of religious phenomena they encourage, leading to flaws in method and explanation which should be apparent from the material surveyed in Chapter 4. Progress in the study of religion was only possible therefore if the underlying identification of natural religion with the religion of reason was questioned as the Enlightenment and its succeeding stages in European thought developed. In this and the following chapter one line of reflection on natural religion which questions this identification will be pursued. No attempt can be made to discuss all or even most of those thinkers responsible for the development of our modern concept of religion. A narrow thread will be traced through Hume, Kant, and a group of writers who influenced or were influenced by romanticism, namely Herder, Schleiermacher, and Hegel. This narrow selection will, however, be found sufficient to raise the important issues about the nature of religion in relation to human nature and history that need to be grasped if the larger movement of thought it illustrates is to be understood. Moreover, the line of reflection selected here will be found to lead to our modern concept of religion. This result will be confirmed in Chapter 7, where we see important ideas from it at work in representative historians and anthropologists who pioneered the study of religion as we now know it. And this line of reflection contains enough to raise some of the critical questions to be discussed in Chapter 8 in relation to modern students and theorists of religion. These questions include: how far does the very business of the study of religion commit one to a fully human, fully historical, fully universal account of religion? Or, how deep is the naturalism behind our modern concept of religion?

HUME ON THE NATURAL RELIGION OF MANKIND

A discussion of Hume's treatment of religion is important for our purposes because he is an eighteenth-century writer who provides strong arguments for the naturalness and humanity of religion, while also arguing equally strongly that the religion of reason is not the original and natural religion of mankind.

A preliminary survey of his views may be given by using the four senses of 'natural religion' distinguished in earlier chapters. I shall consider Senses 3 and 4 first, for it is in relation to these two senses that the most positive emphases in Hume's philosophy of religion come out. It is with respect to Senses 3 and 4 that Hume's treatment of the naturalness of religion and its relation to human nature can be reviewed. In the third sense of 'natural religion', a natural religion is one that is humanly produced or caused, as opposed to a divine or supernatural religion that is instituted by God. I shall concentrate on this sense of natural religion for the moment.

There can be no doubt that when Hume announces at the beginning of *The Natural History of Religion* that he means to treat of the origins of religion in human nature, he is implicitly affirming that religion *does* have its origins in human nature (Hume 1976:25). In this respect he is at one with the deists, even though much of his subsequent treatment of religion seems directly opposed to theirs. In his insistence that religion does have its origin in human nature, Hume may be seen to be repeating and reinforcing a conclusion of the deists' ideas – that all of man's religions are natural religions. Like them he rejects the contrast between natural and divine religions.

Hume may thus be regarded as an advocate of natural religion if by that is meant only that he advances the view that religion is entirely a human phenomenon. This may be seen clearly enough in his treatment of the range of causes behind popular religion in *The Natural History*. But it is equally evident in the essay on miracles in the first *Enquiry*. Hume is here directly commenting on the normative question: 'Could a miracle ever be so well attested as to justify us in accepting the revelation it accredits?' But he is also commenting on the historical question of whether there are grounds for supposing that any religion had a miraculous starting-point. Each of the essay's two sections contributes to a negative answer to this historical question. The first repeats, albeit unconsciously, the deists' general argument against crediting miracle-stories, discussed in Chapter 4 above.[1] The argument of this section allows Hume to conclude that miracles are inherently unlikely and that the historian always has reason for seeking an alternative to supernatural intervention when considering the founding of any religion. The second section of the essay is then able to point to the more mundane and much more probable causes of the growth of miracle stories and the new sects and religions that spring out of them. The historian can give an account of these matters through attention to the kind of societies in which miracle-stories arise – societies which are 'ignorant and barbarous', where custom and tradition rule and which have no sure knowledge of the order of nature (Hume 1975:117–19). In such societies men's natural love of the wonderful and marvellous is not checked by education and the cultivation of good sense, so that their members inevitably live in a world filled with 'prodigies, omens and oracles' (Hume 1975:119). The historian can thus see 'that there is nothing mysterious or supernatural in the case' (Hume 1975:119).

We may therefore put Hume fairly and squarely with the deists in his denial of any divine origin for human religion. This is to agree with those who see the final sentence of the essay on miracles as pure irony. Hume writes that Christianity was not only first attended with miracles

> but even at this day cannot be believed by any reasonable person without one . . . And who is ever moved by faith to assent to it is conscious of a continued miracle in his own person, which subverts all the principles of his understanding, and gives him a determination to believe what is most contrary to custom and experience.
>
> (Hume 1975:131)

There is irony here not just through the tounge-in-cheek description of faith as a possibility, but in the account of the subversion of the understanding as something that is a miracle for religious man. Hume has told us earlier that 'all proceeds from the usual propensity of mankind towards the marvellous', which though it may gain some check from sense and learning remains an ingrained part of human nature (Hume 1975:119). So there really can be no miracle in the origin and persistence of beliefs about supernatural intervention into human affairs.

But if Hume may be classed with the deists in his rejection of the notion of divine religion, there are two respects in which his treatment of this theme is different. One difference arises out of his discussion of miracle; one arises out of the particular way in which he views human nature.

There is a major weakness in Hume's treatment of miracle which is absent from the best deistic discussions. The weakness may be isolated in Hume's statement of the conclusion that miracles are inherently unlikely:

> A miracle is a violation of the laws of nature; and as a firm and unalterable experience has established these laws, the proof against a miracle, from the very nature of the fact, is as entire as any argument from experience can be.

> (Hume 1975:114)

To reason that miracles are overwhelmingly unlikely simply on the grounds that they are against empirically established laws of nature is to ignore the fact they are also held to be interventions of the divine in nature. Their antecedent probability is thus to be assessed differently from that of a mere exception to natural law, and, as we noted in Chapter 4, it remains open to the apologist to argue that some alleged miracles may become antecedently likely when considered as candidates for divine intervention. If the circumstances of these events are considered in the light of the presumed purposes of God, the events may be judged worthy of credit, as Locke and others argued. To ignore this way of assessing the probability of miracle stories is in effect to define them out of existence, since it is to allow their probability to be assessed only under a description (that is, 'violation of the laws of nature') which is misleading as to their true character. What is lacking in Hume is that dimension of criticism we find in Chubb and others which takes the full description of and apologetic for miracles on board and assesses their probability as divinely purposed interventions into history. This in turn means that Hume's treatment does not have the full depth of the deistic investigation of the idea that there might be a divine religion alongside the purely natural ones to be found in human history. We have seen in Chapter 4 that the deistic onslaught on miracles is part of a much larger critical discussion of the justice of God's purposes in selecting some particular culture or epoch to be the recipient of a divine faith. It is a discussion which therefore matches the apologetic in which appeal is made to miracles as a guarantee of the divine origin of religion. We may conclude that, not only does Hume's treatment of miracles unconsciously repeat the range of the deistic criticism of the notion, but also that it is not as full or as sophisticated as that of the deists.

The other difference between the deists' and Hume's treatment of the naturalness of religion can be brought out by considering an important ambiguity in the idea that a naturalistic origin for religion must be sought. This could entail no more than the exclusion of supernatural intervention in history or divine aid in the operation of human powers when seeking to account for the existence of religion. Such naturalism is still quite compatible with setting human nature in the context of some form of religious metaphysics, giving, for example, a divine origin or destiny for human nature. Whereas naturalism might, on a different understanding, entail not only the appeal to human or mundane or secondary causes in the explanation of religion, but also the setting of those causes in a wholly secularized account of human nature. This ambiguity will be important as the survey of the development of the concept of religion proceeds. It will be seen to be connected with the question of whether a naturalistic perspective on religious history is compatible with seeing some overall religious purpose to such history. It also raises the matter of whether a naturalistic perspective is able to take religious categories seriously, or must, because it rests on a secularized account of human nature, be dismissive of them.

If we base the history of religion on human causes, it matters what account we give of human nature. Recent studies by Duncan Forbes have brought out the extent to which Hume's naturalism in ethics, politics and history was radically secularized. Hume set himself the task of banishing belief in the existence of God and any religious metaphysics from the science of human affairs. With them went all allegedly false idealizations they promoted (such as belief in the supremacy of human reason in history). In their place was to be set a wholly secularized and one-dimensional account of human and social facts (see Forbes 1982:194). Among the 'religious' accounts of human nature Hume is opposing may be listed not only the obvious targets – philosophies which urge divine revelation or inscription as the origin of human notions or propensities – but also the deists, who still give an account of human nature from within a form of religious metaphysics. The manner in which this account leads to what is, in Hume's view, a false idealization of the origins of religion will be explored below. The deists, for all their differences from orthodox Christian theology or from the platonism of such writers as Herbert, still give an account of human nature which is religious after a fashion. They set their picture of man within a providential and moral ordering of the world. In this lies the second major difference between their conclusion that all religion is natural and Hume's similar conclusion. As noted above, the clarity of the providential order the deists cling to and the harmony that exists between it and the mind of man is a vital part of the deistic outlook. In this way reason can attain to a religious object, discerning the moral order in creation, and human happiness is completed by a religious mechanism, the apportioning of reward to desert in a life to come. Though it is right to see the deist's critique of revelation and rejection of inscription as decisive moves toward naturalism in the study of religion, a different form of naturalism is involved in Hume's treatment of religion. We shall see below that the deists' form of naturalism can attribute a depth of meaning to religious facts that Hume's cannot.

This second major difference between the deistic rejection of divine religion and Hume's is linked to the fourth sense of 'natural religion', for we shall find that Hume rejects the notion that there is a natural human religiousness, something that deism accepts and locates in reason. This entails that the deists, but not Hume, are committed to the existence of something in human nature that can serve both as the vehicle for discerning a *general* revelation and as the connecting link between a providential order in nature and the human mind. Hume's rejection of divine causes for human religious developments is decidedly not a step toward showing that all religions rest on a core provided by a fundamental religious principle in man which can never be expunged and which unites all religions worthy of the name. To accept this way of tracing the causes of religion to human nature is to grant too much to a religious vision of human nature and to indulge in a false idealization of the causes of religion.

If we now turn briefly to the second and first senses of the phrase 'natural religion', we see further interesting differences between Hume and the deists. These differences emerge from points made already.

The distinction between natural theology and civil and mythical is present only in attenuated form in Hume's writings on religion. *The Natural History of Religion*, the *Dialogues concerning Natural Religion*, and various of Hume's essays describe the basis of popular religious thought as resting upon politically motivated priestcraft and the imaginations of believers – see for example the conventional description of the operation of priestcraft in 'Of National Characters' (Hume 1882a:254). And there is some kind of contrast drawn between this sort of religion and a religion of philosophers. Philo in the *Dialogues* allows the following to count as a description of a philosophical and rational kind of religion:

> The proper office of religion is to regulate the hearts of men, humanise their conduct, infuse the spirit of temperance, order and obedience; and as its operation is silent, and only enforces the motives of morality and justice, it is in danger of being overlooked and confounded with these other motives. When it distinguishes itself, and acts as a separate principle over men, it has departed from its proper sphere, and has become only a cover to faction and ambition.
>
> (Hume 1976:251–2)

None of this amounts, however, to a substantial use of the distinction between a philosophical religion and a religion based on human politics and myth-making. In the first place the true philosophical religion described in the *Dialogues* is all but invisible, as the quotation indicates. It is little more than right moral motives under another name. It is not something added to these, as a philosophical metaphysics founded upon reflection on nature would be.[2] Furthermore, a reading of the *Dialogues*, of § 11 of the first *Enquiry* and of the essay 'Of the Immortality of the Soul' leaves one in no doubt of Hume's belief that rational reflection on nature, the alleged source of philosophic, natural religion, cannot produce any conclusions of religious interest. If a philosophical religion exists alongside the inventions of priests and rulers and the fancies of the human imagination, it is not the result of the observation of nature. How can it be when the only conclusion licensed by any such observation is the religiously useless print that 'the cause or causes of order in the universe probably bear some remote analogy to human intelligence' (Hume 1976:26)?

All this entails that the contrast between revealed and natural

119

religion cannot exist in so clear a fashion in Hume's writings as in the deists'. For the latter the contrast is between one real thing (the religion of reason) and one imaginary thing (revealed religion, which is in essence resolved into the civil and mythical theology criticized by the best pagan philosophers). In Hume neither term in the contrast between revealed and natural religion refers to anything in reality. There is no more a religion of reason than there is a revealed religion, if the vague philosophical or true religion that is identical with the principles of humanity and benevolence is left aside. Thus Hume can, in his essay on miracles, appear as the defender of faith and revelation against the claims of reason (Hume 1975:130–1). If there were to be a religion of reason which might seriously supplant pretended revelation, it would have to add to the normal sentiments behind morality some well-established metaphysical conclusions which made some tangible difference to the conduct of life, principally through having some moral relevance. In his critical assault on the religion of reason Hume whittles his target down to two component beliefs: that the world is the product of intelligent design; and that it continues to be under the government of some morally aware cause. The first of these beliefs is the object of discussion in sections 1–9 of the *Dialogues*. Section 1 applies a general moral about human reason to be learnt from the *Treatise* and the first *Enquiry*, namely that it is quite unsuited to the task of discovering metaphysical conclusions about the ultimate origins and causes of the universe. Sections 2–8 endeavour to show this conclusion about the extent of reason in operation by arguing in detail that the metaphysics of belief in intelligent design behind the universe claims more than anyone can prove, given an unbiased examination of the facts of nature and alternative cosmologies. Section 9 further supports the conclusion about reason's limited extent by arguing that, *a priori*, abstract reasoning fails to make up the gap in our knowledge which reasoning from observed fact cannot bridge.

The second component belief of the religion of reason is the principal object of attack in the final sections of the *Dialogues*, in section 11 of the first *Enquiry*, and in the essay 'Of the Immortality of the Soul'. This belief is absolutely critical for the religion of reason. For unless it can establish that there is a providential (that is morally guided) order in nature it can provide no substitute for the revealed religion it has dismissed. It will yield no conclusion which will do the same job as the belief in gods provided by pretended revelations. In short it will contain nothing of religious significance. The vague cosmological speculation to which design-theology has been reduced by Hume will be useless if 'it affords no inference that affects human life or can be the source of any action or forebearance' (Hume 1976:260). Following the work of Butler in *The Analogy of Religion*, Hume uses the fact of evil to show that outside of alleged revelation there is no ground to suppose that, despite appearances, there is a moral order in nature.

We have already met the deistic response to the objection that the world is not evidently under moral government in discussing Wollaston's ideas on immortality in Chapter 3. In Wollaston the fact that there are 'perturbations in human affairs' is met with the bland response which allows Wollaston to infer that these evils are just sure signs that the workings of providential government will be completed in a life to come; there is a perfect moral scheme evident to reason after all. Hume finds particular relish in attacking this way of arguing, the gist of his reply being contained in these words:

> these arguments are grounded on the supposition that God has attributes beyond what he has exerted in this universe, with which we are alone acquainted. Whence do we infer the existence of these attributes?
>
> (Hume 1882*b*:400)

The attributes justifying the assumption of a perfect providence completed in an afterlife cannot be grounded on revelation if natural religion is said to be sufficient for the discovery of religious truth. If it is sufficient then unaided human reason should be capable of discovering the attributes of God; yet the only material for sense and reason to operate on (the world as we find it to be) shows no consistent evidence of the vital moral attributes of God. The mixture of good and evil in the world in relation to desert allows of no inference to a hidden source of a perfect justice and makes more probable the conclusion that the first causes of things 'have neither goodness nor malice' (Hume 1976:242). Hume's use of the problem of evil against the claims of the religion of reason amounts to a rejection of the idea that there is a moral order in nature and thus of the form natural law ethics took in deism. Natural-law ethics plus some belief in an afterlife cannot serve as a substitute for revealed religion. The religion of reason is not in reality independent of the premisses of revealed religion.

This point of difference with deism over the ability of reason to perceive a moral order in nature must have implications for Hume's interpretation of the history of religion. For the deists saw in the actual religions of mankind an underlying and universal awareness of the naturally given moral law. This underlying awareness *is* the natural religiousness of which forms of genuine religion (excluding the corruptions of religion) are the expression. It is this awareness which unites all forms of genuine religion. To interpret the history of religion in the light of these assumptions must be a false start for Hume. For him nothing with the normal, acknowledged characteristics of religion could be the expression of a rational awareness of moral order. There is no such underlying, universal awareness and there is no natural human religiousness. Religion must have quite other sources in human nature than reason.

The alternative source of religion favoured by Herbert (divine inscription) is ruled out at the beginning of *The Natural History*. In words strongly reminiscent of Locke's discussion of Herbert's ideas in the *Essay concerning Human Understanding* Hume argues that

> Some nations have been discovered who entertained no senti-
> ments of religion . . . and no two nations, and scarce any two
> men, have ever agreed precisely in the same sentiments. It would
> appear, therefore, that this preconception springs not from an
> original instinct or primary impression of nature . . . since every
> instinct of this kind has been found absolutely universal in all
> nations and ages, and has always a precise, determinate object
> which it pursues.
>
> (Hume 1976:25)

From this Hume concludes that religious principles must be secondary products of human nature, the effect in turn of more fundamental principles which work themselves out in different ways in different places. Observation of religious history thus supports Hume's general rejection of metaphysical accounts of human nature in defeating the notion that religion is the universal reflection of direct divine inscription prior to any nurture. The argument is sealed for Hume by his observation that the only point of theology on which consent is even near universal is the vague and infinitely variable belief that 'there is invisible intelligent power in the world' (Hume 1976:37). Hume's arguments against a Herbert-like view of religion as a primary impression in human nature also provide an extra dimension of criticism to the deists' version of belief in a natural human religiousness. Hume's argument that religion arises only in certain circumstances, and then in a variable way, tends to show, if sound, that it does not correspond to *any* kind of primary principal in human nature.

Revelation, reason, and inscription having been rejected as possible sources of religion, the only remaining place to turn to is the human passions. The passions, principally in the form of fear, imagination, and the propensity to adulation, provide the primary principles of which religion is the secondary product in certain circumstances. A similarity and a difference to deistic treatments of popular religion can be seen in this appeal to the passions. Both in general and in detail deistic writers had anticipated Hume in ascribing the religion of large parts of mankind to passional sources, for they naturally regarded popular faith as in many respects a departure from the religion of reason due to the influence of the passions. This general agreement is matched by some striking similarities of detail. Hume paints a picture of the primitive fathers of the human race faced with a world which they could neither understand nor control. Belief in the gods arises out of this desperation, being an attempt through the personification of the unknown causes behind natural phenomena to cope intellectually and emotionally with man's ignorance and fear. Hume repeatedly draws a contrast between this sort of reasoning (if it can be called 'reasoning') and the refined speculations about the intellectual and moral order in the cosmos which are supposed to be the origins of true religion. But in fact the picture of the 'fluctuation of men's minds between hope and fear and the description of how this leads to popular superstition was painted by Toland in 1704, some 40 years or more before *The Natural History* was written (cf. Toland 1704:78 and Hume 1976:33–6). The difference from the deists lies not so much in the admission of the passions as explanatory factors in much of religion but rather in the fact that for Hume they provide the whole of the story, while for the deists they are merely a part. For the deists religion in history is a two-layered cake in which the passions overlay a rational substratum. Hume's picture is so similar because he agrees with and no doubt draws upon their description of the first layer, while ultimately arguing that it is the only layer to the religions of history that there in fact is. His treatment of the causes of monotheism in *The Natural History* §§ 6 ff. is crucial in this respect. For belief in a single divine being in some popular religions could be taken by the deists as a survival of the layer of rational religion in popular faith. But for Hume it is the product of an extra dose of the influence of the passions upon the popular imagination. For monotheism has its roots in polytheism, and not in a separate strand of belief, and arises when our human desire to please by flattery gets to work on the gods of the pantheon. It is thus one further stage removed from the ideal of a religion of reason and not an indication of the reality of that ideal in forms of historic popular faith. Monotheism in popular religion is decidedly not a reflection of the existence of natural religion in the fourth sense we have distinguished – a natural religiousness.

Hume's rejection of any layer in positive religion other than the superstitions founded upon man's passional nature indicates the distinctiveness of the kind of naturalism he espouses. His call at the opening of *The Natural History* to forget religion's supposed foundations in reason and concentrate upon its origins in human nature can now be seen to be an accusation that previous pictures of the actual religions practised in the world have all rested on false idealizations of their subject-matter. In taking religion only as we find it, we are not to suppose that there may be facets to it that lie beneath its outward appearances. Hume's approach may be contrasted with that of Blount's described in Chapter 3 which relies on the distinction between the foundations and super-structure of religion and which takes it for granted that the outward appearances of religion reflect its modes and circum-stances rather than its inward essence. What is in question between Hume and Blount is the extent to which we may seek what I have styled a philosophical, humanist history of religion. This would be a history that attempted to use principles of interpretation in the study of religion which were designed to lay bare something of human and philosophical importance in the record of man's faiths. A philosophical, humanist history will be ready to question the principles of interpretation of any approach which identified man's entire religious life with what might otherwise be regarded as corruptions of religion. Deism, for all its naïveties, does have principles which can bring out something of human importance in the religions of history. It can use the ideas of a religion of reason and of a natural human religiousness to endeavour to show that an awareness of moral law and the supremacy of a transcendent justice lies behind even the most apparently arbitrary jumble of superstitions. Hume's principles of historical interpretation do not allow him to see anything of enduring worth in religion in history.

> 'Tis a matter of fact incontestable that about 1700 years ago all mankind were idolaters.
>
> (Hume 1976:26)

This famous assertion from the beginning of *The Natural History* may mislead us into supposing that the issue joined between Hume and the religious rationalists of his time was primarily a chronological one, concerning the first religion of man. (Was it polytheistic or monotheistic?) In reality it is much more a matter of rival accounts of the forces producing religion *now* and of the sense we can see in the *continuing* history of religion. It is a dispute about the relation of religion to human nature which can be expressed separately from disagreements about the origins of religion in time.

No doubt Hume's specific claim about the extent of monotheistic belief 1700 years before his own century was made with an eye on the rationalistic account of the religion of the New Testament as the restoration or republication of the religion of nature (one of the themes of Tindal's and Morgan's works as we have seen above). If Hume is right in the arguments he offers for concluding that monotheism is a late and uncertain arrival in religious history, then the rationalist interpretation of the religion of Jesus must be mistaken. Hume's claim is similar to Locke's that at the time of Christ a knowledge of the one true God was all but lost to mankind (Locke 1823e:135), while the continuation of Hume's statement seems deliberately designed to refute the only two exceptions Locke allowed to his depressing picture, namely the religion of the Jews and the best pagan philosophy:

> The doubtful and sceptical principles of a few philosophers, or the theism, and that not too entirely pure, of one or two nations form no objection worth regarding.
>
> (Hume 1976:26)

The expansion of Hume's comments on the chronological question amounts to arguing that: (1) if a pure monotheism had once been the religion of man, people would never have been persuaded to abandon it in favour of something obviously inferior; and (2) a just notion of the kind of life led by early man prior to civilization makes it much more plausible to suppose that he was moved by the passional considerations described in Hume's account of the basis of religion than by what Hume represents as the refined speculations leading to an ethical monotheism. Point (1) offers a rejection of the political explanation of the corruption of natural religion favoured by the deists, and (2) provides a dismissal of their arcadian picture of an original free human society. But a deist could, as noted in Chapter 4, accept part of Hume's chronological thesis that monotheism was not the first religion of early man, while still maintaining that religion in history was the product of two conflicting tendencies: the drive to crude animistic beliefs of the sort Hume describes; and the recognition of a transcendent moral order in creation. Provided he resisted Hume's attempts to show that this latter awareness was beyond the reach of the popular mind, then he might still see the faiths of history as having the two-layered structure of a religion of reason and nature overlain by popular superstition. He would, to be sure, need some other means of demonstrating that the religion of reason and nature truly corresponded to the fundamentals of human nature to replace that provided by saying that it was the original religion of mankind. As we shall see below, the notion of progress or evolution can offer such a means of making conclusions about what is natural to humankind stick.

Hume might appear to be the more historically sophisticated – his chronology of religious development is more plausible and founded upon some real attempt at historical research. But it is the deists who have in fact a more profound vision of religious history. They are at least able to see the many vagaries of popular faith down the ages as redeemable, as connected with something worthwhile and important, being the modes and circumstances in which the religion of reason hides itself; whereas for Hume mankind's religious life becomes a kind of blank nothing in the history of the world in which neither he nor anyone else can see any sense. All this follows from the one-dimensional account of religion Hume's particular brand of naturalism forces upon him. This lack is most clearly seen in the famous closing verdict on religion in *The Natural History*:

Survey most nations and most ages. Examine the religious principles which have, in fact, prevailed in the world. You will scarcely be persuaded that they are other than sick men's dreams: Or perhaps you will regard them more as the playsome whimsies of monkeys in human shape, than the serious, positive, dogmatical asservations of a being who dignifies himself with the name of rational.

(Hume 1976:94)

This is to say that there is nothing of human importance in religion because we do not show ourselves to be human creatures in our religious life.[3] In the continuation, Hume describes how all consistency of thought and action is lost when man engages in religion, so that the human self dissolves into incoherence when it participates in this sphere of thought and activity: 'The whole is a riddle, an enigma, an inexplicable mystery' (Hume 1976:95).

One might be inclined to wonder if Hume can see any sense in human history at all, given that he apparently has to write off so large a part of it when it comes to religion. However, from the *Essays* it is clear that he thinks there is sense to be made of some passages of change in history and even a progress from worse to better within some epochs. From such texts as 'Of the Rise and Progress of the Arts and Sciences', 'Of Commerce', and 'Of Refinement in the Arts' we gain a picture of the first ages of the world as barbarous and ignorant and as being without liberty for the individual. The growth of commerce, and with it private wealth and luxury, introduces some movement into history. For commerce promotes contact between nations, and the accumulation of wealth in the hands of private citizens increases their power against the sovereign. Liberty and progress in the arts follow. Slowly government based on humanity and moderation replaces that based on barbarism and zeal. As Duncan Forbes notes, there is no guarantee that this movement will continue forward forever (Forbes 1975:190). However, there is sufficient sense of movement in history to confirm the impression gained from *The Natural History* that religion stands as the dark side of its history, its rubbish-bin, containing all those forces which retard man's advance toward happiness. The various things that will assist the movement of history toward the realization of human happiness (that is, moderation in government, the pursuit of material wealth

127

by private citizens, commerce and contact between nations) are just the things that religion as portrayed in *The Natural History* will hinder. It is no accident that in his own time and nation the factors that make for human progress are present while religion is in marked decline (see Hume 1882a:251).[4]

As far as the development of the concept of religion is concerned, there is a record of both profit and loss to be entered after a study of Hume's writings on religion. On the profit side of the account we may note his exposure of some of the naïveties in supposing that the religion of reason was the first religion of mankind. Hume has also aired some of the difficulties in believing it to be the universal substratum of religion in history. He has suggested an alternative explanation of the presence of monotheistic beliefs alongside popular superstitions and, through the description of the bad effects of popular faiths, he has given reason to doubt if the corrupt elements of those faiths can be regarded as extraneous to the essence of religion. But if these can be seen as worthwhile criticisms of an over-simple history of religions in deism, there are important points in Hume's own account of the workings of religion in history that must be entered on the debit side. The advances in the naturalistic approach to the history of religion which arise out of Hume's criticisms of earlier theories are not secured by the presence in Hume of any alternative account of the nature of religion which enables us to see sense in the history of religion, or which would make religion in history worth studying as a diverse and changing phenomenon. In effect, the deistic criticisms of the faults of popular religion are accepted and declared to be an accurate account of religion in its entirety. False idealizations in the history of religions have been attacked at the cost of robbing us of any motive for studying mankind's religious life. We have reached what might be called the dead-end of naturalism. The demand to describe religion only as we find it has left us without a means for interpreting it as containing anything significant. This undoubted weakness in Hume's account means that he cannot be taken as giving the last word on the relation between religion and human nature.

KANT ON THE PLACE OF RELIGION IN HISTORY

Kant's writings on religion occupy a key place in the development of the concept of religion. They illustrate in a clear way some of the tensions in the Enlightenment's conception of religion which led to its revision. We can see the beginnings of this revision in the way in which Kant himself deals with these tensions.

One of the problems Kant attempts to tackle has been seen to emerge in Hume. The minimum demands of rationalistic humanism appeared to entail a religious outlook which included commitment to natural religion. But this outlook at the same time seems to be clearly contrary to how the world appears to observation. This outlook required belief in a providential, moral order as the setting for human life, but the least admission of scepticism or criticism into metaphysics renders the basis of this outlook weak and question-begging. Kant's solution to this tension between rationalistic humanism and scepticism is to transform belief in the moral ordering of the world from a shaky inference dependent on weak theoretical premises to an immediate certainty of practical faith. Our commitment to a religious, that is providential, outlook is not something which we derive from reasoning about the course of natural events but is the result of a projection, licensed by the demands of practical rationality, of our moral natures onto the world. The importance for the concept of religion of this way of resolving the first tension in the Englightenment's conception of religion will be commented on below.

'We can expect no universal history of religion (in the strict meaning of the word) among men on earth' (Kant 1960:115). This quotation introduces the second tension Kant tackles. Kant's attempted resolution of Hume's sceptical doubts about the certainty of belief in the moral ordering of the world enables him to continue to represent the fundamental beliefs of the religion of reason as the core of true religion. But this creates a further difficulty: how is this conception of the essence of religion compatible with our belief that religion is a part of human history? The essence of religion is identified with something that is simple and uniform through all times and places, and thus religion in its essence seems to have no history (a problem noted above in Chapter 3). Kant recognizes and attempts to satisfy the urgent need to bring the philosopher's account of true religion into harmony with an historical perspective upon religion.

Kant's reflections on the historical character of religion also lead him to comment on a third, and perhaps most important, tension. It is a tension evident in deism. It manifests itself in the obvious difficulty in reconciling the actual progress of religion in history, including its many superstitions and corruptions, with the strong, positive standards of propriety in belief and conduct characteristic of rationalistic thought. Even Hume illustrates this tension, despite his scepticism. *The Natural History of Religion* clearly displays the temptation to write off religion in history in the light of a prevailing ethos committed to sobriety and moderation. Kant, unlike Hume, sees that it would be wrong to dismiss something of such obvious historical and human importance, and this leads him to develop ways of representing religion in history so that it manifests something worthwhile when judged in the light of these positive standards.

Crucial in Kant's attempted resolution of the last tension described above is the means he offers for seeing in a positive light the very fact that religion is diverse and historically changing. The problems Kant tackles are thus linked, since the clashes between religion in history and the positive standards of the eighteenth century occur just where forms of religious belief and worship depart from the simplicities of a universal, rational religion. There are in Kant's writings on religion three very important notions which enable him to see some value in the historically conditioned and changing forms of popular belief. Their importance is not confined to Kant, since we shall be able to see them at work in later writers who are equally concerned to develop an appreciation of the historical. These notions centre upon the progress of history, the relation between religion and the imaginative life of mankind, and the social and public dimension to religion.

The notion of progress is important in that it enables Kant and his successors to avoid a direct confrontation between forms of faith in history and the positive standards of the philosopher's religion. These forms can be seen to be necessary, even though imperfect, for the gradual and progressive realization of true religion in history. A measure of relativity can be introduced into the philosophical historian's assessment of the worth of the phenomena of religion as they are found in history. In Kant this measure of relativity is suitably modest; in other writers we shall comment on it is greater and allows a more developed historical perspective upon religion.

The imagination figures in Kant, and others, as the source of a fresh set of cognitive needs that can redeem features of religion which reason seems to have no need of. Aspects of popular and institutional religion that may be dismissed as unnecessary or distracting for the life of reason may become vital if the imagination is allowed to have a role in the religious life. This point applies particularly to the ritual and mythic aspects of religion. Much of what Kant says about myth and ritual can be seen to bear fruit in nineteenth-century thought. Ritual and shared myth, which seem so conspicuously to escape the net of the religion of reason, can also be redeemed if the public and social purposes of religion are stressed. It is characteristic of Kant that, while remaining committed to leading conceptions and ideals of the religion of reason, he should see a social dimension to the pursuit of those ideals. The social dimension brings with it a rational need for those aspects of popular religion so easily pushed to the sidelines by the deists. Again, later writers take this idea of the social purposes of religion much further.

Kant's novel explorations of the tensions to be found within the idea of the religion of reason and between that idea and an historical perspective upon religion take place within a commitment to much of the content of a deistic idea of natural religion. This can be seen in two works which span the decade which produced Kant's critical philosophy: the *Lectures on Ethics* of 1780 and the *Religion within the Limits of Reason Alone* of 1793. Both reveal an unwavering adherence to belief in a universal and simple religion of reason which serves as the completion of morality, and both regard this religion as something which can be discovered independently of any revelation. Kant's emphasis on simplicity and universality brings him particularly close to the deists. He writes:

> The outstanding characteristic of natural religion is its simplicity. Its theology is such that the least intelligent amongst us can grasp it as completely as the most thoughtful and speculative. Apart from its simple rudiments there are other things in theology but these are no concern of natural religion and serve only to satisfy our thirst for knowledge.
>
> (Kant 1930:81)

His verdict on the link between universality and truth seems to be pure deism:

We have noted that a church dispenses with the most important mark of truth, namely, a rightful claim to universality, when it bases itself upon a revealed faith.

(Kant 1960:100)

However, it cannot be said that Kant straightforwardly sets revealed and natural religion in opposition to one another, embracing the latter so as to reject the former. One reason for this is his belief that natural religion is completed by revealed religion (see Kant 1930:84), a belief pursued further in *Religion within the Limits of Reason Alone*. Furthermore, Kant follows Toland (see Chapter 3 above) in allowing that revelation may be an additional source of information or instruction to reason, though not a separate ground of assent. There may then be no opposition between revealed and natural religion, for whether someone learns of a religious truth through alleged revelation or the use of unaided reason carries no implication about the grounds on which the truth rests. A religion may be '*objectively* a natural religion, though *subjectively* one that has been revealed' (Kant 1960:144). Because of the greater accommodation he is prepared to allow between natural and revealed religion, Kant's account of the ramifications of the religion of reason in the *Religion within the Limits of Reason Alone* is altogether richer than that of the deists and finds room for versions of many distinctively Christian doctrines. Nonetheless, there remains an underlying similarity between Kant and the deists, in that he too regards the core of religion as consisting in a simple, inward, and universal disposition closely tied to the recognition of moral duty.

This religion of inward disposition involves the recognition of our moral duties and the awareness and service of God that flows out of that. It can be said to be the natural religion of mankind, for it is one ·that corresponds to human nature if it is allowed to flourish uncorrupted. Even if it does not outwardly manifest itself as the first public religion of mankind, it is the seed of all religions worthy of the name. It lies behind popular religion, albeit that popular religion is influenced by other factors as well. Earlier by far than popular faith, 'the predisposition to the moral religion lay hidden in human reason' (Kant 1960:102). Kant's general philosophy of course links this moral disposition to reason in its practical dimension. Through the way in which he thus forges links

132

between religion and human nature, we may say that Kant believes in the existence of natural religion in its fourth sense. Religion is a direct, universal, and inevitable outcome of a primary principle of human nature (that is moral disposition/reason). There is a natural human religiousness.

The philosopher's normative religion of reason is closer to the forms of popular faith and the natural religion of mankind than Hume will allow. Kant can see the philosopher's natural religion in popular faith partly because he has transformed the articles of this religion from objects of refined metaphysical speculation into presuppositions of morality which may be immediately grasped. Where there is recognition of duty and the performance of duty for duty's sake then the postulates of freedom, immortality, and God's existence can be grasped. In this way 'morality ... leads ineluctably to religion' (Kant 1960:5). Pure ethical monotheism is thus brought back into popular religion whence it had been banished by Hume. The following illustrates Kant's method very clearly:

> We can hardly question that the Jews, like other peoples, even the most savage, ought to have had a belief in a future life, and therefore in a heaven and hell; for this belief automatically obtrudes itself upon everyone by virtue of the universal moral disposition in human nature.
>
> (Kant 1960:117)

It follows that Kant cannot accept Hume's interpretation of the history of religion. In a brief passage in the *Religion* he appears to dismiss it, accusing such accounts of confusing the origin of religion with that of something else and of ignoring the fact that religion's true nature is only progressively realized in the course of history:

> The veneration of mighty invisible beings, which was extorted from helpless man through natural fear rooted in the sense of his impotence, did not begin with a religion but rather with a slavish worship of a god (or of idols).
>
> (Kant 1960:163–4)

This worship of idols achieves public form in the shape of temple-service, but it attains the religious character of church worship 'only after the moral culture of men was gradually united with its laws'. The genuinely religious forms of faith that emerge are still based on beliefs about revelation in history and on historically-conditioned institutions. Gradually with further moral progress, these historically based forms of faith will be recognized as having value merely as symbolic presentations, and a pure religious faith that is free of dependence on them will be promoted.

The very brief sketch of a natural history of religion provided by Kant fits in with the picture of the progress of history to be found in such works as *The Conjectural Beginning of Human History* and *Idea for a Universal History with a Cosmopolitan Purpose*. These do not deny a passional origin for man's earliest beliefs and practices. Nor do they turn their backs on the extent to which irrational and morally blind forces are at work in human society. But they see such things as part of an intelligible direction in history. According to Kant, the philosopher can conjecture that at the dawn of history man was purely an instinctual creature. He discovers in the course of time, however, the power of choosing his way of life for himself. This brings with it the change from a life of instinct alone to one permeated by rational choice in which man becomes an end in himself; that is to say, his happiness comes to be seen as residing in goals which are the objects of rational choice rather than being provided for him by instinct. The history of man is marked by conflict between the sway of instinct and reason, between propensities to individuality and to sociability. Out of such conflicts comes further progress toward the rational perfection of man. This progress is in turn a moral progress, as the rational awareness of the moral law slowly becomes sufficient for the ordering of human life. When it does so, at some time in the future, the final area of conflict in human society will be removed: the incessant conflicts between different nation states with their divergent systems of positive law will be replaced by a cosmopolitan 'ethical commonwealth' in which humanity will be ruled by the one set of moral laws (see Kant 1963*a* and 1971*a*).

Kant's optimistic vision of human progress provides at least one enduring legacy, offsetting those aspects of it we might be tempted to dismiss as naïve. It brings with it the key idea that man is by nature an historical being. Even if the qualities by which Kant identifies human nature – reason, freedom, moral awareness – link his thought closely to that of the deists, Kant is clear that man needs to be part of an historical process if these qualities are to be realized. They come to define human life only after a sequence of development through conflict has been gone through. Human nature is in a measure a product of history. This entails further that a more charitable eye can be turned towards those aspects of life in history which seem to display these qualities only imperfectly or which seem to run counter to them. They may yet be valuable because necessary for the realization of human nature in history. Rationalism and an historical perspective can thus be reconciled to an extent.

> There may certainly be different historical confessions, only these have nothing to do with religion itself but only with changes in the means used to further religion, and are thus the province of historical research. And there may be just as many religious books (the Zend-Avesta, the Vedas, the Koran etc). But there can only be one religion which is valid for all men and at all times. Thus the different confessions can scarcely be more than the vehicles for religion; these are fortuitous, and may vary with differences in time and place.
>
> (Kant 1971b:98)

These remarks of Kant point both to the problem his account of human nature raises for religion and also to its solution. The religion that corresponds to achieved humanity will be single and universal, just as the social order that corresponds to humanity will be single and universal. But while there can be only one religion, there can be many faiths (Kant 1960:98). Though religion is in a manner of speaking beyond history, because not subject to change, the faiths are historical entities. The faiths are not merely the products of accident or of blind, irrational, and meaningless forces since 'even in the various churches, severed from one another by reason of the diversity of their modes of belief, one and the same true religion can be found' (Kant 1960:98). Religion in fact needs the faiths that are part of history, because, though it is primarily an inward disposition, it has a public goal which can only be realized if the contingent forms of the faiths are used. This goal is part of humanity's general moral destiny – the attainment of the ethical commonwealth – for it is the public union of men in the service of God through obedience to the moral law. Religion is in turn necessary for bringing about the ethical commonwealth (which can also be described as 'the Kingdom of God on Earth'), and so the faiths play a part in the moral progress of humanity (see Kant 1960:139).

The need for rational, moral religion to employ a faith that has a contingent and historical form arises out of two complementary sources: the requirements of the imagination, and the need for the pure religion to assume some public shape. Concerning the former, Kant argues that, though the communication of religion is restricted if it employs some contingent faith or other, 'some historical, ecclesiastical faith . . . must be utilised', the reason lying in men's natural need and desire

> for something *sensibly tenable*, and for a confirmation of some sort from experience of the highest concepts and grounds of reason (a need which really must be taken into account when the universal *dissemination* of the faith is contemplated).

> (Kant 1960:100)

So the myths and dogmas of popular religion can be related to the principles of a 'true' philosophical religion, not just as their corruptions but as their imaginative expressions. Kant goes on to argue that the best teachers of the faiths of history have always tried gradually to bring their adherents to see the 'universal moral dogmas' behind the content of these faiths (Kant 1960:101). Kant thus allies himself to one of the tendencies we have seen to be characteristic of belief in the importance of natural religion, namely the readiness to see philosophical reflection as giving the true, essential meaning to be found within popular, established religion. And like Herbert, he is able to endorse the attempts to see in the gross polytheism of ancient paganism the 'mere symbolic representation of the attributes of a single divine being' (Kant 1960:101).

The *Religion* abounds in further, more central examples of how the forms of historical, ecclesiastical faith illustrate in symbolic fashion universal moral dogmas. Kant's treatment of the moral interpretation of Christianity in Books I and II displays how it falls to the philosopher to give the real meaning of a faith's doctrines and scriptures. One example only must suffice to illustrate Kant's extensive discussion of how imagination can come to the aid of reason. Kant describes in Book II how there is a recognizable conflict between a good and an evil principle in human nature – one within the will of man between his disposition to subordinate the maxims of action to the moral law and his contrary disposition to subordinate them to his desires and passions. The New Testament and the religiously interesting parts of the Old set out this 'intelligible moral relationship' in the form of a narrative. The two principles are represented as persons outside man who battle for his destiny (Kant 1960:73 ff.). Kant refers to this mode of representing rational moral relationships as a vivid one, which 'was in its time the only *popular* one' (Kant 1960:78). It can be divested of its symbolic form to reveal a rational meaning 'valid and binding for the whole world and all time' (Kant 1960:78).

The importance of the faiths of history in playing a part in the moral progress of mankind is increased by the social interpretation Kant gives to that progress. Its goal can be described in terms of the triumph of the good principle over the evil in human life. Kant is clear that such a triumph can only be achieved if men work together to create a certain type of society on earth. Individual progress toward the triumph of the good principle over the evil will always be precarious unless the 'means could be discovered for the forming of an alliance uniquely designed as a protection against this evil' (Kant 1960:100). Out of this in part arises Kant's stress on the need to create an ethical *commonwealth*, something he argues can only be undertaken through religion (Kant 1960:139). But this in turn requires that religion transform itself from a mere inward disposition into a church. A church is religion represented in some visible form, thus enabling the moral orientation which is at the heart of religion to embody a 'public covenant' in the pursuit of the ethical commonwealth. This visible form is at the same time 'a certain ecclesiastical form dependent on the conditions of experience . . . in itself contingent and manifold' (Kant 1960:96). The principles of true religion are inward, necessary, and the same for all mankind. The ecclesiastical/historical faiths are outward, contingent, and varied institutions. But it turns out to be necessary from the standpoint of true religion, and thus necessary for the human meaning of history, that there are such contingent and varied faiths. Kant has not merely reversed the Humean dismissal of established faiths in this passage of argument; he has forged a closer link between natural religion and revealed in doing so.

We shall find the motif of necessity-in-contingency in regard to the faiths of history of particular importance in the further development of the concept of religion. It is to be found even amongst those writers who sharply dissent from Kant's account of

natural religion and its identification with the religion of reason.
Kant has begun what others will take further, namely the
questioning of the equation in deism of the contingent, local, and
changing with the humanly worthless.

Kant's account of the relationship between 'religion' and the
'faiths' seems to involve a significant shift in religious rationalism's
appraisal of the historical. But despite this there remain important
problems in seeing his account as ensuring a respect for religion in
history. In the first place it only redeems some aspects of the
historical forms of religion, namely those which can transparently
be seen to be the vehicle of the moral progress of mankind. For
example, he remains true to the rationalist dismissal of any form of
religious experience or mysticism, describing it as 'religious
fanaticism' (Kant 1960:162–3). It amounts to 'the moral death of
reason'. Moreover, Kant's placing of the faiths in a philosophy of
history based on the idea of moral progress does not even ensure
the comparability of all the religions of history. The notion of
moral progress we have seen to be interpreted by Kant in a
cosmopolitan fashion, entailing the eventual withering-away of
separate nation-states. This means that he is particularly blind to
the link between religion and nationality and finds it hard to
appreciate those religions in history which get their character
partly from the way they have helped to shape a national culture.
This is one of the reasons he writes so scathingly of Judaism in the
Religion (see Kant 1960:116–18). He will not allow it to figure in
any account of the origins of Christianity. Judaism's refusal to fit
into the idea of a cosmopolitan moral goal (among other things)
shows Christianity to be a radical departure from it. Judaism is
castigated as a purely political scheme of thought. It is condemned
for its exclusivity and connection to the life of one particular
nation. The limitations in Kant's appreciation of forms of belief
that are local and time-bound are revealed in the frequent hints
that the historical/ecclesiastical faiths are destined to disappear.
Though necessary, they are only provisionally so; they must be
employed in the minority of humankind but progress will
eventually render them dispensable:

> Hence a necessary consequence . . . of the moral disposition in
> us . . . is that in the end religion will gradually be freed from all
> empirical determining grounds and from all statutes which rest

on history and which through the agency of ecclesiastical faith provisionally unite men for the requirements of the good; and thus at last the pure religion of reason will rule over all.

(Kant 1960:117)

The greatest question-mark over Kant's commitment to the universality and comparability of religion arises from the tendency in the argument of the *Religion* to suggest that, when the faiths of history do wither away, the end-result will be their absorption into a purified Christianity. This faith has always stood above the rest, because it can be considered not merely as an example of ecclesiastical/historical faith but as religion. Its teachings are founded upon reason, and its first intention was to introduce a pure moral faith into the world (Kant 1960:151 and 122). It can in turn be seen to be an example of natural religion, as opposed to revealed, if the true foundation of its doctrines is made plain (Kant 1960:145–51). The Christian portion of the world is that in which the dependence of ecclesiastical faith on moral religion has been first recognized and where the movement to a universal church is reaching completion, making Kant's age and culture closer to the moral goal of history (Kant 1960:115 and 122). Christianity is therefore not merely one faith among others. It in some way speaks for all, containing as it does symbols, doctrines, and narrative myths which transparently encapsulate the principles of the one true religion (Kant 1960:78 and 132–3).

Kant's developmental and moral view of history gives him the ability to forge a link between true religion (natural religion) and the faiths of history. It is plain that he wishes to use this ability to see worth in a number of these faiths (even if he excludes some, such as Judaism). However, his view of history also enables him to pick out one faith, civilization, and age as representing true religion in a uniquely satisfactory fashion. So he can say of Christianity: 'it is intended to be the universal world religion' (Kant 1963*b*:84).

Kant's attempt to see a moral progression in history and to see that moral progression as redeeming aspects of the faiths of history meets Hume's type of naturalism – with its attack on all false idealizations in the study of mankind – head on. The essay, *Idea for a Universal History with a Cosmopolitan Purpose*, contends that history must be able to yield a human sense and that philosophical history must be allowed to exist alongside a narrower, detailed investigation of the past (Kant 1971a:51-2). The kind of perspective on history that Hume's *Natural History* displays in relation to religion is admitted as a possibility *if* a narrow enough view is adopted. 'Folly and childish vanity' do characterize many individual actions. Despite this, the philosopher may hope that what strikes us as confused and fortuitous in the actions of individuals can, in the history of the entire species, be seen 'as a steadily advancing but slow development of man's original capacities' (Kant 1971a:41-2). Kant attempts to enforce this point by citing examples of acts which seem unplanned in the individual case but show a pattern when viewed as part of a larger aggregate. Kant is thus responding to the need noted earlier in this chapter to construe the history of religions as humanly important despite the appearance it might present of unredeemed folly. In reflecting on Kant's efforts to give a philosophical history of religion which meets this need, we have seen the limitations of the principles of interpretation he uses to discover a redeeming sense in the history of faiths. The redeeming thread of moral progress based on a Kantian idea of virtue is in the end much too narrow to rescue much of this history and is tied too closely to the dominant religious ideas of Kant's own culture to avoid making one particular faith the means of interpreting the others.

We noted at the beginning of this chapter three notions in Kant's treatment of religion which contribute to the development of the concept of religion in a direction which enables a more positive appreciation of religion in history. The notions of historical progress, of the importance of the imagination, and of the social dimension to human striving can be seen as ways of bringing the idea of a natural religion, including the idea of a natural human religiousness, into closer contact with the varied and changing religions men have actually lived by. In Kant's hands they begin to show how human nature might need these religions. Kant's continued commitment to much of the substance of the Enlightenment's religion of reason entails inevitable limitations in the manner in which he forges this link. His three notions point forward to the ways in which other thinkers will attempt the same task. For all the imperfections in their accounts of the nature of religion, Hume and Kant between them provide an agenda for the development of the concept of religion through reflection on the legacy of deism.

6

RELIGION, ROMANTICISM, AND IDEALISM

INTRODUCTION

What philosophical and theological significance may we attach to the fact that religion is diverse in its outward expressions and to the fact that it changes during the course of history? How may we account for these facts if we believe that religion is more than a mere result of changing fashions and fancies? How may we account for the notion of truth in religion in the face of diversity and change, or for the assumption that religion is directed to some more-than-human absolute? The answers to these questions given by German romantic and idealist thought are of the first importance historically, for they became enshrined in a philosophical and theological inheritance within which many of the pioneers of the historical and comparative study of man's religions were educated. Much of the work of these pioneers can be shown to be influenced by the philosophical and theological ideas I shall survey in this chapter.

These ideas are in turn intelligible as the outcome of the debate over the status of natural religion our earlier chapters have been tracing. They are an outcome both in respect of being a rejection of some of the claims made for natural religion and in respect of being an acceptance of some of those claims. We have seen how the defenders of natural religion answer the important questions listed above by seeking something of human importance, something we might properly regard as true, behind the diversity and change that marks the 'modes and circumstances' of religion. Much of religion in history thus becomes of no value except as the cloak of an unchanging religion of reason. Scepticism about the real influence of this natural religion then leaves a writer like Hume able to conclude that there is nothing of any importance behind diverse and changing shapes of religion. More modest doubts in Kant about our ability to see the religion of reason as the natural religion of mankind still leave the patterns of historical faith as only temporary requirements for bringing about the public flourishing of a universal and unchanging religion.

The greater sense of the importance of diversity and historical change that romanticism brings with it can be seen as a clear rejection of an interpretation of religious life that turns around natural religion. In this respect romantic thought goes well beyond Kant in seeking to see something important and necessary in diverse and changing forms of belief. The theology and anthropology of deism, as noted in Chapter 3 above, produce the conclusion that the means for interpreting religious history must be found in something that is in the end above history. For what is true in religion reflects the interaction between two terms – human nature and God – which are immutable and untouched by the accidents of culture and history. So a straightforward contrast can be drawn between what is true and worthwhile in religion and what is subject to change and variation. This contrast is only slightly softened by Kant. I shall look briefly at some of the writings of Herder, Schleiermacher, and Hegel to see how this key idea about the source of true religion is reversed. We shall see how they produce a theology and anthropology which entail that true religion must be diverse and changing in its expression. This implies in turn that a serious appreciation of religion can only be attained through a study of its presence in diverse cultures and in history (hence the importance of romanticism and idealism in promoting the global and historical study of religion). The study of man's religious life becomes of human and religious importance: true religion, as arising from man's relationship to the absolute or divine, is to be found *within* the diversity and changeableness of man's religious life. Far from rejecting anything positive in religion as invalid and corrupt because it varies with time and place, the truth of religion is now seen to be contained in its positivity.

J. G. HERDER ON HUMAN NATURE AND HISTORY

The writings of J. G. Herder on human nature and history are vitally important in giving German romanticism and idealism a belief in pluralism and a sense of history. A facet of his longer-term influence can be seen in the writings of Max Mueller, as we shall note in the next chapter.

Herder's essential view on human nature can be explained by contrasting it with Matthew Tindal's assertion that 'human nature continues the same, and men at all times stand in the same relation to one another' (Tindal 1730:20). For Herder this is at best a half-truth. All human beings are possessors of a common humanity, which it is the goal of life to realize fully. But this common humanity only exists at the level of a series of potentialities, which are capable of realization and expression in an indefinite number of ways. The human essence is not ready-made, and its flowering is actually dependent on realizing the full range of its diverse potentialities. From this follows the rejection in Herder of the notion that there is a single, unchanging rational and true religion for all·mankind.

Before exploring this rejection further it is necessary to dispel the impression that the contribution of Herder to the development of the idea of religion is simply a reaction to and rejection of all that is implicit in the notion of natural religion. In fact much of his thought and that of those he influenced builds upon the positive emphases in the use of the third sense of 'natural religion' distinguished in this study. The idea of the humanity of religion preached by the deists is not lost, nor are elements of the naturalism that goes along with that idea. If Herder, Schleier-macher, and Hegel are concerned to see something worthwhile in religion in history it is not by tracing through its course a supernatural religion that is not humanly produced and for that reason infinitely superior to the rest which are; they rather wish to see the religious value of all faiths in their humanity. The room they leave for a divine source for religions is in the context of domesticating the concepts of revelation and inspiration. The applicability of ideas of revelation to a religious development or notion does not then militate against its humanity. This point will be illustrated at a number of places below. They also universalize the – now watered-down – concept of revelation so that it applies in some measure to all faiths. The fact that the positive emphasis within one sense of the phrase 'natural religion' survives in these opponents of deism explains why they can be seen in part as builders upon deism, and why, as we shall see in the next chapter, a historian of religion like Max Mueller can use both the ideas of romantic and idealist thinkers *and* the notion of natural religion in outlining a programme for the science of religion. Their insistence on the humanity of religion also shows their interest in tracing religion back to human nature. The manner in which they do this will show that they are allied to the fourth sense of 'natural religion' in which it refers to a natural human religiousness.

> It is the inner mark of the truth of religion that it is through and
> through human.
>
> (Herder 1892:235)

Similar statements affirming the humanity of religion can be found in other writings of Herder, notably in the *Ideas for the Philosophy of the History of Mankind*, where we are told that in religion lies man's highest humanity (Herder 1887a:161). The message of the humanity of religion is reinforced in Herder's treatment of revelation. It is notable in this respect that he writes about the Old Testament under the title of *On the Spirit of Hebrew Poetry*. It is the ancient poetry of a branch of humanity he is treating of, and it is to be interpreted and explained as such. This does not totally exclude a reference to God, for as he notes in his exposition of 'Hebrew poetry', God is the source of human experience and powers; in this respect the origin of the poetry may be said to be divine (Herder 1880a:6). Yet the poetry is still human as well, following the measure and unity of human experience. We may think of it as the speech of the gods, but it remains human. The title and content of Herder's work on the Old Testament display an early version of the favoured romantic assimilation of divine to artistic inspiration. The human character of revealed documents is shown further in Herder's account of how we are to understand and interpret them. We must do so by recovering their human context. So the nature of such inspired texts as human expressions is confirmed by Herder's request that, for example, we consider the interpretation of the Old Testament in the light of the peculiar lifestyle and perceptions of the people who produced it. In *On the Spirit of Christianity* he tells us that the Old Testament belongs to the childhood of the world. Since a nation or epoch shows its idiosyncrasy in what it regards as divine or spiritual, it is especially wrong to try to interpret such a text by reference to anything other than its unique human context. We should not attempt to explain it according to our own ways of thinking and must even bear in mind that its writings belong to 1000 years of history, so that it would be wrong to interpret them against the background of a single period or state of Hebrew society (Herder 1880b:20). The New Testament must likewise be understood against the background of the way of thinking of its age.

The process of domesticating revelation is here underway most clearly. It is helped by the occurrence in Herder's writings on culture of a metaphysics of God and the world which is set out in a thorough, connected way in *God: Some Conversations*. The contrast between a supernatural, divine cause to a movement in human history and a merely human one can only be drawn if it goes along with the notion that God is not present in all events equally, but intervenes in some to a special degree. This interventionist picture of special divine action gets some support in turn from the belief that God and the world are separate. But Herder preaches a revised version of Spinoza's pantheism, whereby God is ceaselessly present in the world and its activities. The world is not conceived as fundamentally a mechanical ordering of material bodies but rather as an organic system of powers, *Kräfte*. God is its inner sustaining and organizing principle, in virtue of which these *Kräfte* constitute a living *whole*. The contrast between God and the world which might enable us to speak of God intervening in it or in history has gone. It is this which explains Herder's comment on events beyond nature (with reference to the record of the New Testament):

> In nature there are a thousand powers whose inner nature you are unacquainted with, and which you all will still use as children of the great mother.
>
> (Herder 1880b:72)

He gives light as an example of one of these powers. The human mind itself is an instance of the *Kräfte* that make up the world. This being so, we see there is no need to ascribe its inspired utterances to a divine intervention that sets aside its natural workings. God must be continually present in the operation of this system of *Kräfte*, as he must in all systems of powers in the world. So 'inspiration' becomes a word 'to describe the most efficacious workings of [a person's] powers' (Herder: 1880*b*:44). If a Hebraic author says of his works 'Here speaks the spirit of God' he means in effect 'Here speaks the spirit of our constitution and of our worship of God'. We call his and similar works 'inspired books' because they show 'the noblest deeds of the God of man through man'. They show the spirit of God in man and not some 'unnatural exaltation' (Herder 1880*b*:53 and 59).

The great stress on the organic and unified character of the natural world which Herder's metaphysics reveals has important implications for his account of the human mind. Given his picture of the mind as itself a *Kraft* or system of *Kräfte*, he must reject the popular division of the mind into separate faculties or compartments. He cannot accept any rigid separation of reason from other powers of the mind. All the powers of the mind work, develop, and originate together. By giving them different names we do not denote separate faculties in the soul; we just refer to different effects or operations of the one system of powers:

The experiencing and image-creating, the thinking and reasoning soul is one living power displayed in different operations.
(Herder 1881:19)

It is interesting to note how on occasion Herder can link the falsity of the thought that reason is separate and distinct from other operations of the mind with the falsity of the idea that a human existence is self-created, that is, independent of a chain of history, culture, and tradition (Herder 1887*a*:343 ff.). For we have seen in Chapters 3 and 4 how a stress on reason as a distinct and supremely important faculty in the mind is connected with attempts to make the basis of human thought independent of historical traditions. If reason is given timeless, universal truths as its object, then through reason human nature can be separated from its particular place in history, even if less important aspects of human nature remain tied to what is merely traditional. Belief in the separateness of reason is one of the pillars on which possibility of a natural religion transcending all merely local customs, institutions, and ideas depends.

A true account of distinctively human nature must find a characterization of being human which includes all of the operations of the mind or self and shows how they mutually contribute to the realization or development of an undivided nature. Herder attempts such a characterization by picking out the capacity to be reflectively aware of one's states, actions, and so on. The succession of states in the life of a human being is governed by a distinct kind of natural law, that of *Besonnenheit* (or reflective mind). This over-arching characteristic of the human mind is not grounded in any one of its 'faculties' exclusively: all may contribute to the goal it gives to human selves, namely that of achieving true self-awareness (Herder 1891:94). This characteristic goal of human nature is linked to another important distinguishing mark of the human: 'man is created for freedom and has no law on earth but that which he lays down for himself' (Herder 1887a:163). Freedom comes with the capacity of the self to be reflectively aware of its own ideas and thus to be able to mould and shape its own nature. 'Created for freedom' suggests that what is distinctive in our human nature is something which does not necessarily exist in completion but is yet to be fully realized. Herder makes a point of contending that self-awareness is set as a task for us. The full realization and perfection of humanity is a target toward which we aim.

Herder's account of what is distinctive in human nature leads him to contend that man's nature is historical; it is essentially in process. It is of its essence to be changing. By contrast:

> The bee builds in its high age just as it built in its childhood; it will build to the end of time just as it built at the beginning of creation . . . We grow always as if from a childhood, no matter how old we have become. We are always in motion, restless and unsatisfied: the essence of our life is not enjoyment, but always progression, and we have never been human until we have lived to the end of our days. Yet the bee has been a bee from the moment it built its first cell.
>
> (Herder 1891:97–8)

This entails that, even more than Kant, Herder cannot accept a contrast between that which reflects the human essence and that which changes in the course of history.

The sense in which human nature is a creature of history is strengthened by other aspects of Herder's philosophy of man, which add further to his rejection of the notion that the merely historical is unimportant. These further steps down the road of an historical understanding of man come from the way in which he

147

argues that the exercise of *Besonnenheit* in the pursuit of self-awareness and freedom is tied to the local and the traditional. This is because of the culture-bound nature of human life. In Herder's writings on the relationship between human nature and culture there are two complementary themes: that progress towards the realization of humanity by the individual is only possible because he is brought up in a culture; and that cultures are dynamic and diverse. Both themes figure largely in the *Treatise on the Origin of Language* of 1770. This work can be said to contain an argument for the correctness of the first theme in that it asserts that developed human thought is possible only through the acquisition and use of a language. Language is not merely the cloak of thought but its mould, so that nothing like the full emergence of the system of powers that is the human mind would be possible for any one of us unless we inherited a language. This is what ties the development of the human self to some human culture or other, and also reinforces the claim that no single operation of mind (such as reason) is self-sufficient. None allows the individual to escape his grounding in a particular stage of the historical life of mankind. The link between the self and culture which Herder forges via language is even stronger than suggested so far, for he goes on to identify the distinguishing characteristics of the system of powers that is the human self with the ability of man to use language:

> Man is an active being capable of free thought, whose powers operate in progression; on this account he is a creature of language.

(Herder 1891:93)

The human self is characterized by its capacity to be reflectively aware of the actions of its understanding, but this capacity is at the same time the ability to mark and distinguish among those acts. The marking and distinguishing of thought is effected through giving thought its distinct symbolic expression. This is why Herder cannot accept either the thesis that human language is no more than an extension of animal grunts and groans or the thesis that it was given to man by God. Neither thesis explains how language has a distinctively human origin.

The second theme in Herder's account of the relation betwen self and culture is shown in the way he readily accepts the diverse and changing character of culture as an inevitable and natural fact.

Geography, life-styles, and climate establish divergent cultures. Cultures are distinct systems of ideas and institutions linked by a language, the product not of conscious invention but tradition. And like all the products of tradition, culture is rooted in locality and history, and is dynamic in nature.

This set of ideas on the nature of the human self and its relationship to culture and history can be summarized under the heading of 'an expressionist theory of the self'. Expressionism in Herder can be seen both as a doctrine about the nature of the various products of culture and as a doctrine about the nature of the self. It asserts that for a human self to be realized it must be expressed in the products of culture, and that the way to understand these products is to see them as moments in the expression and realization of human selves in history (cf. Berlin 1976:153). Expressionism is a theory of the human self in so far as it tells us that the expression of thought and feeling is necessary for the attainment of the distinctively human qualities of self-awareness and freedom. The objectification of thought and feeling through speech, symbol, and action is the means we have of becoming reflectively aware of them. Accordingly, a theory of culture follows, in that we are bidden to see cultural products as occasions of human self-disclosure. They are thus to be interpreted by reference to the circumstances of those who produced them. Their value is largely to be seen in what they do disclose about the consciousness of their authors.

Some of the implications of expressionism for understanding the products of culture will be illustrated in greater detail below when its application to religious tradition is discussed. But it can be seen at once how it reinforces the notion that human nature as a determinate reality must be diverse and changing. It prevents the standard of truth to human nature being used to reject as merely positive, and thus arbitrary, all that is local, traditional, and time-bound (cf. Chapter 3 above). Each culture and epoch becomes *both* something shaped by tradition and locality *and* a moment in the realization of humanity. If each epoch is such a moment, then no single epoch provides a standard of perfection by which all ages can be judged. Human desires and longings will inevitably be diverse and changing, so that one cannot derive from human nature any law 'for an absolute, independent and unchanging happiness as philosophers define it' (Herder 1891:509).

The above assertion in *Yet Another Philosophy of History* leads on directly to Herder's attack on 'the pet philosophy of his age' (see Herder 1891:527). This is precisely that philosophy we have traced in Kant and which lies behind Kant's way of relating reason and the faiths. It is impossible to see a uniform direction in history leading toward the present, or to measure progress by the single yardstick of the development of the rational life of mankind. No uniform progress could be seen in history if there is in fact no single standard of perfection which might serve to pick out *the* goal of history. Seeing the goal in the flowering of reason compounds the error, for it picks out the goal of history by reference to a standard that belongs to one's own age. Matters get worse still when the arrogant philosopher, not realizing the circularity of this reasoning, locates the value of earlier epochs in the way they contribute to the realization of the modes of life of his own age. This is to treat many of the epochs of history as means only, whereas, says Herder, every age is both a means and an end (Herder 1891:527). Each age is a means to what comes after it in so far as it contributes to the general course of human history and thus to the development of humanity through later modes of life. But it is an end also in that it contains within itself a particular way in which happiness and perfection can be attained. To contend that folk in earlier epochs may only contribute to the attainment of later happiness and human good is monstrous.

The philosopher, says Herder, plays God if he seeks a simple pattern in history based on reading it in terms of the local ideals of his own age (Herder 1891:557–8). It is no accident that Herder presents the presumption of the philosopher of history in this particular way. We must oppose both the error of seeing history as purposeless (equivalent, he contends, to a hopeless scepticism about human affairs) and the error of supposing that its purposiveness can be easily detected or measured by our own standards (Herder 1891:511–13). The error in either case comes from ignoring the providential and divine purpose that there must be in history, even though we might not be able to detect it. The revaluation of history that emerges from Herder's account of human nature encourages him to take up one key doctrine from his Christian theological inheritance – a doctrine which is very much in opposition to deistic thought. This is the idea that God is as much the God of history as he is the God of nature. In opposition to deistic ideas, Herder asks his century how it can believe in God's presence in the laws that govern the construction of nature but not in the course of history:

> If the dwelling-place shows God's 'painting' in its smallest detail, why not the history of its inhabitants? The dwelling-place is merely a decoration, a painting for one view, one scene! The history is an 'unending drama of scenes! God's epic through all the thousands of years, continents and races of men. A story of a thousand forms full of great meaning'.
>
> (Herder:1891:559)

God's movement over the nations is shown in the spirit of their laws, customs, and art, and in the way in which these succeed one another, allowing for the development and preparation of new forms (Herder 1891:562). In the closing pages of *Yet Another Philosophy of History* we find an anticipation of a thought important in later conceptions of the nature of religion: the course of history as a whole is a process of divine revelation to man. It is to God that the 'great book' belongs that stands above all ages and in which we are hardly one letter. Nations are but letters in this 'whole', but there is one who reveals himself throughout its entirety.

The idea of the whole of history being revelatory of God provides a further reason for questioning the equation of what is humanly and divinely important with what is timeless and independent of the movement of history. It also removes the scandal of particularity which the idea of revelation seems to bring with it. Revelation can be accepted as working in all times and places. It need not be thought of as tied to a particular set of ideas if its progressive character and its dynamism are recognized. If the nature of the human understanding varies from one age and place to another, revelation can appropriately be thought of as showing different faces to different peoples. And if its source is thought of as operating within history, its influence upon the varying patterns of human culture, including human religion, can be thought of as something that does not detract from their human character and context.

It might seem as if in Herder's writings on history and culture we have a complete rejection of the ideas embodied in the notion of natural religion, save for the persistent thought that religion has a human origin and basis. Yet Herder's actual conclusions on the nature of religion in some of his mature writings are not as far removed from those characteristic of eighteenth-century rationalism as the changed background to his ideas might suggest. One modern commentator on Herder has summed up these conclusions in the following surprising verdict:

> In many respects Herder's religious views are barely distinguishable from deistic ideas, in particular from those of John Toland and Matthew Tindal.
>
> (Barnard 1965:98)

Support for Barnard's verdict can be found in Herder's essay 'Of Religion, Doctrine and Rites' in the *Christian Writings*. There we find the assertion that the 'religion of the heart' is but one (Herder 1880*b*:238). Religion unifies, because it is one in all men's hearts, even though dogma divides and embitters (Herder 1880*b*:135). The ideal is presented of a religion in which doctrine and dogmas are relegated and conscience becomes primary. Religion thus becomes identical with morality: 'what religion properly and only is: the conscientious performance of our duties' (Herder 1880*b*:210). If Christianity is freed of all its dogmas, it offers something which is close to what a rationalist interpreter of the essence of true religion would have recognized. First, we would find 'the great rule of natural religion': follow the laws of creation. Second, we would find the highest rule of human and folk religion: strive and conquer with love. Third, we would discover the inner rule of the religion of experience: be true to your conscience (Herder 1880*b*:190–1). Here, then, we seem to have the rejection of religious dogmas and the identification of religion with a simple and uniform following of the moral law. Both of these themes are characteristic of rationalism. Moreover, we note the grounding of this law in the creation, which is typical of belief in natural religion.

However, while such remarks might seem to take Herder close to a Kantian vision of an ultimate, single, moral religion for mankind, examination of them in the larger context of Herder's ideas will show that he really wishes to distance himself from the ideal of a religion of reason and that he does have the appreciation of diversity and change in religion that his larger views of history and human nature might suggest. Even in the essay 'Of Religion, Doctrine and Rites' there is evidence of something that distances him from his rationalist contemporaries, namely his sentimentalist understanding of the basis of conscience. In asserting that religion cannot be 'dead laws' or 'self-evident principles without application', he affirms that it is that which 'speaks to our heart compellingly, takes hold of our impulses, awakens our sentiments and binds our innermost conscience' (Herder 1880*b*:237). The presence of this stress on inner experience, impulses, and feeling in connection with the sources of morality and conscience entails that the identification of the unifying core of religion with morality allows Herder a much wider appreciation of the forms of positive religion. The commitment to a unifying core of religion and brotherly impulses which tie human beings together in a community turns out not to be a strait-jacket into which the varying forms of religion in history are to be pressed at the cost of otherwise being dismissed as corruptions of religion. The expressionist approach to culture and the self plays its part here too, since that emphasizes the authenticity of particular ways of expressing the inner core of religion and resists attempts to judge all examples of outward religion by some single, universal standard.

One illustration of the manner in which Herder's criticism of religion shows an appreciation of diversity and thus his true distance from deism can be seen in his recognition of the importance and worth to be seen in the distinctive ways of experiencing the world characteristic of primitive and tribal religion. This recognition involves in part a redescription and in part a revaluation of the same tendencies Hume describes in *The Natural History of Religion*. The main difference from Hume lies in the point that primitive man's apprehension of the world is no longer written off as the superstitious result of ignorance, fear, and the imagination.

Herder's account of the sources of moral impulses links them to our perception of the universe. But this link is not just through the natural-law idea of perceiving a moral order in creation, but also through something much more inward and immediate. In his understanding of religion he can connect the moral impulses that bind society together with our experience of the unity of the world of nature and our sense of belonging to that unity. This is hinted at in one of his definitions of religion:

Religion is this conviction, that is our innermost consciousness of

what we are as parts of the world, what we should be as men
and what we should do.

(Herder 1880b:159)

He describes in *Yet Another Philosophy of History* how religion plays a
part in the origin of a sense of human ties and obligations. The
child's growth into these human ties is enmeshed with a kind of
'religious feeling' (Herder 1891:484–5). For man ideas of truth and
beauty come out of his sense of wonder alone. The source of the
education of the human race into humanity is imagination,
astonishment, and wonder. This is clearly meant to involve a new
appreciation of 'primitive' means of apprehending and responding
to the world. His century, with its 'philosophical deism', is
castigated for blackening the innocence, wonder, and enthusiasm of
this childlike religious feeling with the labels of superstition and
stupidity (Herder 1891:485–6).

Herder's stress on wonder, feeling, and the imagination is
connected with his organic picture of the universe and the
philosophy of *Kraft* that lies behind it. Living, historical religion, as
opposed to systems of dead doctrines or abstract speculations,
preserves through wonder and the imagination a living sense of the
unity of all things – divine, human, and natural. This is why he
can assert that the first and last philosophy has always been
religion (Herder 1887a:162). Ethics – the sphere of social ties and
the readiness to act upon them – is an outcome and expression of
this philosophy. Hence, the link in religion between conscience and
a certain way of apprehending nature. Herder describes the same
process Hume documents in *The Natural History of Religion*. He
accepts much of the Humean account of the origin of belief in gods,
but is able to represent it as the first inkling of truth among human
beings and the beginning of our education into humanity and not
something which demeans us. The readiness to posit intelligent
causes behind striking natural phenomena is our first step toward
the realization of the connectedness of things. It is not fear as such
which makes us invent the gods. Fear merely provokes us to
attempt to understand nature. Religion represents the gods as the
friends of man and seeks to bind him to them. Without the wonder
and astonishment at nature, without the sense of oneness with
things, and without the imaginative capacity to satisfy these
propensities the human understanding would never have been

directed toward its true task (Herder 1887a:161–2). This is why he can affirm that, regardless of whether religion is true or false as a system of beliefs, it has always been the instructor and comforter of mankind. It can be taken to be one of the defining features of man. We can no more expect to find a human community without it than we can expect to find one without language or customs. His affirmation of the necessary universality of religion looks plausible just because he does not identify it with any particular set of doctrines, but rather with our most fundamental way of apprehending the world and our fellows. Here there is indeed a link with deism – through its affirmation of the primacy of religion in human nature.

Herder's predominantly anti-deistic perspective shows through in the full range of his comments on religion, despite his commitment to the unity of all true religion and its grounding in morality. An example of this perspective can be found in his scathing remarks on the rationalist notion (as described in Chapter 4 above) that primitive, mythological religion is the work of priests and their deceitful ways (Herder 1887a:307–8). In general, it is in his treatment of folk religion that the fact of his radically different attitude to religion is displayed, despite the surface similarity of some of his ideas to deism. This is no accident, since this type of religion appears to be the remotest in form and content from the ideal of the religion of reason.

We can illustrate the differences pointed to in the above by looking at Herder's lengthy study of the Hebrew Bible. Where Tindal and others saw something to condemn, Herder saw something to praise. The Old Testament's record of the development of a primitive, folk religion was not to be condemned for its crudely anthropomorphic or demeaning statements about God. The very title of Herder's study, *On the Spirit of Hebrew Poetry*, shows that he is not considering the Bible as an attempt at sober description of God and his dealings with man. It is rather to be judged as an expressive product. Its value lies not in its attempt to state theological or philosophical truths, but in its containing an authentic expression of a people's way of understanding their world. A book such as Genesis is not to be judged as an attempt at accurate statement and then dismissed as lies. It is poetic in form and content, and thus cannot be classed as lying (Herder 1880a:14–15).

Stressing the value of the Hebrew Bible as authentic expression is not the same as saying that it is valuable only as a kind of collective autobiography. Though its utterance is symbolic in form, it may show through its poetry symbols which are important for the whole of the human race. Its simplicity and its unsophisticated character are praised because they preserve a way of apprehending the world and man's relation to it which is valuable for us all and which our civilization has lost. The power of a primitive people's poetry is a function of its simplicity because the images and experiences in it are closer to nature (Herder 1880a:8). Herder persistently praises the Hebrew Bible for its childlike sense of nature's presence and power. In its books we have the poetry of herdsmen whose language is adjusted to the senses and who have a powerful awareness of the proximity of God-in-nature to their lives. The Bible shows in the alleged crude anthropomorphisms for which it is condemned the source of all poetry and the fundamental nature of the human mind. These both lie in the desire to connect and assimilate everything to ourselves (Herder 1880a:2).

His verdict on his century's attitude to ancient scripture and religion is summed up in these words:

> Though this poetry may appear exaggerated to a cold deist, it is yet natural and necessary for the experience of man.
>
> (Herder 1880a:14)

THE CASE AGAINST NATURAL RELIGION IN SCHLEIERMACHER'S *SPEECHES*

We have seen that, despite the general thrust of his philosophy of history and culture, Herder's conception of religion remains to at least some degree equivocal about the role of a universal, natural religion in the religious life of mankind. He retains some inclination to think that each religion can be stripped of its dogmas and reduced to a sense of one's duties or ties to society.

The importance of Schleiermacher's *Speeches on Religion* for our purposes lies in the way they employ an understanding of culture and history similar in a number of respects to Herder's but reject unequivocally the notion that natural religion (particularly in the first two senses of that phrase distinguished in Chapter 1) is a useful term in the analysis and appreciation of religion in history.

We see in him a more consistent and thoroughgoing denial of the deistic picture of religion. Beneath this denial we shall indeed find some points of indebtedness to the notion of natural religion. The thread that links Schleiermacher to belief in natural religion is best explored after his polemic against this notion is set out.

Schleiermacher's rejection of the concept of natural religion reaches its most explicit form in the fifth of his addresses to the 'cultured despisers of religion'. The following is typical of his comments on it:

> The essence of natural religion consists almost entirely in denying everything positive and characteristic in religion and in violent polemics.

> (Schleiermacher 1958:233)

He continues by describing it as the worthy product of its age, showing 'that wretched generality and vain soberness which in everything was most hostile to true culture'. Schleiermacher's grounds for the rejection of natural religion are connected with the general aim of the fifth *Speech*, which is to show that religion is to be found in the religions (Schleiermacher 1958:211). His aim is to offer an account of the essence of religion which leads to the conclusion that religion is pre-eminently to be discovered in the despised positive religions of the world's history. Given an understanding of this essence, we shall see that there can be no universal religion (Schleiermacher 1958:53–4).

In the light of the discussion of Herder it becomes important to note Schleiermacher's refusal to identify the essence of religion with morality. We have traced a line of thought which begins with Herbert's definition of true religion as 'the worship of God in virtue' and leads through to Herder. It is broken in Schleiermacher. He recognizes in the second *Speech* that religion is allied to morality. Moral conceptions can be found in sacred writings, but nothing that is distinctive about religion is explained by noting its connection with morality. The fact is that, just as with the metaphysical beliefs associated with religion, the moral teachings attached to the world's faiths take on a distinctive character from their religious context. It is therefore impossible to explain what is distinctive in this religious context by stressing the connection between religion and morality (or metaphysics). Even if we were to find that some simple beliefs about God and some important moral claims united all faiths, we would still not have found the essence of religion; for we would have passed over whatever it is that gives these alleged common elements the character they gain from being present in religion.

If Schleiermacher is to demonstrate that religion is to be found in the religions, he has to show that it is not merely the corruption of religion that leads to its diverse and positive forms, but rather its essence that produces these. The identification of the essence of religion with feeling is meant to show just this. The contrast between feeling and doing and knowing is meant to secure the distinctiveness and autonomy of religion. Further, by identifying the essence of religion with something inward (a disposition to apprehend or respond to the world in certain ways), Schleiermacher secures the point that religion always needs to be expressed if it is to exist as a concrete reality. People's beliefs in moral and doctrinal formulae are but manifestations of this underlying disposition of feeling. Should there be any universally shared moral or doctrinal beliefs, they could be identified with religion itself only on pain of confusing a mere manifestation with the essence of religion. This point is most clearly set out in the *Christian Faith*:

> If the expression 'Religion in general' be employed, it cannot again signify such a whole [that is a community of believers]. Nothing can be fitly understood by it but the tendency of the human mind in general to give rise to religious emotions, always considered, however, along with their expression, and thus with the striving for fellowship i.e. the possibility of particular religions . . . It is only that tendency, the general susceptibility of individual souls to religious emotion, that could be called 'religion in general'.
>
> (Schleiermacher 1928:30)

Schleiermacher argues that the logic of the phrase 'natural religion' cannot be at all like that of 'the Christian religion'. If it is used to refer to that which underlies all the religions, and therefore something that is independent of the various modes and circumstances of culture and history that influence the shape of the religions of history, then it cannot also refer to a communion of belief that unites people together across the boundaries of culture and history. What unites all specific communities of belief cannot itself be a community of belief because beliefs are the result of the expression of some underlying disposition and dependent as expression on the determining influences of particular cultures. What is natural – that is to say, separate from these cultural determinants – is merely a disposition. This disposition cannot be reckoned to be a universal religion that may be compared with, or contrasted with, or discovered behind, specific religions such as Christianity or Islam. Natural religion is at best an abstraction to be drawn out of the specific religions in history and not something that competes with them (Schleiermacher 1928:48). Schleiermacher appears to be prepared to admit that there is something called 'religion in human nature' and in this respect he implicitly affirms the existence of natural religion in one sense (that is, the fourth we distinguished). The mistake lies in identifying this with a particular set of beliefs and notions.

The details of Schleiermacher's account of religion as feeling add further weight to his critical discussion of the notion of natural religion. This can be seen most clearly in the version provided in the second of the *Speeches*. There Schleiermacher avoids tying the essence of religion too closely to monotheistic belief – a failing to be seen in the account of the essence of religion as the feeling of absolute dependence in the *Christian Faith*. Amidst the many unclarities of the central description of feeling and religion in the second *Speech*, a number of comprehensible lines of thought can be distinguished. One is an extension of the kind of thinking about the unity of the world that we saw in Herder and that is widespread in German thought at the very end of the eighteenth century through the revival of interest in Spinoza and the influence of romantic aesthetics. The world is not thought of as a mere aggregate of discrete things but as a unity, bound together in the manner of an organism. As an organic totality, a single living principle runs through it. Human wholeness is to be attained through unity with this living principle and thus through the overcoming of the barriers that separate man from the universe that surrounds him. Feeling is that through which this unity can be achieved. Through feeling we not only become aware of the connectedness of all things as expressions of a single, unbounded living principle, but we also become at one with this principle. We recover both our sense of the unity of things and our sense that we are part of this unity. Our emotions may be so disposed that through them we become united with orders of being outside ourselves. Thus 'patriotic feeling' may refer to an emotional disposition that unites someone to the life of a nation; 'family feeling' to a disposition that unites someone to the life of a family. 'Religion' refers to an emotional disposition which unites the pious individual to the infinite, divine life that runs through all things. If someone has patriotic feeling he will respond to events in the life of a nation not in a way which rests upon the significance those events have for the individual's own concerns, but for their significance as expressions of the life of the nation. In religion we have the ultimate manifestation of this ability to respond to events other than for their relation to one's own immediate concerns. We respond to them in the light of their significance for the whole or as expressions of the divine (cf. Brandt 1941:182–3). Schleiermacher describes this conception in the following terms:

> every occurrence . . . is an operation of the Universe upon us. Now religion is to take up into our lives and to submit to be swayed by them, each of these influences and their consequent emotions, not by themselves but as parts of the Whole, not as limited and in opposition to other things, but as an exhibition of the Infinite in our life . . . The sum total of religion is to feel that, in highest unity, all that moves us in feeling is one.
>
> (Schleiermacher 1958:49–50)

Religion-as-feeling is so defined by Schleiermacher that its essence is different from any set of propositional judgements. It is a mode of apprehension that is pre-conceptual, though discursive thought can serve as its vehicle or expression. No amount of propositional knowledge about the world will bring with it the 'sense and taste for the Infinite' Schleiermacher sees at the heart of religion. Discursive moral thought is equally removed from the unity with the life of the universe that is recovered in religion. Not even religious doctrines and opinions are identical with the sense and taste for the Infinite. When the cultured despisers of religion criticize the fantastic opinions that may be associated with religion, they merely criticize the externals of religion (Schleiermacher 1958:14). What matters in religious doctrines is whether they stand firmly grounded upon feeling (Schleiermacher 1958:46–7). From Schleiermacher's general account of its essence, we see that if religion is to be true to its nature it must act powerfully on and in the life of individuals. It must genuinely function to shape the way in which they apprehend all the events that impinge upon them. The conceptual and institutional vehicles of religion must be vitally connected to those things which shape a person's life in society if they are truly to serve the ends of religion. This means that the concepts of religion must be related to the elements of the individual's culture, those conceptions and relations which are the immediate and inherited framework of his existence. It would serve no purpose if religion were to be expressed by beliefs or institutions which were the product of standing back from the culture in which the believer was set. The necessary potency of religion would be lost, and it would cease to be vitally related to concrete human existence.

It is now possible to summarize exactly why the natural religion of eighteenth-century rationalism cannot be taken to be the essence of religion. First, it defines religion by reference to moral and metaphysical claims which, though related to it, are not identical with it. Second, it mistakenly regards principles and opinions in religion as capturing its essence when in fact discursive propositional claims can only be outward expressions of religion's essence. Finally, it picks out a single 'correct' expression of religious feeling, which is moreover alien to the conceptual structures of living cultures. The favoured expressions of religion in natural religion are philosophers' abstractions, which, if they could be adhered to, would deaden religion and thus deny its point – to place individuals in living relationship to the universe and the life that runs through it.

The effect of Schleiermacher's description of the nature of religion is to tie living, worthwhile religious expression to cultures. More clearly than Herder he contends that the true religion for any people will be the one that corresponds to its culture. Religion in general needs the many religions because they provide the necessary mediation between it and the many diverse cultures of history. The religions of history 'are just the definite forms in which religion must exhibit itself' (Schleiermacher 1958:217). Instead of the variety in religion introduced by its connection with diverse cultures being something that is corruptive of religion's truth, it turns out to be something that is necessary for religion's truth. The objection that no particular religion in history can be true because it is tied to a particular epoch or place is deflected by transforming the truth of religion into something that is largely a matter of its authenticity. It matters that the religion of any people expresses, in its doctrines, usages, and institutions, a living relationship with the divine. The truth of religion in general can then reside in particular but divergent manifestations, and there is no problem in conceiving how a number of these could each be true.

In Schleiermacher the idea of progressive revelation, which occurs in embryonic form in Herder, is fully worked out. We can take from Schleiermacher the message that no complete truth could have been given to man at the beginning of history, for he would not have understood it and it would have been religiously valueless. Nor could any universal revelation have been received and understood, bound as men are in their thinking by the categories of their varying cultures. Each of the positive religions becomes in a way necessary as one of the forms God's revelation had to take to be comprehensible to man. As Schleiermacher clearly states, each religion is one of the forms which mankind, in some region of the earth and at some stage of development, has to accept (Schleiermacher 1958:216).

All that we have seen in Schleiermacher's account of religion so far entails a revaluation of the historical character of religion and of its positivity. With regard to religion and history, he notes that the proponent of natural religion wishes to separate religion from history altogether:

> So little is any special cultivation through the positive to be thought of, that its most genuine adherents do not even wish the religion of man to have any history of its own at all or to commence with any notable event.
>
> (Schleiermacher 1958:231)

Schleiermacher sets himself in opposition to this deistic view and also to the arguments outlined in Chapter 3 for the conclusion that true religion must be unchanging. There we saw that deistic thought wished to identify true religion with that which grew out of the relation of man and God. Since the character of that relation was unchanging, so must be true religion. Alleged religious beliefs or observances that change with the course of time can only be expressions of a departure from the divine-human relationship and the result of things which are quite extraneous to that relationship (such as political whim or the ebb and flow of fashion and fancy). For Schleiermacher, in contrast, there is no single relation between

God and man, and religion is to be identified with 'the sum of all relations of man to God' (Schleiermacher 1958:217). Connected with the notion of a progressive revelation of God to man is the idea that the divine-human relation evolves. To speak of this relation is not to speak of something that is fixed for all time but of something that exists only as a growing and changing entity. So true religion is not a unitary, indivisible whole, but a series that has diverse members and depends upon their divergent characters to exist. Schleiermacher writes:

> The whole of true religion can only be actually given in the sum of all the forms possible in this sense. It can, therefore, be exhibited only in an endless series of shapes that are gradually developed in different points of time and space, and nothing adds to its complete manifestation that is not found in one of these forms.
>
> (Schleiermacher 1958:223)

With this notion of an evolving series of relationships between God and man the deistic contrast between what is essential in the divine-human relation and what is subject to change vanishes. Change is not necessarily the mark of corruption from without, for it may be the sign of evolution from within. History is not alien to religion; rather, religion needs its involvement in history if it is to bear witness to the sum of relations between man and God. Schleiermacher can therefore acknowledge with a welcoming voice, and not as a sign of criticism, the fact that religion 'bears traces of the culture of every age and of the history of every race of men' (Schleiermacher 1958:235).

The re-appraisal of the positivity of religion follows from the conclusions on history and religion just noted. We have in the many positive religions of the world definite and distinct forms of the relation of God to man, severally necessary for religion to exist in completeness. These forms of religion will be in part defined by their cultural and historical settings. They will thus be like all traditional products of culture in being dependent on contingent facts for their existence and identity. They will characteristically have definite starting-points in history, contingent origins which any one joining them will have to accept as given. The deists would see these features as marks of the essential arbitrariness of positive forms of faith and see a corruption of the intellect in the necessity to accept their defining features as given. Schleiermacher, in contrast, contends that such features are essential to the religions, being living forms of relation to God, and the acceptance of these features by the religious individual is also essential if he is to be party to a living, definite form of relation to the divine. We might compare his contention with the riposte one could make to anyone foolish enough to complain that to learn to speak and express his own thoughts he had to accept the contingent and arbitrary forms of a particular human language. The contingency and arbitrariness he complains of is of course essential if he is to acquire a means of communication at all and to share a living relationship with others through that. To attempt to construct a language on rational first principles is not an alternative to first accepting what he dismisses as arbitrary and merely positive. Schleiermacher's conclusion on the rationalist's rejection of reliance upon and acceptance of the forms of positive faith is as follows:

> Hence their resistance to the positive and arbitrary is resistance to the definite and real. If a definite religion may not begin with an original fact, it cannot begin at all ... And if a religion is not to be definite it is not a religion at all, for religion is not a name applied to loose, unconnected impulses ... Suppose someone were to object to come into the world because he would not be this man or that, but man in general! The polemic of natural religion against the positive is this polemic against life and it is the permanent state of its adherents.

> (Schleiermacher 1958:234)

The effect of Schleiermacher's teachings concerning the historicity and positivity of religion is to remove the opposition between what is humanly and divinely important, on the one hand, and what is affected by the diversities of history and culture, on the other. What is important in religion is its embodiment of the relationship between human nature and the Infinite. This is now portrayed as an evolving relationship, which must change with culture and history because at least one of the terms in the relationship – man – must use the changing forms of history and culture to enter into and express the relationship. It might now appear that Schleiermacher is completely divorced from the tradition of understanding religion in terms of natural religion. Yet, just as in Herder, we can see in Schleiermacher an acceptance of the utility of the notion of natural religion in its third sense, for, like Herder, Schleiermacher accepts that religion must be rooted in human nature. We see again that 'domestication' of revelation which allows the contrast between natural (human) religion and divine religion to disappear. Acceptance of this third sense of natural religion is also linked to the tacit acknowledgement of the fourth sense (a natural human religiousness) that we have already noted.

Early on in the first *Speech* Schleiermacher announces his intention to show the human source of religion, 'the human tendency' from which religion proceeds (Schleiermacher 1958:11). If in the final *Speech* he argues for the superiority of Christianity over other faiths, it is on the ground that it displays this human tendency to the most perfect degree yet encountered. It does not stand out as something which, in its origins or course, exhibits exceptions to the normal laws or causes which produce human religion. These laws and causes in turn do not disturb our normal expectations of nature or human psychology. Religion, says Schleiermacher, leaves physics and psychology untouched (Schleiermacher 1958:88). We have seen how the contrast between divine and natural religion depends on seeking a miraculous or supernatural origin for one faith as against others. This ceases to be a ground of distinction within religion in the *Speeches* because the contrast between the miraculous (or supernatural) and the natural vanishes. 'Miracle' becomes merely the religious name for an event. Any event can be seen as a miracle, for a miracle is merely a sign of the Infinite, and all events are potentially signs of this sort. The notions of revelation, inspiration, and grace are similarly domesticated (Schleiermacher 1958:89–90).

Schleiermacher shows in his treatment of miracle, revelation, and prophecy that, for all that he undoubtedly rejects the notion of natural religion, he is indebted to the Enlightenment's critique of religion. He is seeking an origin of religion in human nature and, with that, endorsing the comparability of all religions and the universality of the concept of religion. In like manner, his account of doctrine and dogma in religion displays clear indebtedness to the criticisms of the externals of religion provided by the Enlightenment – hence his concern to show that such things are not the essence of religion, but are merely expressions of that essence. The naturalistic perspective on religion remains, and so therefore, tacitly, does the concept of natural religion in one of its guises. Also present is the distinction between the foundations of religion (that is, the human tendency from which religion springs) and the superstructure of religion (provided by expressions or realizations of religion). Through the polemic of Schleiermacher's case against natural religion there emerges, then, a positive if tacit endorsement of Senses 3 and 4 of the notion of natural religion. The endorsement, for Sense 3, is present in the denial of the existence of divine religion and the affirmation of the naturalness of all forms of religion; the endorsement for Sense 4 in the commitment to the existence of a natural human religiousness.

Questions can rightly be asked about the precise character of the naturalism to be found in the *Speeches* and in *The Christian Faith*. There is no question, however, that J. Forstman is right in his verdict on the account of religion within the *Speeches*: 'It is religion within the limits of human perception' (Forstman 1977:79).

HEGEL ON RELIGION IN HISTORY

No attempt can be made here to offer anything like a full survey of Hegel's philosophy or even of his philosophy of religion. A brief treatment of a few selected themes can, however, add in important respects to what has been found so far in the romantic reaction to and development of the concept of natural religion.

The continuity between Hegel's thought on the character of religion in history and that of Schleiermacher's and Herder's is marked. This can be seen straightforwardly if we interpret the account of *Geist* and its relation to history in such works as the *Lectures on the Philosophy of History* and *The Phenomenology of Spirit* as a description of the human essence and its unfolding. *Geist* is minimally a way of referring to the essential characteristics of human nature, even if it has additional senses in the Hegelian system; so that a statement like 'Spirit is self-contained existence' (Hegel 1956:17) is at least a way of affirming that a peculiar kind of freedom is one of the defining characteristics of humanity. To tell us that history is the unfolding of spirit is minimally to affirm that the distinctive characteristics of humanity need to be realized through historical process and that human history is intelligible as a whole because it is shaped by this gradual realizing of human nature.

Interpreted as a philosophy of human nature Hegel's account of *Geist* shows its similarity and indebtedness to Herder in a number of key respects. First, there is a common emphasis on freedom as the distinguishing mark of human existence; second, there is an insistence on the dependence of freedom on self-knowledge; and third, there is the joint assertion that such distinguishing characteristics are not given but are to be realized. They can only exist as actualities at the conclusion of an historical process. In the *Philosophy of History* these linked ideas are expounded in Hegel's gloss on the defining characteristic of *Geist* – self-contained existence:

> Now this is freedom exactly. For if I am dependent, my being is referred to something else which I am not . . . I am free, on the contrary, when my existence depends on myself. This self-contained existence of Spirit is none other than self-consciousness – consciousness of one's own being.
>
> (Hegel 1956:17–18)

He continues by asserting that *Geist* makes itself actually what it is potentially. The realization of the essential properties of *Geist* by human beings is the key to understanding the general course of world history:

> it may be said of universal history, that it is the exhibition of spirit in the process of working out the knowledge of that which it is potentially.
>
> (Hegel 1956:18)

The similarities between Herder and Hegel become even more marked when we note the crucial role of expressionism in Hegel's account of the realization of *Geist* in human nature. The process of the slow achievement of self-consciousness and freedom on the part of humanity is effected by the succession of national cultures in history. Such cultures are the necessary vehicles for the attainment of self-knowledge, because it is through expressive activity in culture that man knows himself. Self-consciousness arises out of the bodying-forth of ideas, desires, and values that we find in the creation of a culture. There is a further respect in which the distinctive achievement of *Geist* – freedom – is realized by humanity through life in national cultures. Through the creation of culture man comes to live in a human world. He comes to occupy an environment which is not alien to him, but which reflects his ideas and values back to him. He slowly approaches a self-contained existence, in so far as the world comes to reflect his will. In and through culture man can create a world which is his and thus attain a radical freedom which distinguishes creatures in whom *Geist* can be realized.

The detailed arguments for Hegel's application of the expressionist notion are to be found in the famous discussion of the master-slave relationship in *The Phenomenology of Spirit*. Just two themes from that discussion need to be noted here. One is contained in Hegel's assertion that self-consciousness only exists when it is exercised for another – that is, when it is acknowledged (Hegel 1977:111). If one accepts that consciousness of one's own thoughts can only exist or achieve stability if those thoughts can be recognized by others, then their bodying-forth in outwardly recognizable forms is necessary if this defining feature of mind is to be realized. Expression of mental contents becomes a condition of their knowability. A further important theme is signalled in Hegel's defence of the idea that work is the means whereby permanence and significance is given to mental contents. Work, or purposive activity in general, fixes mental contents in objectivity and permanence. Further, it transforms the objects on which it is directed from alien things into objects that are not separate from the self. Through work the world of objects ceases to be seen as opposed to the subject of consciousness but becomes something that belongs to him (Hegel 1977:118).

It is through these linked ideas that Hegel can claim that history is the development through successive stages of the idea of freedom, and connect this idea with expression and the successive national cultures of history:

The very essence of spirit is activity; it realizes its potentiality – makes itself its own deed, its own work – and thus becomes an object to itself; contemplates itself as an objective existence. Thus it is with the spirit of a people: it is a spirit having strictly defined characteristics, which erects itself into an objective world, that exists and persists in a particular religious form of worship, customs, constitution and political laws, in the whole complex of its institutions, in the events that make up its history.

That is its work – that is what this particular nation is. Nations are what their deeds are.

(Hegel 1956:73–4)

Out of this understanding of history and culture comes a version of the idea of progressive revelation found in Herder and Schleiermacher. One of the functions of the idea of progressive revelation is to provide a deduction of the necessity of different forms of positive religion in history. For Hegel this necessity follows from the need of *Geist* to be realized through the stages of human expression and freedom represented by successive national cultures. Religion must exhibit movement through successive and distinct stages because it is conditioned by, and indeed is a part of, the general progress of *Geist* through cultures. The specific forms of religion in history correspond to specific points in the progress of *Geist*. Each religion contributes to, and is in turn shaped by, the stage *Geist* has reached in that religion's particular geographical and historical setting. Behind and within each religion is an historically conditioned form of human self-consciousness and freedom. Each religion makes a vital contribution to the stage of self-consciousness in which it is embedded and is in turn shaped by it. Each religion is in a manner of speaking inescapable and each helps to forward, through the connectedness of stages of *Geist* in history, a larger historical process.

The points of agreement between Hegel and the other writers considered in this chapter can now be summarized. From the very brief sketch offered of the elements of his philosophy, it is apparent that he joins with Herder and Schleiermacher in seeing the diverse religions and cultures of history as stages in the achievement of expressive wholeness on the part of mankind. The necessity of the historical character of this process is secured, as in the other writers, through a developmental idea of human nature and through the linking of expression to culture. In sum, we find Hegel in agreement with the point that there is human worth in the history of religions.

There would be no purpose in attempting even a very brief sketch of Hegel's thought on religion if we could not find in him distinctive ideas and emphases, which could be seen to influence the way the history of religions has been conceived and which provided additional reflections on the theme of natural religion. Three such distinctive emphases will be outlined here. They concern the role of reason in religion, the link between religion and political institutions, and the relationship between the humanity of religion and the divinity of God.

In the various transcripts of his *Lectures on the Philosophy of Religion* Hegel comments on and rejects the thesis that religion is essentially founded upon feeling (Hegel 1984:271 ff. and 390 ff.). He concedes that it is important that the believer have God in his feeling, just as it is important in the moral life to have the good in one's feeling. No mere determination of feeling, however, can be identified with the essence of religion, because feeling in itself is blind and fleeting. It gains a determinate object and some measure of stability only when informed by some content or other. This means that feeling must be guided by thought and directed by concepts to be worthwhile. Conceptual and rational thought is necessary as the director of feeling if it is to be anything other than arbitrary. Hegel puts this point in the following way:

> The content must be true in and for itself if the feeling is to count as true. For that reason it is also said that one's feelings or one's heart must be purified and cultivated; natural feelings cannot be the proper impulses to action. What this says is precisely that what is genuine is not the content of the heart as such, but instead what ought to be the heart's *goal* and *interest* – this content and these determinations should become and be what is genuinely true. But what is the genuinely true we first learn through representations and thought.
>
> (Hegel 1984:395–6)

Hegel's criticism of Schleiermacher's route to the discovery of the essence of religion is one source of his insistence that the process of the generation of religion in human life and history, and of culture in general, should be seen to be the work of reason. Hegel affirms that however complicated and arbitrary the formation of religious conceptions in history may appear to be, it must be rational. He connects its being the embodiment of the work of reason with its being a human process (Hegel 1984:198–9).

The emphasis on reason as the operative cause behind changing conceptions of the divine in religious history is part of a larger insistence on Hegel's part that history consists in the rational and necessary course of *Geist* (Hegel 1956:10). Whatever else is intended in this assertion, it affirms at least that history is fuelled by human reason and thus embodies an intelligible process. Hegel is contending that the expressive processes that produce the national cultures which are the basic building blocks of history could only serve in the realization of *Geist* if they are controlled by conceptions and ideas. These processes of expression cannot be the work of blind feeling or unreason if they are really to advance man in his journey to self-knowledge and freedom. Hegel's general understanding of history thus demands an emphasis on purposive activity (activity embodying conception and controlled by reason) because that understanding displays history as a journey in knowledge. Only such activity helps consciousness become aware of itself. When we are told in the *Lectures on the Philosophy of History* that reason reveals itself in the world (Hegel 1956:9), the statement gets its sense from the notion that reason shows itself in purposive activity and work. This understanding of the function of reason is connected with the more restricted conception to be gleaned from the pages of *The Phenomenology of Spirit*. There reason is given the task of overcoming the partial and limited apprehension of things that is due to the operations of the understanding. Reason in its larger role as the controller of expressive activity is also concerned with the overcoming of divisions and limited apprehensions, because through reason in history the division between ourselves and the world is slowly conquered. Reason's target here is again a partial and limited understanding – of ourselves.

Reference to reason as behind expression in religion and other aspects of culture helps us both to see more clearly why Hegel should so consistently portray history as the history of ideas and to discover some minimal sense in his affirmation that history is a dialectical process. For, like a sequence of ideas, history is intelligible from within and proceeds according to a pattern that is determined by a set of internal relations between its component parts. It is self-determined (Hegel 1956:63–4). Hegel does not need, therefore, any agent outside history to be its controlling force or drive.

Hegel's discussion of the role of reason in our conception of God in the *Lectures on the Philosophy of Religion* displays some attempt to save part of the Enlightenment's conception of religion. Indeed the entire discussion of the relation between feeling and reason in religion tries to draw out a compromise from within the conflicting tendencies of previous philosophies of religion. However, we can see that Hegel on reason in history and religion achieves a decisive shift away from the Enlightenment's use of reason as a source of beliefs and notions in human culture. Hegel's invocation of reason as the origin of religious conceptions is not, for example, the appeal to a faculty which will produce timeless, universal beliefs about God. Reason is still thought of as a faculty that is directed towards the discovery of truth, because, among other things, it is related to the achievement of self-understanding. Yet this and other tasks are performed from within a particular place in the development of *Geist*. Reason as one of the component powers of *Geist* is indeed bound up in *Geist*'s progress through history. For a number of reasons, then, Hegel's philosophy can relate true religion to the work of reason without thereby contending that religion must be beyond historical change or cultural variability. More than Kant (as described in the previous chapter), Hegel offers us an evolutionary account of reason. This is of great importance in the development of the concept of religion and of the historiography of religion.

We have seen that the Enlightenment's conception of reason not only encourages a contrast between the religion of reason and historically varied forms of faith, but also between such 'natural religion' and those manifestations of religion that are the product of the human imagination and/or political institutions. The romantic revaluation of the imagination, illustrated in this chapter by reference to Herder, removes part of the force of this latter contrast. Some of this revaluation is preserved, in my opinion, in Hegel's broadening of the notion of reason and more generally in the great stress he repeatedly places on art as an agent in the realization of *Geist* in history. There is in Hegel in addition a matching revaluation of the significance of the political. Like the revaluation of the imagination this too opens up a larger portion of the religious life of mankind in history to positive appreciation as something humanly important and necessary.

In general terms it is easy to see why the political structures of nations should be important in Hegel's account of the realization of *Geist*. Once we grasp the connection between *Geist*, self-knowledge, expression, and freedom, we can see that *Geist*'s realization is served by its involvement in the life of states.

Geist in man will be realized through his membership of human society. The master-slave discussion and other aspects of Hegel's argument establish in his system that the journey towards full self-knowledge and freedom must be a corporate one. The translation of those elements of a human society's culture which distinguish it and bind it together into forms of law and government is a necessary step in this corporate journey. Laws, constitution, and government are essential means whereby a society objectifies and reflects upon its fundamental values and conceptions. They are thus the means through which it can achieve full self-knowledge of those values and conceptions. Through their objectification in law and institutions, a society's values come to have greater reality in shaping the world in which its members live. The creation of political realities is thus an agent in forming a world which is not alien to human consciousness. Hegel's understanding of political life in states enables him to represent political institutions and structures as important elements in the expressive activity of the human self in society and therefore as central agents in the achievement of self-contained existence on the part of *Geist.* It is by reminding ourselves of these ideas that we can understand those seemingly paradoxical statements in Hegel to the effect that living under law is the completion and realization of freedom (see Hegel 1956:38). Freedom is not the mere absence of external restraint but the attainment of self-contained existence. The work and life of human beings in society is completed with the stages in objectifying society's values that come with the institutional expression of those values in law and government.

The force of Hegel's views on the importance of the political can be seen by considering his remarks on the state of nature in *The Philosophy of Right.* These remarks are relevant to our theme because some earlier accounts of the state of nature represent in extreme form the kind of thinking about the corrupting effect of political society on human nature we have encountered in the deists' portrayal of man's loss of his original natural and rational religion. It is of the essence of the type of picture of the state of nature Hegel is attacking that it portrays man in the state of nature as a rational and moral being. His move to living in political society is to be justified only if it secures ends which his rational and moral nature already makes him aware of. In Hegel's view, however, it is fundamentally wrong to see political society as supervenient on, or extrinsic to, an original, pre-social rational and moral nature. For it is only through man's growth in developing political societies that he comes to have rational will. He develops as a moral being in such societies. By nature – that is, considered in abstraction from the kind of relationships and forms of self-consciousness which membership of such societies makes possible – he is not a rational or moral creature at all – he has not risen above the level of animality. We cannot in Hegel's opinion consider what is proper to human nature by seeking those properties man has in a state of 'nature' divorced from social and political institutions. The institutions we live under are not in the normal case to be considered as foreign or alien impositions on our humanity (though of course in particular cases social and political institutions can be alien or corrupting). We can now see why Hegel should comment dismissively on the idea of a natural origin for rights (Hegel 1942:116). There can be no natural rights, if by these we mean rights that arise from an a-social or a-political condition. A similar point surely applies to the idea of a natural religion, if that too refers to something arising from individual consciousness in abstraction from a social state. The contention that rational and moral will is a creation of life in political society is destructive both of belief in a natural origin for morality and of belief in a natural origin for religion. 'Natural religion' does have a use in commentary on Hegel's survey of religion. It can refer to those religions which concentrate on the natural world as the locus of the divine, but they are not natural in the sense of being a-social or a-political.

Hegel's portrayal of the importance of religion in national cultures complements his general account of the necessary growth of *Geist* in a framework provided by evolving political societies. He writes of the identity between a people's religion and their political constitution. If their constitution is the most realized form that their collective awareness of their shared values and notions takes, then this constitution is in turn expressive of their conception of God and dependent on that conception. Their religion will contain an expressed consciousness of the most fundamental values which bind them together as a people, and in this respect their religion will be one of the foundations on which their constitution rests. 'The conception of God constitutes the general basis of a people's character' (Hegel 1956:50). The link between religion and constitution forged in Hegel's writings provides the most forceful critique of that disparagement of civil theology and religion we have found to be characteristic of the elevation of natural religion.

Hegel's view of the social and political character of realized human nature complicates any account of how he stands to the fourth sense of natural religion distinguished in this study – a natural human religiousness. It follows from what Hegel affirms about the vital role of religion in the progressive realization of *Geist* in successive national cultures that religion is a universal phenomenon for Hegel and that religion is the expression of primary principles in human nature. But any 'natural religiousness' we have is something which needs an institutional, social, and political setting to flourish. Human nature does not contain religion, if human nature is somehow abstracted from historical and social life. (The relation of religion and human nature in the light of a necessary social understanding of human nature will be further considered in Chapters 7 and 8 below.)

Hegel's teaching on the importance of political culture reveals him to be the source of radical criticisms of much that is implied in earlier uses of the notion of natural religion. We have already seen, however, that he is allied to the belief in the humanity of religion and to some form of the belief in a natural human religiousness. He thus endorses some of the traditional emphases contained in the notion of natural religion. (His insistence of the role of reason in religion would be another point of at least formal agreement with earlier beliefs in the centrality of natural religion.) Two points have emerged in Hegel so far in support of the theme of the humanity of religion: the argument for the rationality of religion from the premiss of its humanity, and the account of history as a self-determining process which accordingly requires no external moving force. In his commitment to the humanity of religion he is in agreement with the thought of Schleiermacher. However, in his treatment of this theme it is possible to see a major criticism of Schleiermacher's account and this leads to an important difference between Hegel and any writer we have considered so far. With this difference comes an interesting development in the concept of religion.

Hegel's departure in the manner in which he treats the humanity of religion can be brought out if we remind ourselves of the way the romantic outlook in Schleiermacher explains the existence of religious diversity. The divine-human relationship is held to

produce its varying results because of man's irreversible involvement with culture and history. God's revelation varies because it is
always cast in the terms provided by man's diverse and changing
cultures. Reminding ourselves of Schleiermacher's reference on the
first page of the *Speeches* to 'the eternal and holy being that lies
beyond the world', we might be moved to ask of this account of the
dependence of religion on culture 'But what is the divine really
like, what is the *truth* about the divine?' It seems that no answer
can be given unless the immanence of God is more unequivocally
stressed than Schleiermacher allows. All knowledge of God has
been relativized to cultures. These are in danger of becoming an
impenetrable barrier between man and an absolute which lies
beyond them. The divine seems set to become an unknowable
thing-in-itself of which we only ever perceive appearances. To
avoid this it seems we need a God whose reality lies within culture
and history and not beyond them.

The important criticism noted above of the romantic failure to
integrate its picture of the humanity of religion with its view of the
relation between religion and God can be found in the Introduction
to Hegel's *Lectures on the Philosophy of Religion*. He points out
how his contemporaries are content to say that 'we can know only
our relation to God, not what God himself is' (Hegel 1984:163).
Human religion can be studied and followed, but not God himself.
Hegel hints at a fundamental contradiction in his contemporaries'
thought about God and religion. They must posit in their general
account of religion an essential connection between human
consciousness and God, for otherwise the concept of religion would
be devalued in their eyes. Yet, they must, on the other hand,
separate God from the consciousness of him contained in religion if
they are to maintain that in religion we have only our relation to
God and not God himself. This point of criticism is immediately
followed by a reminder of the expressionist understanding of the
self that Hegel shares with his protagonists. God is *Geist* (spirit)
and the essence of *Geist* is that:

> spirit is a self-manifesting, a being for spirit. *Spirit is for spirit* and
> of course not merely in an external, contingent manner. Instead
> it *is* spirit only in so far as it is *for* spirit. This is what constitutes
> the concept of spirit itself. Or, to put the point more
> theologically, God's spirit is present essentially in his community;

God *is* spirit only in so far as God is in his *community*.

(Hegel 1984:164)

If we say that God manifests *Geist* most perfectly then our account of his nature must follow our understanding of the key qualities of *Geist*. If this understanding rests on the expressionist conception of the self, then we shall have to conclude that God's nature cannot be fixed independently of his relationship to other manifestations of *Geist*. His involvement with others, his communication with them and expression of himself found in human history, and particularly religion, must be essential to the realization of his nature. If the absolute is *Geist* then its existence and character must be bound up with its expression and thus with human culture and history.

A consistent application of the expressionist understanding of the self appears to lead to the conclusion that God cannot exist totally separate from the human phenomenon of religion. Human religion must in some sense be the locus of the divine. On some occasions Hegel takes this thought to the extreme of identifying God with humanity and religion:

> there cannot be two kinds of reason and two kinds of spirit, a divine and a human reason or a divine and a human spirit ... Human reason ... is the divine reason within humanity. Spirit, in so far as it is called divine spirit, is not a spirit beyond the stars or beyond the world; for God is present, is omnipresent, and strictly as *spirit* is God present in spirit.
>
> (Hegel 1984:130)

He continues these remarks by affirming that religion is not an invention of human beings but an effect of the divine at work. This assertion of the divine character of religion is compatible with that of its human character, if we take the bringing of God into the human world seriously. Doing that, we could not treat religion as an *invention* of human beings, since that would be to attribute the wrong significance to the work of reason.

Obscurity and a maze of conflicting interpretations surround Hegel's precise conception of God. Much of this obscurity centres on the question just broached of how close his conception is to the traditional notion of a transcendent being. No attempt can be made in these pages to sort out the difficulties that beset a clear and consistent reading of Hegel's many comments on the relation

177

between *Geist* and the idea of God. The general tendency of Hegel's comments can at least be indicated and with sufficient definition to enable a contrast with deism to be drawn. We have seen how the deistic belief that positive religion must be corrupt is based not only on a belief about the independence of human nature from culture, but also on a belief that God is manifested in an unchanging series of laws and relations. God's being is quite independent of, and unaffected by, his involvement with culture. As well as endorsing the alternative conception of man offered by writers such as Herder and Schleiermacher, Hegel brings into greater prominence a direction in thinking about the character of the divine that is implicit in the work of some of his contemporaries. Hegel's use of *Geist* to interpret the notion of God implies at the very least that the divine is not an unchanging entity which is complete in its reality prior to its involvement in history; the divine is being assimilated more to an immanent principle within human history. Change and evolution are accordingly of the essence of that which Hegel refers to as 'God'. God's self-realization is to be found within the evolving life of mankind. The positivity which characterizes man's historically conditioned life in culture can no longer be rejected, not least because the tendency of Hegel's account of God as *Geist* is to sanctify or divinize this historically conditioned life.

There are many aspects of Hegel's philosophy of religion which I have not touched on. But enough has been said to show how Hegel's idealism, reinforcing and going beyond romanticism, provides a rejection of one of the key ideas behind belief in natural religion. This is the idea that if religion is the embodiment of the divine's dealings with what is fundamental in humanity, it should preach the same method of salvation wherever and whenever it exists and regardless of political or social context.

CONCLUSION

The kind of perspectives on religion arising from the representatives of romanticism and idealism we have discussed brings us close to the achievement of the modern concept of religion, whose rise we have been attempting to illustrate. These perspectives were extremely influential on those nineteenth-century scholars in whose hands the historical and global study of religion reached maturity.

Such conclusions on the significance of the ideas discussed in this chapter can be illustrated if we consider what thoughts about the nature of religion we would have if we went along with the characterization of religion given by the writers discussed in it.

First, we should expect to see in religion an historical reality that can only be studied through the medium of history. All three writers would lead us to think that forms of religious expression inevitably change and that these changes are connected with the larger changes within human culture and institutions.

Second, we should expect to see in the historical record of the religions more than a mere tale of the base and the trivial. This is in fact how the more extreme critics of religion in history such as Hume did represent it, and how Christian theology has often represented the history of non-Christian religions.

Third, and more positively, we should expect to see in religion the presence of central aspects of man's life in society. All the writers discussed in this chapter try to locate in religion irreducibly fundamental aspects of man's awareness of himself as an individual or social being. As a consequence, man's participation in religion makes, according to their views, an essential contribution to the full realization of a proper human life in society.

Fourth, because they root religion in a fundamental aspect of human awareness, they represent all faiths as expressions of one underlying human phenomenon. All become the outward manifestations of the one set of human powers or modes or perception. This point is most clear in Schleiermacher and Hegel. Though these two authors, like Herder, argue for the superiority of Christianity in the history of faiths, they still conclude that it belongs to the same order as other expressions of mankind's religious capacities. It has a similar explanation to other faiths, similar objects and goals.

The third and fourth points in this summary seem to be testimony to the manner in which the concept of natural religion bore important fruits in the development of the concept of religion even among those writers who were critical of some of its implications.

Finally, if we accepted the general picture of religions arising out of romanticism and idealism we would be committed to the ultimate intelligibility of religious change and development. The idea that religion involves the progressive revelation of God, or the unfolding of an absolute characterized by reason, suggests, to say the least, that there will be a discoverable rationale behind the major developments of religion in history. Commitment to the existence of such a rationale need not be incompatible with accepting the presence of accident and contingency in the history of religions. Hegel, for one, does not deny the existence of unreason or merely personal ambition in history. But we could hardly accept the vision of religion in history of a Hegel and regard such factors as the major ones in the determinations of religion's course. We should expect, given the beliefs about the rationale to religion's history that we have documented, that overall this history should add up to a *story*. We should expect that a large enough view of the history of religion should reveal some movement, direction, or evolution in man's religious life. The kind of sense in the history of religion should become clear once its basic facts have become known, even allowing for those passages in the history that will stand as exceptions to it. To a large extent this sense can be seen as deriving from the evolution of man's natural religiousness within and behind the outward details of religion in culture.

When we think of the consequences of the romantic and idealist philosophies of history, we can see why they exerted such a potent influence on the early development of the study of religion. Not only did the terms of these philosophies demand that religion should be studied historically if its full reality was to be understood, but they held out the promise that the study of human religion would be important in achieving a full understanding of human nature and would be successful in discovering some overall sense in religious history.

7

NATURAL RELIGION AND THE SCIENCE OF RELIGION

INTRODUCTION

Looking back to Chapter 6 we see the importance of the romantic and idealist reaction to deistic thought in the development of our modern concept of religion. What emerges with romanticism and idealism is a form of naturalism which is capable of treating all religious developments historically. This is allied to a plea for history as the medium through which religion comes to fruition and for the study of history as the indispensable means for understanding religion. But history is not seen merely as the sphere in which particular religious facts emerge and specific forms of religion develop. It also shows the slow evolution of something that underlies any particular religion – this being the essence of religion itself. A form of human consciousness which is 'religion' in the singular evolves along with the outward forms of 'religion' in the plural. The evolution of religion in the singular behind the progress of the many particular religions enables writers such as Schleiermacher and Hegel to expect a general logic or pattern to be seen behind that progress. This pattern has two aspects: in one light it is the logic of the unfolding of humankind's natural religiousness, and thus reflects a dynamic in human nature; in another, it is a form of general revelation, reflecting the dynamic of the divine's dealings with humanity.

We should expect to find, if our account be correct, that those responsible for founding the scientific and historical study of religion should show clear evidence of the influence of this inheritance of ideas. A brief glance at two of the most important

181

founders of the history of religions bears this out. P. D. Chantepie de la Saussaye and C. P. Tiele share a basic commitment to a naturalistic approach to the study of religions. Tiele affirms as a fundamental principle of the study of religions that 'all changes and transformations are the results of natural growth, and find in it their best explanation' (Tiele 1877:2). Chantepie likewise affirms that it must be possible to explain religion as part of the mental and social development of mankind, praising Hume for pointing out the necessity of a natural history of religion as he does so (Chantepie 1891:10–12). Religion can only be realized as a product of the natural and essential characteristics of man; supernatural explanations are to be excluded.

Chantepie links this plea for naturalism to a threefold account of the necessary conditions for the emergence of a 'Science of Religion'. In the first place a philosophy of religion independent of the specifics of Christian dogma is required. Kant, Schleiermacher, and above all Hegel are credited with the creation of this. Next, students of religion require the backing of a philosophy of history which enables them to make sense of the history of culture and civilization, one which will allow the study of history to be more than the documenting of isolated, outward events and more than the study of political acts. Herder is given credit as the founder of this philosophy of history. Finally, the science of religion requires the availability of material facts about religion to fill out this framework. The science of religion divides into the connected disciplines of the history and the philosophy of religion. Both support each other – philosophy of religion needs the facts provided by history to give it content, while the history of religion requires philosophy for its definition and interpretation of religion. The object of this twofold science is the study of religion in its essence and manifestations (Chantepie 1891:7–8). The commitment to a 'religion' behind the religions is clear in this, as it is in Chantepie's statement that 'religion is the specific and common property of mankind' (Chantepie 1891:14). The many religions cannot be this property; only something unitary and underlying them can. This capacity for religion enables Chantepie to reconcile naturalism with a religious perspective on the study of religions by introducing general revelation as a controlling factor in the growth of religion: 'To . . . us religion seems to spring from the very essence of men, but under influences and circumstances wherein the activity of God is manifest' (Chantepie 1891:33).

To see how the inheritance influencing the pioneers of the historical and scientific study of religions works in greater detail it is necessary to turn to the writings of the man whom Chantepie credits with the greatest claim to be the founder of this study: F. Max Mueller.

F. MAX MUELLER

A number of writers associate Max Mueller's name with the foundation of the modern study of religion (cf. Wach 1958:3). One reason for this is the extent and importance of his efforts as a translator and editor of religious texts. This aspect of his work is not our concern in this study. Another ground of his fame – though perhaps we should say 'notoriety', given the scorn heaped upon it – is his account of the nature of mythology. Mueller today still appears to receive greatest attention as the author of a theory of myth which rests upon the notion that mythology is a disease or corruption of language. This aspect of his work was the subject of much critical attention during Mueller's working life at the end of the nineteenth century. But the general discredit into which his theory of myth has fallen does not detract from the main thing upon which his claim to be the founder of the science of religion rests – that is, his systematic account and defence of the aims, methods, and presuppositions of the historical and comparative study of religion. As an apologist for the study of religion Mueller was unmatched in his day, and his apology did much to gain the discipline respectability and attention.

Mueller's apology for the study of religion rests upon accounts of the nature of religion, history, revelation, and human nature that show clear indebtedness to the thinkers on the nature of religion whose ideas are documented in earlier chapters of this book. The line of indebtedness stretches back through romantic and idealist German thinkers of the nineteenth century to Kant and the deists. Mueller's work on the science of religion provides the necessary detailed proof that reflection on natural religion in relation to the nature of religion provided the concept of religion on which the modern study of religion was built. He signals his own indebtedness to the philosophical traditions in question in his account of the intellectual training which lay behind his discovery of religion and its place in history. Herder, Hegel, and thinkers of the romantic movement occupy pride of place in this account (Mueller 1889:17, 261–2). His relationship to such thinkers becomes clearer still when the content of his portrayal of the nature and presuppositions of the science of religion is examined.

In Mueller's voluminous writings there is a cumulative attempt to build a complete science of human thought, starting with the scientific study of language and proceeding through the study of mythology and religion to the science of thought proper. The science of religion makes its contribution, therefore, to a larger study of human nature – a fact which alerts us to Mueller's refusal to see the science of religion as being confined to the assembly of external facts about particular religions. He defines its aims succinctly as being 'to find out what religion is, what foundation it has in the soul of man, and what laws it follows in its historical growth' (Mueller 1893a:7). The first two of these aims match Chantepie's first branch of the discipline, the philosophy of religion; the third aim obviously fits the second branch, the history of religion. Mueller himself gives the science two branches, which he calls 'comparative theology' and 'theoretic theology'. The former is said to deal with the historical forms of religion, and the latter has the task of explaining the 'conditions under which religion is possible' (Mueller 1893a:16–17). Sometimes Mueller associates these branches of the science of religion with, respectively, the science of religions (in the plural) and the science of religion (in the singular) (Mueller 1889:53).

Both comparative and theoretic theology call for further explanation. The necessity of the comparative and historical study of religions involved in the first of these is entailed by the need to discover the laws religious history follows, implying the need for historical knowledge which will be general in form and not confined to one particular religion. Mueller reiterates time and again the fact that 'religions change and must change with the constant changes of thought and language in the progress of the human race' (Mueller 1889:275). The depth of his thought on the necessary historical character of religion will be clearer later. The necessity of the comparative character of knowledge of religions is affirmed in the use of the famous tag, derived from Goethe, 'He who knows one, knows none' (Mueller 1893a:13). The essential thought behind it is that the nature of any religion is only truly seen when it is viewed as part of a larger whole. This involves two things: first, seeing it in the context of a larger human history that extends beyond it, something that is only revealed when a knowledge of many religions is gained; second, seeing it in relation to aspects of human nature that again only become clearly apprehended when many manifestations of human religion are studied. To know only one religion, we may say, precludes knowing it as an example of *religion*. This takes us to theoretic theology. Discovering the conditions under which religion is possible is clearly related to discovering what in essence religion is and what foundation it has in the human soul. The Kantian language used to describe theoretic theology's task is no accident. A close student and translator of Kant, Mueller was gripped by the thought that there must be something in the human mind that is the precondition of religion in history and which makes it possible, just as Kant argues that the Categories are preconditions of empirical knowledge and thus make it possible. Mueller is in effect affirming that there is a religious *a priori*, something that must be rooted in the original, cognitive endowment of the human being. It is the task of the philosophical-cum-psychological branch of the science of religion to uncover it. This is something it can only do well after sufficient data about the manifestations of religion in history have been gathered by comparative and historical study.

The nature of theoretic theology's task leads on to Mueller's definition of 'religion', which displays with great clarity the double use of the term noted in Schleiermacher. It can be used to refer to a body of religious doctrines, in which case it obviously has a plural and in which case we can contrast one religion with another. Yet Mueller also notes that thinkers wish to affirm such things as 'Religion is the distinguishing property of human creatures' (cf. Chantepie 1891:14, quoted above), but they cannot then be affirming that possession of a particular body of doctrines or form of faith is peculiar and essential to human beings. There seems to be a common recognition of the point that there must be an underlying and universal cognitive capacity specifically 'designed' so that we can come to embrace particular forms of religious faith. This is 'religion' in the singular. For Mueller considerations parallel to those which enable us to distinguish a use of 'language' in which it only has a singular (referring to the capacity for speech and for learning the many languages) justify us in thinking that there is a proper use of 'religion' in which it only has a singular. It then refers to the faculty of faith (or the faculty of the infinite) which underlies the many religions that exist in history. It is this that the Kantian branch of the science of religion will uncover and anatomize (Mueller 1893a:13–14). It is this faculty which is the primary 'condition of the possibility' of the existence of the plural forms of religion in history. What the faculty of faith enables us to do is apprehend the infinite in the finite (no doubt a conscious echo of Schleiermacher) and the definition of 'religion' in the singular is accordingly given as 'Religion consists in the perception of the infinite under such manifestations as are able to influence the moral character of man' (Mueller 1889:188).

There are manifest problems in becoming clear about the nature of the faculty of faith and the definition of religion that it prompts. Mueller's language might suggest belief in a separate compartment of the mind devoted to religious awareness. Though he does speak in these terms in some of his earlier works, referring to a *sensus numinis* behind religions (Mueller 1861:436), by the time of the writing of *Natural Religion* he fights shy of any such implications. He describes in that work how the ordinary apparatus of human thought and perception gives rise to the apprehension that limited, finite objects of experience are pointers to a reality beyond themselves. We are aware of finite objects in space and time as limitations of a greater reality. Ordinary perception and conception, and not a separate faculty, is thus the ground of our sense of the infinite (Mueller 1889:124–5). The clearest example of this that Mueller can give is the manner in which perception of powerful and awe-full natural objects and forces, such as the sun, can give rise to the apprehension of an unbounded, unlimited reality beyond them. He writes: 'a river or a mountain, and still more the sky and the dawn, possess theogonic capacity, because they have in themselves from the beginning something going beyond the limits of sensuous perception' (Mueller 1889:148). This explains why Mueller's account of the essence of religion should be labelled 'nature mysticism' (that is being able to see a mystical, numinous depth in natural objects), but this label is misleading, as we shall see below, for he also contends that experience of things other than the natural world can give rise to the apprehension of the infinite. We have at the least a commitment to a general mode of religious experience or spirituality that is excited by ordinary perception and thus is universal. 'Infinite' is used by Mueller as a – no doubt vague – gesture toward the content and focus of this general religious experience or spirituality, preferable to anything more specific such as 'God' because it is not tied to the conceptual structure of any particular religion and allows non-theistic forms of faith to manifest the underlying human correlative of all religion. 'Unbounded' and 'unlimited' are the chief connotations of 'infinite' in Mueller's description of primal spirituality. It should be noted, however, that he does not contend for the absurdity that all people are born with possession of a discursive and explicit concept of a religious infinite. As he notes, such a view is open to the obvious objection that many cultures may lack a word for this concept (Mueller 1889:125). 'Infinite' is the scholar's word for a mode of experience; how folk conceptualize this experience depends upon culture and history. Discursive, explicit religious concepts are not innate. There is development and change in religion as peoples grow and develop in the way they conceptualize the primal religious awareness. It is in this way that the history of religion, in its underlying nature and its varied manifestations, is enmeshed in the larger history of mankind.

Mueller's commitment to the existence of the faculty of faith, the ability to sense the infinite, brings with it a use for the notion of natural religion. In the first instance it is the fourth sense of 'natural religion' that Mueller's belief in a religious *a priori* invokes. The description of the faculty of faith is his way of referring to a natural human religiousness. This natural human capacity for religion provides the best answer in his view to the question of how religion can be assumed to have arisen in the human mind. A frequent target in his discussion of this point is the belief that what lies behind the many forms of religion that exist today is some primeval revelation, from which present-day religions are a corruption. This cannot provide the key to understanding how men have been able to understand and choose between competing religious notions, because this primeval revelation would itself have had to be understood and accepted. Any 'supernatural religion' (that is, religion of special revelation) needs a background of natural religion, presupposing the existence of a natural human capacity to understand and discriminate between religious ideas. Natural religion in this sense is described as 'the solid rock' on which all religion, be it revealed or otherwise, is based (Mueller

1891:331, 1893*a*:76). It is the instrument of choice, of testing between different religious notions that arise in history. It is, therefore, that which makes the larger religious life of mankind possible.

Natural religion in this sense has three branches, corresponding to the three fundamental ways in which the faculty of faith can be excited to receive apprehensions of the infinite:

> Natural religion . . . manifests itself under three different aspects, according as its object, what I call the Infinite or the Divine, is discovered either in *nature*, or in *man*, or in the *self*.
>
> (Mueller 1891:1)

To these aspects there correspond three different branches of natural religion: respectively, physical religion, anthropological religion, and psychological religion. Each of these merits a separate, large volume in Mueller's huge corpus. We have already met the thought that the natural world provides apprehensions of the infinite, so physical religion needs no further introduction. Experience and reflection on human nature also gives rise to perceptions of the infinite, and this is the concern of anthropological religion, while inner experience of the self provides perceptions of the infinite for the purposes of psychological religion. Each branch is associated with distinct notions and therefore with different types of religious beliefs. The notion most obviously arising out of physical religion is the concept of deity. From anthropological religion comes the concept of the soul in relation to the body and thus the belief in personal immortality. Psychological religion gives rise to the notions associated with mysticism and particularly to the concept of a union between human soul and the infinite (see Mueller 1891, 1892, 1893*a*).

Exploration of the three branches of natural religion described in the volumes of Mueller's lectures shows that they serve to extend the notion of natural religion further. Their existence shows that Mueller is unequivocally committed to the existence of forms of religion that are not dependent on revelation but arise out of the unaided use of human faculties. The branches of natural religion show how mankind could have come to a substantial body of religious thought without the assistance of any putative special revelation. Natural religion gives us access to certain fundamental tenets, however inchoate they may be, which 'cannot be absent in any religion' (Mueller 1893a:76). In speaking of natural religion as the means we have of understanding and testing religious notions, he seems to have in mind some 'shopping-list' of fundamental notions which arise naturally in the human understanding when it is awakened by experience of the natural world, human nature, and the self (even if the precise form of their expression depends on social and cultural developments). These are the solid rock on which any 'supernatural religions' build.

We are now in a position to see that Mueller's commitment to a natural, human religiousness takes him close to the position of the deists. There are certain fundamental religious notions which arise naturally out of the human mind's reaction to the world around it. These are common to all religions worthy of the name because they are the means of testing whether any religion is fit to be embraced. They are not innate. What exist prior to experience of the world are the capacities which enable everyone to acquire these notions subsequent to experience. To be sure, these capacities are not well summed up for Mueller by the word 'reason'. His comments on Kant show his readiness to add to the powers of the mind conventionally allowed in rationalist thought (Mueller 1893a:14–15). Kant is circumvented much in the manner adopted by Schleiermacher by declaring Kant to be right about the limits of the cognitive powers he describes, but wrong in ignoring a generalized spirituality or capacity for religious experience, which once added to the Kantian system provides the possibility of a route into religion. But then we are given a deistic twist to a romantic description of the powers of the mind through the belief that, when this generalized spirituality is directed upon the objects of experience, it will provide free of revelation common, minimal religious foundations for all, something that is not so dissimilar from deism. This gets clear expression in the preface to Mueller's collected essays:

> The elements and roots of religion were there as far back as we can trace the history of man; and the history of religion, like the history of language, shows us throughout a succession of new combinations of the same radical elements.
>
> (Mueller 1867a:x)

The notion that there are naturally produced religious radicals brings us close to the heart of deism. All in all, Mueller appears to have effected a remarkable fusion of deistic and romantic thought on the nature of religion.

To bring out Mueller's exact relation to deism we need to ask if he could accept the possibility that a religion consisting solely of these radicals might exist independently and therefore function as a rival to any 'supernatural' or historical form of faith. In the *Introduction to the Science of Religion* Mueller does countenance the possibility that the notion of a natural religion consisting solely of the universal, radical elements has a role to play in the scientific treatment of religion. He suggests that it corresponds to the linguist's ideal of a general grammar – a collection of self-evident rules supposed to be hidden in every language. But just as no linguist supposes that these universal self-evident rules ever exist in isolation and in their purity, so we cannot suppose that any actual religion has consisted exclusively of the principles of natural religion. To think is said to be one of the major errors of deism (Mueller 1893a:71). A religion wholly natural, in reflecting nothing but these pure principles, exists 'in the minds of modern philosophers rather than of ancient poets and prophets'. In history we never find a race where reverence for the infinite is not mixed with 'mythological disguises' (Mueller 1893a:77). With the deists Mueller shares a belief in a common religious endowment which is natural to human beings, and like them he believes this will entail common elements in all religions worth the name. However, he is committed to thinking that any actual religion will be rooted not just in a common natural inheritance, but also in a particular historical and social setting. His guide in thinking about the nature of religion is frequently language, as we have already noted. Analogies with language suggest a common, natural facility for 'acquiring' religions and also some common elements in all religions. Equally they suggest that actual religions will be diverse products of history.

Mueller shows in his criticisms of deism that he will not accept for the purposes of the science of religion a classification of religions that distinguishes one wholly natural religion from many religions of history and revelation. Each religion is a structure built on the rock of natural religion. Can we make distinctions for the science of religion between the nature of the structures built on these common foundations? Mueller makes frequent reference to the traditional distinction between Christianity and Judaism as revealed, divine, or supernatural religions and all other faiths as merely natural. He must, in the first place, query part of this distinction in so far as he has advanced the thought that no religion could be wholly supernatural – the bedrock of each is natural. Yet he also questions the belief that the superstructures of different faiths might have divergent sources. Comparative theology and the science of religion must treat *all* faiths as natural – that is, as humanly, historically produced extensions to the fundamental starting-point provided by the faculty of faith and human experience. From the standpoint of the science of religion the uselessness of any distinction between natural and revealed religions is evident, not least because *all* religions characteristically claim that their key elements are the product of revelation or inspiration. The fact that they make this claim is merely another fact about them and about religion in general which the science of religion must explain. Each claims a unique kind of authority. The science of religion cannot side with any particular religion in the comments which faith in that religion offers on the authority of another (Mueller 1893a:69, 1891:51–2). In our third sense of natural religion Mueller regards each and every faith as natural. To see why this is so in greater detail we need to explore Mueller's beliefs on history, revelation, and miracle.

We have already had occasion to note Mueller's commitment to the historical character of religions. Throughout his writings on the science of religion he pleads for an historical treatment of religious questions. What is important for present purposes is the unitary view of history he advances. The unity of human religious history cannot be broken either by the appeal to revelation or by the plea of certain religions to stand outside it. If we examine the history behind the notion of revelation, argues Mueller, we shall see that 'in the beginning truth made revelation'. It was the sense that something was overwhelmingly true in religion that led to its association with special divine inspiration or sanction, so that by a process itself historical we can see how human psychology led to the beliefs that some truths were specially, divinely communicated and that revelation made truth (Mueller 1889:236). Christianity and its claim to revelation can be assigned a place within the natural history of religions. Mueller sets in opposition, on the one hand, viewing Christianity as something unreal, and, on the other, viewing it as an integral part of human history (Mueller

1892:383). The divinity claimed for Christ might appear to prove that if Christianity is 'real' then it cannot be an integral part of human history and cannot be comparable to all other religions in this respect. However, Mueller contends that the divinity of Christ is itself something that must be put in the context of universal religious history. When this is done it is seen to be an instance of a general truth about the relation between the human and divine. There is a universal relation between the divine and the human whereby the latter participates in or partakes of the former. Christian claims about the divine sonship of Jesus 'serve to sum up nearly all that has been thought on the Divine element in human nature, on the Infinite in man' (Mueller 1892:390).

Claims for the uniqueness of Christianity as something that 'stands altogether outside the stream of history, and beyond the reach of any comparison with other religions' (Mueller 1892:390) are particularly to be avoided because they lead to the unchristian dismissal of other religions as worthless and false and the tacit or explicit damnation of whole nations of people. For Mueller the true character of Christian beliefs and Christian scriptures will be seen only when these are placed in the general context of the history of religions and the specific historical contexts surrounding Christian origins. Only then will their true meaning be brought out. As with all religions, the real truth of Christianity and its scriptures will only be discovered through historical study (Mueller 1893a:206).

The opinions of Mueller on revelation surveyed so far entail that he must domesticate the notion of revelation in the manner of a Herder or Schleiermacher if he is to retain any use for it at all. In effect Mueller collapses special revelation into general revelation, allowing the latter to be expanded by the course of human history.

The faculty of faith, we have noted, finds materials for its apprehension of the infinite in the world around it. This enables Mueller to contend that the whole world was a miracle and a revelation to early man. A special revelation was not needed. No more powerful revelation than the whole world imbued with the infinite could be imagined (Mueller 1891:141–2). All our experience of the environment is thus capable of being revelatory, much as described by Schleiermacher. History, the medium through which apprehension and particularly conceptualization of the infinite evolves, is the completion of this general revelation. It is the manifestation of the participation of the infinite in the life of mankind, and thus can be spoken of as a process of the divine education of the human race. All religions contribute something to this process and are representations of it in particular times and places (Mueller 1893a:151). Each religion is in some sense true and necessary, 'being the only religion which was possible at that time, which was compatible with the language, the thoughts and the sentiments of each generation' (Mueller 1893a:190)

Special revelation in Mueller seems to be no more than the occurrence of important moments of inspiration within the historical evolution of a particular faith. This domestication of revelation has its counterpart in his dismissal of miracles as traditionally understood. Here his teaching again follows Schleiermacher's in reducing the proper use of 'miracle' to the name for events occurring within the course of nature but which are of special religious significance. His attack on the traditional conception is geared to rebutting arguments from the special status of key events in Christian salvation-history to the unique and exclusive truth of Christianity. Thus he urges his readers to accept that the miraculous wrappings surrounding the incarnation are unimportant for its significance and likely to detract from that significance (Mueller 1892:379). Likewise he contends that a scientific explanation of the main elements of the story of the resurrection will be found some day. This event can be taken to be historical fact, but one that has been 'miraculized' and misinterpreted from the earliest days of Christianity. That it has been treated in this way shows the operation of processes common to the foundation of religions everywhere. The historian will have to stand back from these processes, just as he must stand back from the accompanying literalism in the interpretation of a religion's fundamental scriptures (Mueller 1892:xvi-xix). The true meaning of these events and of the life of Christ will only be arrived at once they are seen as integral parts of human history. Christ stands as a fulfilment of religion's searching after the divine or infinite in man (Mueller 1892:383).

The summary of Mueller's views on the basis of the science of religion shows the extent to which they are dependent on the philosophical inheritance documented earlier. Other illustrations of his use of ideas from that inheritance could be given, but enough has been done to see how he moves from these philosophical ideas to a defence of a historical and comparative study of religions. We note how his apologetic for the science of religions inevitably ties it to a particular philosophical and theological interpretation of the phenomena of religion. In particular, Mueller has not been able to produce a conception of the study of religion in which it is separate from theology. The labels for his two branches of the science of religion are significant in this respect. In his concern to show a predominantly Christian audience how the comparative and historical study of religion is essential and not subversive of religious commitment, Mueller in effect turns that study into a theological enterprise. Its value is seen to lie in the *religious* understanding it brings. He has to remove the obstacle presented by the thought that a study of religion truly historical and global will be ungodly and distracting from the unique truth of the Christian message. He achieves this only by arguing that this study is important because, though critical and in this respect 'scientific', its object is the complete revelation of God to man. Mueller has, in other words, to represent the whole of religious history as revelation and the ultimate goal of the science of religion as being to uncover this fuller revelation. What a Christian dogmatics does uncritically and only in part, the science of religion does critically and by basing itself on the entirety of revelation. The object of the science of religion is a *story*, an evolution with a pattern of growth and fulfilment, and it is a religious story:

> We believe that there is nothing irrational in either history or nature, and that the human mind is called upon to read and to revere in both the manifestations of a Divine Power. Hence, even the most shattered pages of traditions are dear to us.
>
> (Mueller 1867b:6)

Though Mueller has the global and historical perspective on religion that must underlie any critical treatment of it, he has this perspective in combination with views which fit ill with the demands of critical study. What we need to distinguish are the demands of historical study of religion themselves and a theological interpretation which the religiously committed might like to put upon the results of this study. Mueller may need to present the possibility of this theological interpretation in advance to counter the theological biases of those who are too wedded to an extreme position on the uniqueness of Christianity, but one should not maintain that accepting this interpretation is a precondition of the science of religion.

Mueller's theological interpretation of the study of religion depends in the first instance on his commitment to a natural human religiousness and the gloss he places upon this (what we have called his 'religious *a priori*'). An important question here is whether *any* belief in a property or ability in human nature which uniquely corresponds to the religious behaviour of mankind is bound to lead us in this direction. From this natural religiousness he moves to a belief in general revelation and some form of universal incarnational theology (the two of course complement one another). We have noted before, in relation to the deists, how the move from positing a natural human religiousness to a religious interpretation of human nature is easily made. Seeing the direction in which one can travel from positing a natural human religiousness, it is tempting to refuse the starting-point. However, Mueller's religious *a priori* is related to other elements in his account which are not so easily dismissed. For example, it is an important root of Mueller's insistence on the universality of religion in human life. Is it important to maintain this insistence? If so, can it be done without committing ourselves to a basic religiousness in human nature? From the starting-point of a religious *a priori* in human nature Mueller's theological interpretation of the study of religion proceeds via the religious gloss he places on the evolution of religious life. There are again two sorts of doubt a critic might place against the movement of Mueller's thought. He might wonder about whether we need some general pattern in religious history at all. Even if that is accepted, he might regard the religious gloss placed on whatever pattern is there as unwarranted and unnecessary. The rejection of the search for pattern, for large-scale meaning in religious history would stop Mueller's programme in its tracks, but we will want to know if any version of the *history* of religions (as opposed to chronicle) is possible without commitment to a search for meaning at this level.

In Mueller we can see how the romantic and idealist interpretation of religion in human nature and history produces in its wake a major disadvantage: it tends to unite the study of religion to theological purposes. It may seem to many that a condition of the emergence of the critical study of religion is that it be separated from theology, and perhaps also from the philosophy of religion. We have discovered the importance of two questions (about the existence of some kind of a natural human religiousness and the existence of some kind of overall meaning to religious history) which jointly appear to raise the question 'Can or should the critical study of religion be separated from the philosophy of religion?' Chantepie, we noted, thought that the answer to this was 'No'. It is a question which will be taken further in the next chapter. But we shall find that it is also profitable to pursue all the questions raised about Mueller's programme for the science of religion by briefly examining the thought of some of his most important contemporaries, the ethnographers of religion of the late nineteenth century.

NATURAL RELIGION IN TYLOR'S *PRIMITIVE CULTURE*

Our aim in this section is not to attempt a full survey or summary of nineteenth-century anthropological thought about the nature of religion. Rather, we wish merely to pursue the important questions about the nature of religion in history that arose out of the discussion of Max Mueller. Mueller shows one way in which the legacy of deism bears fruit for the scientific study of religion. The deistic notions of religion as the product of human causes and of the existence of a natural human religiousness lead, under the influence of romantic and idealist thought, to a theologically loaded picture of religious history. The meaning of man's natural religiousness and naturally produced religious history is interpreted as implying the working-out of a general revelation, making human nature and the entirety of the global history of religions into a vehicle of revelation.

We have already encountered significantly different ways of coping with the deistic legacy in Kant and Hume. Hume's response to it is of particular importance as illustrating the possibility of a more stringent form of naturalism, which clearly avoids setting religious history within a theological vision of history's meaning. However, the correlation Hume makes between religion and human nature is so crude as to rule out the possibility of seeing significant meaning or point to religious history. Tylor serves to illustrate a means of coping with the legacy in a modified Humean fashion, showing how a more stringent naturalism than Mueller's can give a relatively sophisticated grounding of religion in human nature and discern some meaning in religious history.

Thus the route to seeing religion in human nature and history as general revelation is avoided.

Two things immediately stand out from Tylor's anthropological approach to the nature of religion. They are his commitment to the possibility of treating the history of culture as an inductive science (see Tylor 1865:160) and his concentration on primitive life as the key to this inductive science. Both these major assumptions depend on his evolutionism. Given the belief that there is an evolutionary history of man from animal origins to life in sophisticated civilizations and that the human intellect has evolved along with this, then two things appear to follow. There ought, in the first place, to be empirically discoverable laws which control this evolutionary history and the evolution of the intellect and culture which it contains. Furthermore, in the outline of the evolutionary history of culture pride of place will have to go to a reconstruction of a hypothetical state of primitive culture from which the rest flows. This will provide the basis for understanding the nature of the process of descent with modification that explains the course culture has taken to the present. Thus the primitive as it is found in the present becomes of vital significance in the science of culture, being the means by which the hypothetical origins of culture can be reconstructed. If religion is then given the role of defining the nature of the human intellect in its original state, then it is provided with both a central place in the economy of human nature and an importance in the scheme of history.

The very brief sketch of Tylor's ideas offered so far points to many of the assumptions which later anthropological theorists have come to reject. They would no longer accept Tylor's account of the basis of their subject and his evolutionary portrayal of religious history. These assumptions include the beliefs that there is a near uniform evolution of culture, that this is determined by a corresponding evolution of the intellect, that contemporary primitive peoples represent early stages of the evolution of culture and the intellect 'frozen' for us, that religion uniformly corresponds to early stages in these evolutionary processes. In textbooks on anthropological theory it is common to write off Tylor and other evolutionary anthropologists on the grounds that such assumptions are either false or totally unprovable (Evans Pritchard 1965 provides a compendium of criticisms on these lines, while Mueller 1888 contains many of them in embryonic form). There is no need to go into or rebut such criticisms here. Despite them, it remains true that Tylor's thought on the nature of religion is an important way of illustrating one way of coping with the legacy of deism.

The clearest way in which Tylor shows the legacy of deism is in his naturalistic approach to the treatment of religion. This is a simple and inevitable consequence of his presumption that religion can be explained and interpreted from within an inductive science of culture. It must therefore be capable of being regarded as a human phenomenon and as an outcome of natural causes. It is this naturalism which is summed up in a statement of Tylor's which we have used in defining one of the senses of 'natural religion' important for this study:

> First as to the religious doctrines and practices examined, these are to be treated as belonging to theological systems devised by human reason, without supernatural aid or revelation; in other words as being developments of Natural Religion.
>
> (Tylor 1903a:427)

Anthropological theorizing about religion can only treat of the 'forms of natural religion', as Frazer calls them (Frazer 1926:16). Tylor still feels it necessary to combat what he describes as 'medieval ideas' in the history of religion (Tylor 1903a:24). The medievalism referred to insists that forms of higher faith and civilization could only have come about with the assistance of revelation and divine intervention. Tylor is in general fighting speculative treatments of the origin of culture and civilization which assume that the achievements of civilization could not have been produced by human hands alone. A typical target is the kind of view quoted from Archbishop Whately in *Researches into the Early History of Mankind*:

> For, all experience proves that men, left in the lowest, or even anything approaching to the lowest, degree of barbarism in which they can possibly subsist at all, never did and never can raise themselves, unaided into a higher condition.
>
> (Tylor 1865:160–1)

Tylor's commitment to the tenets of Darwinism gives him both a reason for denying any such non-naturalist explanation of the origins of religion and civilization and a model for providing a convincing alternative account. While it might appear inconceivable that higher forms of faith could emerge if we suppose a sudden transformation from 'barbarism' to sophistication, it becomes entirely plausible if we adopt Darwin's preferred solution to problems of historical descent – namely, simple primeval forms and the slow accumulation of many minor changes over a long period of time to produce complicated end results. It is just this procedure that Tylor adopts. He avoids the gross implausibility of supposing with the deists that the first, natural religion of mankind is a sophisticated ethical monotheism. Tylor settles on animism – the simple belief that there are spiritual beings – as the first religion produced by human reason. This form of natural religion is the product of reason, and basic because it corresponds to the first philosophy of life and nature that mankind was able to devise. It represents that mode of thinking about the world that the earliest stage of the evolving human intellect was able to muster. It is a philosophy based on belief in souls in man and nature, which enables primitive man to give answers to the most fundamental explanatory questions with which he was faced. What explains the difference between a living and a dead human body? What are the human shapes and forms that appear in dreams? What accounts for the difference between animate and non-animate things in nature? The process whereby man peoples the world with spirits in order to provide him with a coherent way of understanding the operations and facts of nature is a conscious echo of Hume's *Natural History* (see Tylor 1903*a*:477). However, an important difference should be noted. Tylor speaks of a religion devised by human *reason*, indicating the primacy of the intellect, not the passions, in the creation of the natural religion of mankind. There are practical problems which engage the passions influencing the content and function of animism, but its moving force is primarily the intellect and its desire to solve explanatory problems. This emphasis on reason enables Tylor in the end to give religion a role in the advancement of humanity. In a sense he is closer to the deists than Hume in seeing natural religion as the product of human reason, but unlike them he has an evolutionary conception of reason and its operations. Its discoveries need not therefore be the same in all times. There is an evolution in human nature.

Despite the fact that Tylor has an evolutionary conception of the nature of human reason, and can therefore accept variation with time in a natural religion of reason, he remains close to deism in other aspects of his treatment of the uniformity of human nature and religion. Notwithstanding the fact that there are great varieties in the expression of human nature in culture, there are striking uniformities which the evolutionary anthropologist must explain. Variety is in the last resort the reflection and not the negation of a law-like sequence in the progress of culture. It invites explanation in terms of uniform causes operating at differential speeds. There is a single ladder of human culture, reflecting a single sequence in the development of the human intellect from barbarism to science, but different stages on this ladder can be found in existence at any one moment in history. It is the existence of underlying uniformity in diversity that provides another fundamental condition for the possibility of an inductive science of culture (Tylor 1903a:1–6). From the fact of the underlying uniformity in human nature and culture there follows the underlying uniformity of religion. Just like Mueller, Tylor employs the word 'religion' in two ways: one way as a common noun which has a plural, another way as a proper noun having a singular only. In the latter usage it refers to the whole or the essence of which particular religions are parts or expressions. Like Mueller, he affirms that individual religions cannot be understood unless they are seen in relation to the underlying unity – religion. Unity exists, in the first instance, because of the basic tenet of animism – belief in spiritual beings – unites all forms of religion. It serves as the essence of all religions. In this manner all forms of faith, no matter how late in human evolution and sophisticated in ritual or theology, are united to the first, natural religion of human reason and are descendants from it – much in the manner in which deism claimed. All faiths are linked 'in an unbroken line of mental connection' by a system of religious philosophy having common elements (Tylor 1903a:501–2). What divides faiths appears to be nothing more than degrees of sophistication and elaboration in this philosophy. For example, early animism is strictly amoral, whereas later forms of faith become linked to notions of retribution and justice and thus to ethics.

As well as preaching the uniformity of religion Tylor also regards it as universal. No more than Mueller will he credit tales about native peoples who allegedly lack any form of religion (Tylor 1903a:417–19). His attempt to preserve the universality of religion is one reason why his definition of religion is cast in such broad terms. As with Mueller and other authors treated here, he appears to regard religion as a central, important aspect of human nature. It is a mental set or outlook which is universally the beginning of the attempt on the part of man to understand himself and his world. All cultures are offsprings of the primitive, first societies which were defined by the animistic character of their thinking. Religion is thus the clue to the original state of the human intellect and of culture. It is the key to the understanding of man. It would appear from all this that Tylor is committed to embracing another part of the legacy of deism in the notion of a natural human religiousness. However, vague though we have found that notion to be, it does have certain limits which Tylor appears to breach. As we defined it in Chapter 1 it included more than the belief that the religions corresponded to an important, even universal feature in human nature. It entailed that this feature was ineradicable in human nature and that its proper expression was always to be religion. In sum it is a means of bringing out the belief that there is a one-to-one correspondence between religion and some permanent and universal feature of human nature, so that wherever human nature finds expression there will also be religion. But in Tylor religion corresponds only to a universal and uniform *stage* in the expression of human nature. Religion is an expression of primitive life, which it in part defines. Existing cultures may all show their indebtedness to primitive roots, but there is every prospect that forms of culture will emerge which will have left this past behind them. While religion corresponds to a permanent desire to have a philosophy of life and nature that will enable us to understand the world around us, animism will in the end give way to materialism – a philosophy of nature flatly opposed to the idea that the concepts of soul and spirit are useful in explaining human or natural phenomena (Tylor 1903a:502).

Tylor's claim that primitive culture is defined by a commitment to animism and his assertion that modern culture is defined by a commitment to materialism, together with his linking of the essence of religion to animism, clearly entail, though he may be shy of stating this explicitly, that religion has no future. If all religions are but forms of animism, religion must be a survival in our culture. In a book on primitive culture, it is ominous to find that most space is devoted to animism and religion as the component parts of the primitive. Tylor concludes his account by describing anthropology as a reformer's science: in showing how the evolution of culture has proceded it can point to the pattern which must be taken further if society is to progress. The office of the evolutionary ethnographer is to impress the idea of an evolving culture on contemporary minds and to 'expose the remains of crude old culture ... and to mark these out for destruction' (Tylor 1903*b*:453). This seems to entail a clear message for religion.

We have seen how Tylor answers two of the important questions posed by Mueller's account of the history of religions. To the question 'Is religion a universal phenomenon?' his reply is 'Yes, but not permanent.' This determines the reply that his account implies to the question 'Is there a natural human religiousness?' There is something in a stage of the evolution of human nature that religion corresponds to, but the permanent, ineradicable feature behind this – man's desire and need to explain nature and life – only produces religion under certain circumstances – the conditions established by and surrounding the operation of the primitive intellect. In the last analysis religion does not represent, in the terms of Hume, a primary principle in human nature. We are now able to see from the discussion immediately above that Tylor gives the basis of an affirmative answer to another question posed by Mueller's work: 'Is there a pattern to religious history?' His portrayal in the opening chapters of *Primitive Culture* of anthropology as a science which discovers a unformity behind the diversity of history rests on the fact that universal and unvarying laws are at work in the evolution of culture. Pattern and meaning to the changes in the shape of religious history, as of all aspects of culture, is thereby guaranteed. The underlying pattern is presented by the evolution of the human intellect as this is determined by the circumstances of life and the survival of the fittest. This pattern amounts to the growth of the intellect from barbarism to sophistication and knowledge. Yet the place religion gains from its role in this larger pattern to human history and evolution determines a sharply negative answer to a final question that can be drawn from Mueller: 'Does the pattern to religious history have a religious meaning?' The meaning reflected in this pattern is determined by something outside religion and which spells its end. It is not that Tylor's evolutionism implies that religion is everywhere a delusion or the result of folly, as Hume's portrayal of the natural history of religion might suggest. A correct summary of

Tylor's position would surely be that religion is rational in its originating context and also an important stage in the progress of mankind from ignorance to knowledge. The worth and value of religion in relation to its appropriate place in evolutionary history is affirmed, but the meaning of that history tells of the primitive and temporary nature of religion.

In his Hibbert Lectures of 1888 Mueller did his best to contend against the kind of picture of primitive religion represented by Tylor among others. He rightly saw that the outlines of this picture came as much from the continued influence of Enlightenment ways of characterizing religion and the powers of the human mind as from the contentions of Darwinism. Placing religion primarily in the sphere of reason as Tylor does, the way is open to see it as a temporary phenomenon, to be replaced in due course by more sophisticated ways of understanding the world. If, alternatively, other forms of cognition or consciousness are allowed as the home of religious life, then it ceases to appear as something that must give way to increasing knowledge of the world and to theoretical sophistication in our ability to explain nature. And so he repeats Schleiermacher's fight for a distinct form of spirituality or spiritual awareness as the true source of religion. Both Tylor and Mueller preserve aspects of the deistic legacy. Some of these aspects they share, as in the case of their fundamentally naturalistic approach to religious phenomena and their belief in some underlying unity to these phenomena; others they do not. Tylor has the intellectualism and rationalism. Mueller has the belief in the primacy of religion in human nature and all that flows from that. Common acceptance of the usefulness of the notion of natural religion imposes some similarities, but enables radical differences to flourish. It provides a shared agenda, that of basing an interpretation of the history of religion on a picture of the relation between religion and human nature, but it does not entail any agreement on the working-out of that agenda.

CONCLUSION

Mueller and Tylor present reactions to two different types of material available in great quantity for the nineteenth-century study of religion. Mueller responds to the great mass of philological and written historical evidence about religions; Tylor to the newly found discoveries of ethnography about tribal, non-literate cultures and the palaeontological and archaeological evidence about the remote human past. That they are responding to different types of material in the scientific study of religion helps to explain in part the competing programmes they offer for it. For Tylor the scientific study of religion will be part of an inductive science of culture whose links will be with evolutionary biology. For Mueller the scientific study of religion will be a form of critical history with close links to philology and of course theology. Tylor appears to offer the possibility of a history of religions that is free of theological assumptions and aims but only at the cost of basing it on an anti-theology, since the organizing principles for the history of religion that he takes from evolutionary biology are naturalistic in a sense which implies 'anti-religious'. This might appear to offer the history of religions a depressing choice, one which militates against the assumption that the history of religions is a properly scientific – that is, critical and objective – discipline. Yet the necessity of the choice between a theology and an anti-theology to provide the organizing principles for the history of religions, and the source of the meaning and pattern it sees in religious history, would appear to be entailed by something we have established. This is the need to make some connection between the nature of the history of religions and a conception of how religion stands to human nature. For either that conception flows from a religious vision of human nature, as with Mueller, or an anti-religious vision, as with Tylor. If the concept of human nature *is* important in the conception of religion that organizes and stimulates the historical study of religion, then it forces a theological choice to be made at the starting-point of the discipline.

The question of the relation between conceptions of human nature and the organization of the scientific treatment of religion is something which we must briefly comment on in our concluding chapter when we consider the relevance of the notion of natural religion to contemporary issues in the study of religion. Before closing the present discussion on the nineteenth-century birth of the historical-scientific treatment of religion, there is a certain naïvety in the remarks made about the relation between religion and human nature in this chapter which must be dispelled.

Talk of a natural human religiousness or of correspondence between religion and some ineradicable feature of human nature appears to ignore the point persuasively made by Herder and Hegel (documented in our discussion of them) that it is human nature *in society* that makes religion. The mediation of society between human nature and religious expression has been lost in discussion of Mueller and Tylor, and thus an implicit return made to one of the most limiting and naïve aspects of deism. Tylor's stress on the intellect and the solution of its problems in understanding life and the world as the source of religion is markedly individualistic. He also appears to conceive of culture as a mere additive product of the actions and thoughts of its individual members. Social life and action is the sum of individual life and action. The classifications and explanations of human culture thus relate to the classifications and explanations of individual psychology (Tylor 1903*a*:13). The evolving human intellect can thus appear as an external moving force behind social and cultural change. Though the static human nature of the deists has gone, the human nature that transcends culture has remained. Mueller's insistence on a primary, generalized spirituality located in our ability to apprehend the infinite in the finite might also appear to be markedly individualistic. This is probably a misleading impression, given the fact that he places so much stress on the necessary schematization of apprehensions of the infinite through concepts. Concepts are inseparable from some mode of linguistic expression and are thus tied to the socially created products of a shared language. There are many passages in Mueller reminiscent of Herder and Hegel on the relation between culture, language, and society (for example Mueller 1889:281 ff. and 353 ff.).

From a concentration upon Tylor and the foundation of the scientific study of religion it is hard to conceive how social anthropology and sociology developed as important contributors to religious study. The origin of these approaches to the study of religion and also a necessary corrective to Tylor in the embryonic anthropology of religion can be illustrated from W. Robertson Smith's *Lectures on the Religion of the Semites*. Primitive religious life is not based, according to Robertson Smith, on a philosophy or theory put forward as an answer to an intellectual problem. Ritual and practice were the sum total of primitive faiths (Smith W. R. 1923:20). Primitive religions existed in the first place because their rituals and practices were necessary means of securing the identity and existence of primitive societies (Smith W. R. 1923:28–30). They were maintained thereafter by tradition and custom. Religion and society in primitive life were one and the same. Men identified social ties through religious symbols and practices, and the force of those ties in turn maintained religion in being.

Robertson Smith supports his identification of primitive religion and primitive society with an interpretation of primitive religion as a form of totemism and of primitive society as clan-based. The totemic rites of the former are then represented as the means by which the identity of the latter is secured and maintained. This leads on in an obvious way to the account of religion offered in Durkheim's *Elementary Forms of the Religious Life*. The parallels are striking, and Durkheim freely acknowledges the indebtedness (Durkheim 1976:89 ff.). From both accounts it follows that the study of primitive religion and the study of primitive society are one.

The idea of society and culture as a mediator between religion and human nature does not destroy the possibility of arguing for a correspondence between religion and human nature or of contending that there is a natural human religiousness. It merely complicates these tasks. Similar conclusions to Mueller's on the link between religion and an ineradicable aspect of human nature can be reached while acknowledging that only in society is religion possible. Whatever facet of human nature is chosen for the job of being the source of a natural religiousness, it has to be one that forever shows itself in all societies. Even a Durkheimean identification of the source of religion and the source of social bonds can make a connection between religion and a human nature that is universal and ineradicable. Given that we take seriously his hints that wherever and whenever there are social and moral forces, so there will be religion (Durkheim 1976:427), it will follow that there is a natural human religiousness. This is none other than those facets of human nature that impel man to live in society. Religion appears to be a natural concomitant of those. So granted that we accept in some form the thesis that the expression of religion is necessarily social, it does not follow that we must deny that man is religious by nature rather than by circumstance. This is a point we will take further in the next, and final, chapter.

8

THE CONTEMPORARY STUDY OF RELIGIONS

INTRODUCTION: THE LEGACY OF DEISM

During the course of this study we have located the legacy of deism primarily in its contribution to the development of the concept of religion, and through that to the development of the study of religion. We have argued that it stands at the head of a movement of thought which is a vital influence on the emergence of the historical and global study of religions. Its chief contribution to that movement is its assertion and defence (by way of its promotion of the concept of natural religion) of the historical, natural, and universal character of religion. The previous chapter illustrates how this assertion and defence were important in the writings of the nineteenth-century pioneers of the history and anthropology of religion. We must now offer some comment on the question of how far this legacy of deism still plays a role in the contemporary study of religion.

Since the contemporary study of religion is notable chiefly for the diversity of the approaches it offers to the subject-matter of religion and for the confusion and disagreements in method it displays, we cannot hope to survey it fully here. But we can isolate a number of key questions about the character of the conception of religion it employs – questions which are of crucial importance in a wide range of approaches to religion in contemporary scholarship. Discussion of these questions can serve to throw light, not on every branch of the study of religion at the present time, but on a number of leading approaches within it. The legacy of deism for twentieth-century scholarship is to be noted above all in the very fact that these questions are prompted by the inheritance of thought about religion that earlier historians and philosophers of religion derived from the notion of natural religion.

By the time we come to the way in which the deistic inheritance bears fruit in Max Mueller we can see that, as transmuted through the reflections and criticisms of romanticism and idealism, it boils down to a number of key assertions about the nature of religion and the programme for the scientific study of religion. The more important of these are:

(1) It is important to maintain the universality of religion in human culture.

(2) We cannot maintain this without also affirming the existence of a natural human religiousness.

(3) Sense can be made of the notion of a natural human religiousness, even though the social character and foundation of religion is also recognized.

(4) It follows from (1) to (3) that the historical study of religions is inseparable from the philosophy of religion.

(5) We have in fact to organize the science of religion around some conception of human nature or other.

(6) Whatever account of human nature or organizing principle is used, a basic naturalism must be assumed in the study of religions.

The chief component parts of the deistic legacy can therefore be seen to lie in linked assertions about the universality of religion, its relation to human nature, the crucial role of philosophy in providing a framework for the study of religions, and the importance of a minimally naturalistic approach to the details of religious history. It is also true that in writers such as Mueller and Tylor there is more to the deistic legacy than listed above. The affirmation of the existence of a natural human religiousness is linked in many nineteenth-century students of religion to the idea that there is an underlying human core to all religions. This core provides the engine which drives the historical development of the many religions. Belief in a religion behind the religions thus leads to attempts to discern or prescribe a pattern to religious history prior to or independent of the detailed study of religion. Belief in a religious *a priori* feeds the notion that some theologically or philosophically significant pattern is to be traced behind the facts of religion. The history of religions then becomes a study which is the means of promoting some message about religion, be it theological or anti-theological.

The drive to see meaning in religious history of the sort described above is evident in the thoughts we have traced in the deists themselves and in a series of other writers: Kant, romantic and idealist writers on religion, and Mueller and Tylor. This aspect of the legacy of deism meets with considerable scepticism today. Principally it offends against a contemporary insistence on the autonomy of historical enquiry and a matching scepticism about grand philosophies of history, whether they focus on religious history or not. Hand in hand with affirming the autonomy of historical enquiry in general comes a concern to separate the study of religion as a scientific discipline from theological or philosophical glosses on religious history. Critical reaction to the legacy of prescription of a pattern of religious history will be amply illustrated in the sections which follow. At the same time, some defence is offered of the more modest items in the legacy of deism listed in (1) to (6) above. We offer some contemporary reflections on these affirmations in three sections. First, the universality of religion and contemporary scepticism about the concept and category of religion are discussed. Second, the notion of a natural human religiousness and the role of philosophy of religion in the historical study of religion are treated. Third, the status of naturalism in the study of religion is explored.

THE CONCEPT OF RELIGION AND THE UNIVERSALITY OF RELIGION

The question of whether the phenomenon of religion is a universal one connects, we have argued, with the important matter of the relation between religion and human nature. At first sight it might appear that this question is straightforwardly an empirical one. We have recorded various opinions on whether religion can be found in all human cultures in the course of this study. For example, Herbert, the deists, and Max Mueller answer the question in the positive; Locke and Hume in the negative. The question can surely be settled by recording the latest results of archaeological, historical, and sociological research on the evidence of religious beliefs and practices in the variety of human cultures. It can easily be shown in the defence of religion's universality that the reports, which someone such as Locke relies on, to the effect that this or that remote people lack any semblance of religion represent no more than the blindness of initial impression. Because Europeans lacked any insight into or sympathy with the cultures in question, they could see nothing in them that obviously resembled the forms of Western religion and concluded that religion was absent from these peoples altogether. This is in essence how Mueller tackles 'evidence' for the conclusion that religion is not universal (see Mueller 1889:86–7). On the other hand, those who argue in opposition to religion's universality can point to the knowledge born of the twentieth century that social and political systems can be founded with the intention of excluding religion from any role in the life of a people – apparently with some good measure of success. A society can be built on the basis of a rejection of religion and yet still survive. Moreover, the very success of the efforts of scholars such as Mueller has confirmed the extent to which many important strands of the Eastern world-view are built on the denial of theistic outlooks, with the result that it may become more tempting to conclude that what we recognize as religion is not really exemplified in Buddhism or Jainism.

It is quite misleading, however, to suggest that the question of religion's universality is a straightforwardly empirical one. Contemporary scepticism about religion's universality is likely to rest not so much on the impression made by modern attempts to found societies on a-religious lines, nor on the results of modern research revealing the uniquely different character of the 'non-theistic' religions of the East. What will drive the contemporary opponent of Mueller's assertion is much more likely to be scepticism about the concept of religion itself. This scepticism centres on the belief that the concept of religion is likely to lose any clear meaning if it is so defined as to leave open the real likelihood that religion is to be found in all cultures and epochs.

Scepticism of this sort can start from the historical point that the notion of religion is distinctively Western in origin. To this day many languages have no precise equivalent to our word 'religion'. The Western origin of this word is indicated in Aquinas' definition of 'religion' (quoted in Chapter 3 above) to the effect that religion consists in rendering due observance and obedience to God. This draws on the classical Latin meaning of the word as 'rendering due reverence to the gods'. This sense of the word carries with it the implication that religion is a separate aspect of or institution in human life. Given that Western thought about the gods (or God) provides religion with a focus which is distinct from ordinary objects, defining 'religion' in terms of the service of God tends to turn religion into a value- and action-system different from other, 'everyday' value- and action-systems. But without this meta-physical background, enormously strengthened as it was by monotheism and the Christian doctrine of creation, the very idea that there is a distinct aspect to human affairs called 'religion' may never have arisen (cf. King 1987:282). This origin to the notion clearly stays with it during the course of the development of the concept of religion illustrated in the preceding chapters. In Herbert and the deists the notion that religion consists in paying due observance and obedience to God is not radically abandoned; rather, the requirements for what may count as proper service and worship of God are loosened. This is the effect of counting the pursuit of virtue as the main measure of the proper service of God. The ties between the concept of true religion and the details of Christian doctrine, so evident in Aquinas' account of religion as a form of the virtue of justice, are thereby loosened, with the prospect that religion can be found universally. Radical attempts to break with this tradition are to be found in Schleiermacher and Mueller, as we have seen. But their attempts to define 'religion' in terms of an ability to sense the infinite in the finite are open to an obvious objection. Their talk of the 'infinite' helps to give the notion of religion some clear sense if it carries with it the implications of the God-idea; but in that case they have not broken with the older tradition, which even when expanded through deism faces refutation at the hands of apparently non-theistic religions. If the 'infinite' does not carry the content of the concept of God with it, then definitions which use this notion give 'religion' a universal denotation only at the cost of using a central defining feature that is irredeemably vague and thin.

A particularly clear instance of this kind of scepticism about the ability to use the concept of religion to denote a universal phenomenon is to be found in M. E. Spiro's influential paper 'Religion: Problems of Definition and Explanation' (Spiro 1966). We see in Spiro an argument built around the twin points, first, that we must be true to the Western origin of the concept of religion if it is to have a clear sense and, second, that if we are faithful to this origin religion cannot be reckoned to be a universal phenomenon. Spiro's definition of 'religion' is proffered with the aim of meeting what he alleges is the key need any such definition must meet for the purposes of the study of religion: it should unambiguously provide a denotation for the term and thus clearly demarcate what are the proper subjects for investigation in the study of religion. A definition must meet two further criteria. It must exhibit 'cross-cultural comparability' (that is be successfully testable against a range of examples of religion from different societies). It must also possess 'intra-cultural intuitivity' (that is, match the key features of religion found in the central cases of religion we are familiar with in our own culture) (Spiro 1966:91). This latter criterion entails that belief in superhuman beings who have the power to help or harm man must be an essential element in any successful conception of the nature of religion. The force of the interpretation of the need for intra-cultural intuitivity favoured by Spiro is, of course, to tie the concept of religion firmly to its theistic roots, since it ensures that a version of theistic belief becomes an inescapable defining condition of religion. Spiro's ultimate definition is to all appearances a sanitized, neutral version of the ancient notion that religion consists in rendering due obedience and service to the gods. The normative elements have gone, but the thrust of the older tradition is preserved: 'I shall define "religion" as "an institution consisting of culturally patterned interaction with culturally postulated superhuman beings"' (Spiro 1966:96).

By ensuring that 'religion' can only refer to belief-systems that have some theistic content Spiro also guarantees that his definition has the discriminating power vital for the task he sets it. His major complaint against definitions that do not specify a lowest common denominator of belief-content for all genuine religions is that they are irredeemably vague and allow anything and everything to count as religion. This is a charge that he levels against functionalist definitions of 'religion' in particular (those that define 'religion' in terms of the kind of role it serves in individual or social life). But his point would apply with equal force to the type of experiential definition we have seen in Schleiermacher and Mueller. With Spiro's criterion of clear demarcation it becomes a positive merit that 'religion' as defined will not necessarily denote a universal class of human institutions. Universality cannot be expected to follow in the absence of any arguments to show that a form of theism is essential to personal or social life whenever and wherever we find it. Spiro is therefore quite happy with the possibility that a system such as Buddhism could be excluded from the class of religions even though it provides the world-view of a number of human cultures. (We should note that he does in fact think that *living* Buddhism exhibits a belief in superhuman beings – Spiro 1966:92–4.) He draws attention to the many forms of human organization which anthropologists and others study which are not found in all communities regardless of geography and development. He asks 'Does the study of religion become any the less significant or fascinating if it were discovered that one or two societies did not possess religion?' (Spiro 1966:88).

Spiro's criticism of non-theistic definitions of 'religion' does not cast doubt on the general terms of the global and historical perspective on religion that is the chief feature of our modern concept of religion; it merely suggests a substantial limitation on that perspective. Spiro's argument implies that if the concept of religion remains true to its history it cannot have true universality. We have seen attempts in Schleiermacher and Mueller to break from elements in the history of the concept of religion so as to give the concept full universality. Other attempts, often based on functionalist definitions of religion, can be found in twentieth-century writing on the nature of religion. Such theorists break from the deistic legacy in one respect (religion is no longer tied to the service of God, not even through the mere practice of virtue), while trying to preserve another aspect of that legacy (religion's universality). This must simply be a muddle if Spiro is correct.

A more radical scepticism still about the concept of religion can be found in the writings of Wilfred Cantwell Smith. His argument in *The Meaning and End of Religion* (Smith W. C. 1978) is that the history of the concept of religion has given birth to a monster – a concept which not only fails to fit non-Western religions, but disastrously distorts the theistic traditions which it was originally designed to encompass. Smith's entire argument stresses the fact that the concept of religion is one with a history tied to the cultural and intellectual development of modern Europe. It has resulted, fundamentally, in two false poles in the concept of religion: one whereby it refers to various overt systems of belief and practice, and another whereby it refers to religion in general – a generic something or other which underlies these various overt systems (see Smith W. C. 1978:48–9; here I simplify Smith's analysis somewhat). This is indeed the result we have found to accrue from the romantic reaction to Enlightenment philosophy of religion. It matches the normal dictionary definitions of religion. *The Shorter Oxford English Dictionary*, for example, gives the following as the two primary, current senses of the word: 'a particular system of faith and worship' and 'recognition on the part of man of some higher unseen power as having control over his destiny'. The essence of Smith's manifold critique of this concept of religion lies in the manner in which, for him, it places stress on 'externals' (that is, doctrines and prescribed practices and the human capacity to produce and embrace them) as the heart of living faith. He distinguishes sharply between these externals of religion, under the heading of 'cumulative traditions', and the individual believer's relationship with the transcendent focus of religion, what he calls 'faith'. This latter is the primary, because most important, element in what scholars call 'religion'. But it cannot be defined by any explicit doctrines or formulae and the entertaining or embracing of such externals is neither a necessary nor a sufficient condition for having faith. Any concept, therefore, which seeks to approach the reality of religion by reifying or stressing such externals can only falsify that reality. One of the gravest falsifications produced by the concept of religion is the notion that there are distinct religious entities in the world, things picked out by such European labels as 'Hinduism' and 'Buddhism' and generated out of some primal, generic tendency to embrace religion on man's part.

Smith would have the joint concepts of faith and cumulative tradition take over the work of the concept of religion. One advantage of this would be that it would prevent the tendency to ossify and reify distinct religious traditions in the world. If we think about the cumulative traditions behind such labels as 'Christianity' and 'Hinduism' we would have to recognize their shifting, varied character, and incidentally see the essentially secondary, derivative nature of the externals of a religious tradition. From this would flow the advantage that our attention would be drawn to the individual's relation to God, which must be what is important in any 'religion', even though it cannot be defined by anything external. A further advantage of this step would be that it would take us away from what Smith calls, in *Toward a World Theology*, 'the unproven naturalism' of the modern approach to the study of religion (Smith W. C. 1981:124–5). Thinking of the reality of religion as contained in what is picked out by the concept of religion (as that has been defined by the history we have touched on) inevitably confirms the idea that religion is a human institution whose being and nature can be explained along the lines of any other institution in history. But to distinguish faith from cumulative tradition tells us, first, that the visible part of 'religion' in history (cumulative tradition) is only an aspect, secondary and external, to the whole, and, second, that the heart of religion is something that goes beyond a mere human institution. Faith embodies a relation between two terms, man and God, one of which cannot be confined in any human institution. Religion is an outsider's concept, which belongs to those who observe faith's outward expression (Smith W. C. 1978:129–31). In fact, the reality behind religion is 'a dialectical process between the mundane and the transcendent, a process whose locus is the personal faith and lives of men and women, not altogether observable and not to be confined within any intelligible limits' (Smith 1978:187).

The anti-naturalism of Smith's approach to the understanding of religion is something that must be taken up later in this chapter. From his criticisms and the other points noted so far we can draw up a cumulative case for saying that the concept of religion born of the Enlightenment and nourished by nineteenth-century thought is: (1) too closely tied to particulars of the history of European thought about religion to be truly universalizable and (2) too ready to introduce a false reification and ossification of non-Christian (*and* Christian) responses to the realities felt in faith.

A reply must be attempted to these criticisms of the deistic legacy of belief in the universality of religion. This will involve a defence of the coherence and usefulness of the concept of religion itself. Rebuttal can begin with the point that the fact that a certain concept has a history, or has its home in a particular historical setting, does not entail that it cannot transcend this history or setting. It may be that, for all that the concept of religion is parochial in its origins, it has been the means of uncovering a genuine aspect of human belief and behaviour, which reflects real facets of human nature. Many of the concepts used in description and criticism of human life are alike in being Western in origin and in lacking precise equivalents in some of the cultures to which they are applied (concepts such as art or literature may be mentioned here). This reflects the fact that cultural criticism is itself a peculiarly Western product in many respects. In this survey we have seen efforts made to transcend the limited origins of the notion of religion and thus to tackle the objection that the notion of religion is too closely tied to its parochial origins. The deistic definition of religion in terms of morality ('The pursuit of happiness through reason and truth' – see Chapter 3) is one means of doing this. It enables the details of Christian theological belief to be discarded from the notion of religion and attempts to cut the application of 'religion' clear from any items of doctrine over which the cultures of mankind might disagree. The net effect of all this, however, is to tie the concept of religion down to a new set of limited and local ideas, since both the content of and the prominence given to the notion of virtue themselves reflect peculiarly eighteenth-century European concerns. The turning-away from this concern with virtue as the means of defining a universal notion of religion in the nineteenth-century, romantic-inspired tradition is an attempt to cut the concept of religion free not just from Western theological ideas but also from Western moral systems. We have previously noted that such attempts in Schleiermacher and Mueller to find a common basis for the applicability of the concept in the notion of experience face a serious dilemma. The root of the limitation of such groundings of the concept of religion lies in the difficulties inherent in the notion of a generic religious experience. On the one hand, if this is to be a truly universal basis for the notion of religion it must be free of any connections with particular religious concepts or doctrines; on the other, if it is so divorced from any such concepts it appears contentless. As such it cannot serve to point to a similarity that unites all those things we want to call 'religions'. (See Byrne 1988:18–19 for a fuller discussion of experiential ways of unifying the concept of religion.)

That these ways of justifying the extension of the concept of religion outside its original home do not appear to work is not to say that none can be found. One such means is through the notion of function and a functionalist definition of religion. Defining and extending the category of religion through a functionalist definition of it has the evident advantage of serving as another means of cutting the concept of religion free from any particular doctrinal or conceptual content. Because functionalist definitions turn their backs on seeking a particular theological content to all examples of religion they too can be met with the charge that they are irredeemably vague and without substance. This precise charge is made by Spiro by way of further defending his claim that the concept of religion must be tied to its original theistic connotations at the price of its universality.

Spiro takes as typical of a functionalist understanding of religion one which defines 'religion' as any system or institution focusing on what is of ultimate concern to an individual or members of a group. This is the content he can find in Durkheim's characterization of religion as concerned with the sacred. All such functionalist definitions are met with the complaint that 'it is virtually impossible to set any substantive boundary to religion and, thus, to distinguish it from other sociocultural phenomena' (Spiro 1966: 89–90). This charge is supported by the claim that even if, as is the case in modern American society, the stockmarket, baseball, or sex were the ultimate concern of some social group or other this would not make these things into religions for these groups, since they lacked any central preoccupation with god-like beings (Spiro 1966:96). Non-theistic systems may and do serve the function of providing individuals, groups, or whole communities with objects of ultimate concern around which their lives are ordered and knit together, but this is not something which tends to show that these systems are at all analogous to religion.

Part of Spiro's concern in these arguments is to prevent any firm link being made between religion and those human needs which appear to be universal. If fundamental needs are found which it is religion's function to fulfil then the universality of religion is a likely, if not automatic, outcome. So we find him complaining of attempts to link religion to the functions which flow from the very nature of socio-cultural systems (Spiro 1966:90). If Spiro's essential point is that functionalist definitions buy religion's universality too cheaply by associating it with universal needs which may be met by the most heterogeneous social phenomena, then an adequate reply will have to begin from a tight account of the specific, defining functions of religion, which then can independently be shown to relate to universal or near-universal human needs. The beginnings of such a reply can be seen in J. M. Yinger's important distinction between systems which are directed toward ultimate concerns and those which are directed toward utilitarian or mundane concerns (Yinger 1970:6 ff.). Utilitarian concerns may be defined as those which result from contingent needs which can be satisfied through ordinary human effort. Ultimate concerns are those which relate to needs which are in some sense necessary and foundational in the human condition and which ordinary human effort cannot satisfy. What lies behind ultimate concerns as the functionalist defines them is not merely what happens to concern a society or individual most of all. He has in mind a certain range of limited facts about the human condition which both threaten people's sense of security and which yet cannot be overcome given the very nature of human existence. Yinger lists here such facts as that human striving always falls short of the goals and standards we set ourselves; that we always long for more than we can achieve; that the actuality of suffering and death can never be escaped despite all our best efforts; that all joint efforts and forms of social existence can fall prey to hostility and disharmony between human beings. With our memory of the past and anticipation of future evil and disharmony we cannot fail to be aware of human finitude and failure. The problems which are a mark of this finitude and failure cannot go away yet threaten both the individual's sense of life's meaning and the group's sense of unity and purpose. Religion's function, according to Yinger, is to offer a residual way of coping with such ultimate problems (at least emotionally) through symbolic systems which relativize the finitude and limitation in human life which lie behind them. Religion's symbolic systems interpret these problems as part of some larger good which is beyond them (Yinger 1970:15). Yinger's definition of religion is then:

> Religion, then, can be defined as a system of beliefs and practices by means of which a group of people struggles with these ultimate problems of human life. It expresses their refusal to capitulate to death, to give up in the face of frustration, to allow hostility to tear apart their human aspirations.
>
> (Yinger 1970:7)

Yinger's functionalist characterization of religion depends on two factors: the fundamental character of the problems and concerns he calls 'ultimate', and the readiness of people to hold beliefs which express some sense that mankind can be saved from these problems. It is a conception of religion which can allow variation in the content of the symbolic systems men construct to cope with such ultimate problems, variation which reflects the differences in the societies in which they live. At the same time it suggests the universality of religion, being based on the premiss that 'All men feel these wrenching difficulties' (Yinger 1970:7). It is not a definition that lacks a cutting edge, as Spiro's case suggests, since a distinction can be drawn between theoretical and practical systems which are not devoted to such ultimate problems (no matter how important the objects of these systems may be in individual or group life) and those which are. Manifestly, baseball can be ruled out as a religion on this score.

Yinger's definition appears far removed from a deistic understanding of religion, being in some ways more outwardly akin to Hume's in its stress on the role of religion in providing some emotional security in the face of human limitations. Yet it does contend for religion's universality and relate the existence of religion to ineradicable facts about human nature and the human condition (a point which distances it from Hume's and which will receive greater attention below). It also argues for common elements in religion underlying doctrinal differences. The existence of these common features shows an overlap between Yinger's functionalism and the roots of the modern concept of religion in deism. Three features of religion in general follow from his account of its nature. (1) In religions failure, death, frustration are symbolically reinterpreted. They are presented as not what they seem. (2) Religion brings people into fellowship with one another, emphasizing shared experiences and values. (3) The values offered by religions are super-empirical and therefore beyond easy refutation by everyday facts of immediate experience. Belief in these values goes beyond the facts of experience in consequence.

It does not follow from what Yinger says about the humanly fundamental nature of the concerns which religion deals with that the universality of religion at all ages and places can be guaranteed in an automatic fashion. In fact, he comments on the difficulty of offering any clear proof or disproof of this universality (Yinger 1970:104). His account indeed suggests that a stimulus, in the form of some basic needs, exists which prompts the development of religion in all cultures, but this is not to say that this cannot be overridden in some. Here he refers to the avowed attempt of some ideologies to construct the societies which they dominate on anti-religious lines. Yet one or two examples of successful attempts to banish religion from social and individual life would not necessarily refute the univerality thesis, since it would have to be established that these societies were enduring and permanent to a degree, rather than mere transitional states. Any society which had offered to banish religion would in due course face the human failures and limitations that provide the concerns which motivate religion (Yinger 1970:104). Apart from the vagueness introduced into the universality question by the issue of whether apparently non-religious systems are transitional arrangements of human social life or not, there lies the inevitable degree of uncertainty in applying any definition of 'religion'. There could then be room for debate on whether a given system of belief and practice was functionally equivalent to admitted examples of religion and whether, if so, it had sufficient features in common with those examples (particularly that of having beliefs and values going beyond empirical evidence and refutation) to be judged to be worthy of being called 'religion'. A functionalist understanding of religion cannot then finally settle the universality of religion. It can, however, provide a presumption in favour of that universality and a means of showing that the concept of religion is not inevitably tied to its Western, theistic roots.

A recent survey of the sociological debate about the universality of religion concluded that, while modern sociological approaches had established that religion cannot be understood as an extraneous social phenomenon that will wither away in the course of social evolution, the question of whether religion is an inevitable part of any form of social life remains open (Hardin and Kehrer 1984:17).[1]

Two further suggestions for concluding that the concept of religion is not inevitably tied to its theistic, Western roots and may have universal applicability may be mentioned here (both come from Bianchi 1987). They are that the concept of religion can be thought of as one that is extended to new instances outside its original context of use by analogy and that in the course of so doing its meaning can be thought of as being modified and extended. The first suggestion amounts to the notion that the use of the word 'religion' need not be governed by the possession in all its exemplifications of a common property or set of properties. The second suggestion amounts to the contention that the notion of religion can be modified in use as it is found helpful to extend it through the admission of systems which are importantly analogous to the original cases the notion was based on.

These two features of the concept of religion are found in other concepts in use in the humanities. They will result in the word 'religion' being one with a family-resemblance meaning. If its meaning is extended through tracing analogies which branch out from some central cases of religion, then we should not expect that all the resultant examples we place in the class of religions will share a single set of identifying properties. As we move through the spectrum of things we call 'religions' we shall find its members connected together by an overlapping, evolving series of relationships rather than a set of relevant properties that remains unaltered through each example of religion. The class of religions will then be what Southwold calls a 'polythetic' one: there is a linked set of properties characteristic of members of the class, but it is not necessary that all the attributes in the bundle be possessed by each and every member of the class. Inclusion in the class is possible if only some of these attributes are displayed in any one case, but which particular selection of the bundle examples do display varies from case to case (Southwold 1978:369; cf. Byrne 1988:10–12). Family resemblance allows for the open-endedness of a concept such as religion, thus recognizing that in the course of applying it away from its original context of use we are testing how far it can be modified to take into account new phenomena which bear real and important analogies with the paradigms to which it was once tied. The business of the global and historical study of religion is at one and the same time a matter of collecting and interpreting empirical facts about religions *and* a matter of exploring and determining the sense the concept of religion has. The structure of the concept of religion cannot therefore be settled totally in advance by the kind of *a priori* theorizing about human nature that we have seen in the deists and their successors. To that extent the legacy of philosophizing about the concept of religion that derives from them is misleading. However, *a priori* reflection is needed to give an initial shape to the concept of religion and the character of that initial shape is vitally important to the possibility of later extending and refining the concept through reflection on empirical investigation. In this latter respect contemporary family-resemblance (or functionalist) understandings of the concept of religion remain indebted to the more abstract attempts to give the concept of religion a universal scope that we have documented earlier.

Allowing the notion of religion to be extended through investigation is not tantamount to abandoning Spiro's demand for it to retain some clear discriminating power. Even if this extension results in a family-resemblance understanding of the concept, it will not leave just anything to count as religion. Southwold's account of the polythetic nature of the class of religions rests on some twelve characteristic attributes which are exemplified within it (Southwold 1978:371–2). Nothing can count as a religion unless it shares a significant number of these attributes. If the judgement as to what falls into this class is finally a matter of weighing the strength of analogical connections between existing and newly proposed members of the class of religions, then it cannot be governed by strict rules. Analogical thinking cannot of its nature be reduced to the application of formal principles. But if such thought is said to be arbitrary on this ground, it would not merely be the history of religions that suffers as a consequence, but the whole range of the human sciences.

The question of the universality of religion appears to come down to the issue of how far we are prepared to go in allowing 'real' analogies between central, accepted instances of religion and newly proposed ones in the study of history and culture. What is counted as a 'real' analogy in such cases will be importantly related to how far we feel that new examples of religion can be treated by the same modes of interpretation and explanation as existing ones. This point illustrates one aspect of the importance of the analysis of the basis of religion offered by Yinger, in that it points to a common account of the human needs behind religion and the possibility of similarities in the explanation of a wide range of outwardly different phenomena. The weight to be given to similarities in interpretation and explanation for judging the extent of religion's universality takes us back to the relation between religion and human nature. It highlights the need to see similar human traits lying behind the things we call 'religions'. The belief in the universality of religion and the belief in a common religiousness are then mutually supporting.

The more radical scepticism about the concept of religion aired by Smith has still to be addressed. His proposals for doing away with the concept of religion altogether have been the subject of much critical debate – most, it must be said, hostile – and they have not in fact been acted upon. The concept of religion survives in the usage of historians and students of religion in general. No attempt can be made here to provide a full review of the debate Smith has provoked (see Wiebe 1981 for a fuller treatment). Two aspects only of Smith's critique of the concept of religion will be distinguished and addressed.

One of Smith's charges against the concept of religion is that it falsely reifies and ossifies the spiritual life of mankind. Because we think of the general class 'religion' having a number of specific religions as its members, so we come to take it for granted that there are discrete, static systems into which spiritual life must be pigeon-holed. This leads to a radically misleading impression of the spritual life of, say, India, for there is no discrete, static entity corresponding to our term 'Hinduism', yet the use of this coinage is forced upon us by the logic of 'religion' and its plural 'religions'. We think that the world must abound with particular systems of faith and worship, waiting only for the scholar to come to classify and define them. Many of Smith's most scathing comments in *The Meaning and End of Religion* are reserved for this attempt to find static, discrete systems of belief where in reality there are only fluid and overlapping ways of expressing mankind's dynamic relationship to the transcendent.

This dimension of criticism against the modern concept of religion I should like to set aside as essentially minor. It points to a rigidity in thinking about religious traditions but not the complete futility of the concept of religion. After all, one can still talk of there being 'religions' in history and culture, while acknowledging that the primary reference of this common noun is to fluid and overlapping traditions. If the word contains any tendency to ossify and overly systematize the actual realities it is supposed to denote this can easily be resisted, once pointed out. Smith himself, as Wiebe notes, thinks that there is something in history that corresponds to the scholar's talk of 'Hinduism', 'Islam', and so on (Wiebe 1981:133; cf. Smith 1978:63–4). Smith thinks of there being a class of things called 'cumulative traditions' which has its specific members. The warning not to see whatever we call these shifting and interconnected cultural traditions as static, wholly discrete entities is modest enough. The actual history of the concept of religion amply shows how aware those who contributed to its formation were of the changefulness and traditional character of the things we call 'religions'. This is one of the crucial points about religion that deism and its legacy has tried to wrestle with. It can hardly be argued, then, that reifying and ossifying religious traditions is an inescapable consequence of using the concept of religion.

Much of the force of Smith's complaint against the tendency of the concept of religion to strait-jacket the realities of religious life must come from the second strand in his critique that I wish to consider briefly. Smith's distinction between faith and its outward expression in the cumulative traditions, and his emphasis on the individual character of faith, argues much more strongly for the conclusion that the treatment of religious life under the heading of 'religions' is misleading. If the true reality within religion lies in faith, and faith cannot be classified because of its character as something inward and individual, then the systematizing, reifying tendencies implicit in the notion that religious life is to be studied through a class of religions distinguished by their doctrinal, institutional, and practical dimensions would appear vicious. His emphasis on the separateness of faith and on its primacy entails that there is much else that is misleading in the concept of religion, as was noted earlier in this section. His account of faith has come under fire on a number of grounds (see Wiebe 1981:134–5, and 1979:232).

The chief point to be tackled in relation to the concept of religion is the degree to which faith can be separated from its external manifestations in belief and so on. Smith himself is not altogether clear on this point in *The Meaning and End of Religion*. He cannot totally divorce faith from cumulative tradition without producing paradoxical results: faith would then become completely unknowable in the public world. Cumulative tradition would be turned into something of no interest, either to those who have faith or to those who wish to learn something about human religious life – it would be religiously dead. Smith comes down to saying that belief is an expression of faith which implies that something of faith is preserved in belief, while belief is not identical to faith and decidedly secondary to it in the religious life of individuals. This is sufficient to gain his point that the religious life of individuals cannot be found wholly or directly in the historical realities scholars study under the name 'religions', but can only be known, if at all, by inference from those realities to the faith that underlies them. Radical scepticism about the utility of the concept of religion can be drawn from all this if both the separation between outward manifestation and inner faith and the primacy of inner faith are interpreted in a radical way. The difficulty with so taking Smith's claims is that which derives from the intentional character of religious awareness, already reflected in comments above on Schleiermacher's and Mueller's search for a generic religious experience.

Religious experience is intentional in nature. It presents itself as awareness of an object. It is not just blank feeling, but, putatively at least, experience of something: Yahveh, Allah, Krishna, or whatever. In this respect it is analogous to experiences which present themselves as perceptual, rather than to objectless moods (such as anxiety). It is this characteristic which enables perceptual experiences and states like them to have the character, if they are veridical, of placing the subject in a relationship with something beyond himself – a character Smith himself stresses that religious awareness has. As intentional states, perceptual experiences and things analogous to them are accordingly defined by the beliefs that acompany them. What makes my perceptual experience of a refrigerator an experience of that sort is partly the fact that it is moulded by beliefs of the right kind. These beliefs are those which enable my experience to contain an element of recognition that I am looking at a refrigerator. An intentional experience only latches onto its object via the subject's more-or-less correct and more-or-less full belief about what he is experiencing. By the same token, religious experience – in so far as it is analogous to perception – reaches beyond itself to an object only if it is moulded by religious beliefs. Belief makes experience possible, even though experience may add to and enrich belief. If intentionality is important to religious experience and it does present itself as experience of an object, then the contrast between the experience as inner and primary on the one hand and the beliefs of the surrounding tradition as merely external and secondary on the other must go. In the end this whole manner of talking about personal experience in religion must be misleading.

A number of contemporary writers have argued for the understanding of the relation between belief and experience in religion defended above (see Katz 1978 and Geach 1969).

However, it is noteworthy that in essence the point of view just advanced does no more than repeat the argument about the relation between conception and feeling from Hegel summarized in Chapter 6 above. Hegel's contention that without the contribution of concepts from reason feeling would be arbitrary makes the same point that the affective side of religious cognition gets its worth from being directed toward the right kind of object. It can only be guided to this object if it is clothed in the right kind of conceptual content, hence reason is necessary for religious feeling to be of value. If Hegel's argument as summarized in Chapter 6 is correct, then the outward, cultural institutions which surround religious feeling cannot be viewed simply as the cloak which hides true faith as personal feeling and experience underneath. These must rather be the very moulds which give form and therefore value to faith. The historian's or philosopher's preoccupation with religions as systems of belief and practice is not in that case an aberration.

RELIGION AND HUMAN NATURE

The theme of this section is provided by two linked elements in the deistic legacy: the commitment to a natural human religiousness and the refusal to separate the historiography of religions from philosophical reflection on religion. The link between these two themes lies in the way in which belief in a human religiousness ('religion' in the singular) behind the religions invites philosophy to undertake two important tasks in relation to the historiography of religion. First, it offers itself as a source of reflection on the data of the history of religions. These data should add up to a portrayal of the character of our natural religiousness which it is philosophy's job to produce. Second, since philosophy can provide a sketch of our religiousness, it can provide a framework for the work of historians of religion, giving them principles of meaning and interpretation which will guide them in their more detailed study. The framework enables a pattern to be discerned in the history of *religions* by enabling these histories to evince the evolution of *religion*. Both these modes of connection show themselves in the work of a paradigmatic deist, such as Blount (see Chapter 4 above). We have noted his commitment to a philosophical history of religion which can provide a gloss on the data of religious history. Equally, the deist conception of the structure of religion in human nature gives Blount, and others, a prior scheme into which the data of religious history must fit.

The connections between the concept of a natural human religiousness and the effort of philosophy to give meaning and pattern to the history of religions have been the target of considerable scepticism in the contemporary study of religions. Before this scepticism is outlined and discussed it is important to underscore two points relevant to this theme that have been raised already. One concerns the universality of religion. We have seen belief in the universality of religion to be a natural partner of belief in a natural human religiousness. Belief in some strong connection between religion and human nature is one means of establishing a presumption in favour of religion's universality, while at the same time the fact that religion can be treated as a universal phenomenon supports the notion that religion is grounded in human nature and not merely in human circumstances that may come and go. As a further point we must consider the social character of religion. The comments about social theories of the character of religion made at the end of Chapter 7 are vindicated by contemporary exponents of religion's universality. Attention may be turned away from an unmediated connection between religion and human nature toward religion as the expression of social life, because of some theory about its social function. But this will in many respects serve the same purpose as a belief in a natural human religiousness, if it also carries a commitment to the truth of the notion that religion is a *necessary* expression of social life. Yinger's ideas, which come close to asserting that religion is necessary in some form in any society, illustrate this parallel (cf. Stark and Bainbridge 1985). His expectation that religion is likely to be found in all functioning human societies is dependent on the location of certain human needs which any society has to satisfy if it is to have a long-term future. But that is to tie religion to human nature, rather than to contingent human circumstances. Yinger clearly envisages that the expression of religion as symbolic system will vary according to the societies in which it is located, so there is no unmediated link between religion and human nature, yet the very existence of religion is not the result of contingent social circumstances, but of features of the human condition itself which no society can ignore. Though the notion of the social character of religious symbolism complicates any discussion of the relation between religion and what Hume refers to as 'primary' or 'original' instincts in human nature, it can still provide something like the belief in a religion behind the religions if the necessary existence of religion in society is posited. Behind the details of the history of religion will lie the pattern and meaning to be discerned through tracing the evolution of an inextinguishable drive behind the symbolic activity of man in society (cf. Bellah 1970).

Scepticism about the ability to see such meaning through positing 'religion' as an element in the human condition which lies behind religions is forcibly expressed in Rudolph's *Historical Fundamentals and the Study of Religions* (Rudolph 1985). The essence of his criticism is contained in the proposition:

> 'Religion' in the singular is an abstraction; like all abstractions it is an a-historical phenomenon, which historians must leave to philosophers and theologians.
>
> (Rudolph 1985:91)

In history we find nothing called 'religion' in the singular, only religions. Rudolph warns historians of religions away from this concept on the grounds that it is an 'abstraction of metaphysics', which has been inherited from the age of rationalism, romanticism, and German idealism. Any historian who adopts it ends up dependent on a philosophical or theological theory (Rudolph 1985:34). The philosophical and theological loading that comes with the concept of religion in the singular encourages an illicit fusion of the discipline of the history of religion with philosophical speculations. Rudolph accuses pioneers of the history of religion such as Tiele and Mueller of fundamental error in not separating the history of religion from philosophy in their work (Rudolph 1985:23–4). A particularly striking form of this error occurs when the growth and development of religions as outward, historical phenomena is made subordinate to the growth and development of religion in the singular, conceived as the inner essence or kernel of religion which is manifested in the religions of history. Two mistakes (among many) result from this error. One is that the history of manifest religions is made out to be determined by something inner, something hidden within religion and separate from the external, cultural and social facts which surround it. The historian is then seen as dealing with something merely external or secondary if he confines himself to ordinary historical facts. A second mistake is that an *a priori* picture of religious change takes over. As philosophy or theology supplies the missing account of the nature of the religion which is manifested in the religions, they force the historical account to be bent to the results which are indicated in advance by the theory of 'religion's' development offered by speculation (Rudolph 1985:83–5). The belief in a religion behind the religions and the notion that this internal thing is developing according to its own unique logic soon leads on to a theory of general revelation. The historical study of religions is then illicitly converted into collecting evidence to confirm the pattern of general revelation assumed to be manifested in the outer forms of religion.

Rudolph's cure for the disease of subsuming the history of religions under a pre-given account of general revelation is to insist once more on the separation of the scientific history of religions from philosophy and theology. In particular, the idea that change in outward religions is driven by an internal process of develop-ment of some inward religiousness must go, and in general, a concept of development must be constructed free from philo-sophical and theological overtones, and belonging to the empirical study of change in human affairs (Rudolph 1985:89–90).

It must be conceded that many of Rudolph's strictures against approaching the historical study of religions guided by the thought that there is a human religiousness to be seen beneath the outward forms of religion strike home. In the search for a philosophical history of religions displayed by the writers discussed in this study, and in the attempt to discover pattern and meaning in the history of religions which this search entails, we see frequently the *a priori* imposition of theory on fact. In fact we find the manipulation of evidence to fit philosophical and theological conceptions. Clear though it is that Rudolph's case fits a large part of the inheritance we have described, it does not follow that the two main parts of the deistic legacy which we are now examining must be rejected. These two elements are that the history of religions as a discipline cannot be separated from the philosophy of religion, and that there is a religiousness underlying the religions. There appear to be three main charges to be distilled from Rudolph against the inheritance of ideas derived from deism: (1) the historiography of religions must be independent of philosophical reflection on religion; (2) a natural religiousness denoted by 'religion' in the singular cannot in principle be discovered by historical, empirical investigation; and (3) attempts to use philosophical conceptions of the nature of 'religion' in humankind to order the historical study of religion inevitably promote the most hopeless 'a priorism'. These three charges, though interrelated, will be considered in turn.

Charge (1) gets its force from the contrast to be drawn between the *a priori*, normative and abstract, character of the philosophy of religion and the empirical, descriptive and concrete, character of the history of religions. There is no doubt some force in these contrasts. If we consider a straightforward factual question in the history of religions about the sequence of events in the history of some faith, it may be easy to separate in our minds the factual enquiries and narrative descriptions needed to answer it from any consideration of the truth of religion or of the relation between religion in general and other abstractions such as morality or experience. However, matters are not so simple as this; indeed, the tasks of the history of religions are much more varied and ramified. It is the job of the history of religions not merely to describe series of events but to explain and interpret them. Indeed, the normal subject-matter of this, as of any form of history, is the sphere of human action, thought, and belief in the past. Human action, thought, and belief from the past cannot be described without their sense and meaning being reconstructed and rendered intelligible. R. G. Collingwood's statement that 'All history is the history of thought' (Collingwood 1961:215) is an over-simplification but it still captures an important measure of truth. To understand human action is to grasp the intentions and reasons that lie behind it, which in turn entails grasping the sense of the beliefs and concepts which inform it. Something akin to the exercise of the philosophical imagination is required, therefore, critically to reconstruct human action in the past. Granted that an understanding of ideas and the relationships between them is a necessary part of the exercise of critical history, it may still be urged that the judgemental, normative, and theoretical aspects of philosophy (here, the philosophy of religion) are alien to the historian's task. The truth or otherwise of religious notions is not an issue for the historian of religion, neither does his work presuppose or lead up to a grand theory about religion's place in human nature or culture. A description of religious action – and the minimal explanation that comes from setting this in the context of an intelligible narrative knit together by an account of the reasons, intentions, and beliefs of religious actors – is all that an historian, as opposed to a philosopher of religion, can or should provide.

The problem with the above, 'minimalist' interpretation of the task of the history of religion lies in the fact that it ignores the explanatory task of any scientific (that is, critical and organized) treatment of religion. It should be the job of the science of religion, even if concerned mainly with the history of religions, to explain as well as describe. If it is an explanatory exercise, it cannot avoid the philosophical questions about the status of religion in human life, which Rudolph apparently wishes it to ignore. The reason for this is succinctly given by Donald Wiebe as follows:

> An explanation of religion as an illusion will be vastly different from the explanation of religion as a true picture of reality. To provide an explanation of it one must judge first whether it (religion) is . . . right or wrong, true or false, a vision of reality or a mere projection of the human mind.
>
> (Wiebe 1981:80–1)

Since philosophical questions about the status of religion as either a picture of the truth or an illusory projection of the mind appear to bear upon its character in important ways, they cannot but be included in an explanatory science of religion. Only philosophical arguments can settle these questions, so any scientist of religion who deals in more than simple descriptions must be at least implicitly a philosopher of religion.

There are two objections that those who wish to defend the independence of the history of religion from the philosophy of religion might urge at this point. First, they might contend that the appraisal of the truth or otherwise of religious conceptions has no bearing on any explanations of how they are acquired. Questions of truth are, crudely, questions about the relationship between the content of what is believed in religion and reality. But to explain religious beliefs as they are held by religious individuals is to account for how these individuals come to acquire them. The matter of what kind of intellectual, social, or emotional background explains this or that historical phase of religion is nothing to do with whether the beliefs and conceptions of that phase are ultimately true or not. We must distinguish questions about *what* is believed and its relation to reality from questions about *how* it comes to be believed. The latter are questions about human motivation and the historical background to human beliefs. Historians can only deal with questions of this sort, and they are completely separate from the philosopher's questions about the content of what is believed. A second point in defence of the autonomy of the scientific history of religion might be that Wiebe's ultimate questions about the truth of religion are only to be raised at the end of historical enquiry, because they concern the status of religion as a whole. Of course, someone must consider how religion as such stands in the sphere of human knowledge. But the historian's focus is always upon some specific phase in the historical life of religion. The question of whether religion as a whole affirms anything that adds to the stock of human knowledge, and whether any particular phase of religion contributes to the sum of truth in religion, can be ignored by the historian considering simply the facts about this specific phenomenon.

Both these objections to the link between philosophy and the history of religion can be met by considering the arguments of Alisdair MacIntyre's 'Rationality and the explanation of action' (MacIntyre 1971). MacIntyre initially distinguishes between questions about the *truth* of beliefs/institutions in history and questions about the *rationality* of beliefs/institutions. These are distinguished as, respectively, questions about what is believed and questions about how it is believed (MacIntyre 1971:248). But this is of no help for those who want a history of religion (or of any other form of social institution) that is divorced from a philosophical understanding of human nature. For the rationality or otherwise of a set of beliefs is vital in deciding how they are to be explained. We typically, and rightly, expect rational beliefs and actions to be explained in a quite different way from irrational ones. Irrational beliefs are ones which may be accounted for in a way which sets aside the avowed reasons of those who hold them, for to judge them to be held irrationally is to judge that such 'reasons' played no part in their production and are at best rationalizations or cloaks for whatever factors truly moved folk to accept what is in fact contrary to their reason and understanding. MacIntyre shows how this difference in approach is clearly displayed in an historian's approach to, for example, the European witch-craze of the sixteenth and seventeenth centuries (MacIntyre 1971:244 ff.). To judge this complex of belief, behaviour, and experience to be irrational in character is to invite an explanation quite different from that required of a rational institution in history. It is to seek some explanation that goes beyond the terms in which the participants saw themselves; it is to look for causes which might explain a mass delusion and defeat of reason. By contrast, a complex of human belief and behaviour that is rational in its origins is one that can be explained in its own terms. It is intelligible as comprehensible response to a range of evidence or human experience. The connections between its component beliefs and concepts are rational and therefore intelligible ones. The reasons for the belief and behaviour of individuals within it are not mere rationalizations but intelligible as providing a genuine account of why what is believed is believed. But note that here we see how explanation of a particular historical phenomenon is dependent on judgements which involve the application of rational, and thus to an extent philosophical, norms to it. There is no alternative to a judgemental, normative, and philosophical under-standing of this historical phenomenon, granted that how beliefs and actions are related to human reason is vital in seeing how they are to be explained. If we accept the case for the asymmetry in the explanation of rational and irrational belief/action so briefly summarized here then two vital elements of the deistic legacy are preserved. One is that the concept of reason is vital in the study of human life (including religion) in history. A second is that such a study cannot be separated from, because it must include elements of, a philosophical understanding of human belief, action, and motivation.

Wiebe's point that explaining religion as a true picture of reality is different from explaining it as an illusion can be seen to have some sense to it once we note that judging the rationality of beliefs is often connected with judging their truth. A belief that is acquired irrationally may turn out to be true; a belief that is acquired rationally may be proved false upon closer investigation of the facts. Yet one important mark of many of the beliefs we say are held irrationally remains that they are so clearly false that no one could have come to believe them through the operations of reason. Judging religion or some form of religion to be an illusion (where there is an indicator of radical falsity) may well be then an important guide in determining how it is to be explained.

Suppose it be accepted that there is an inevitable philosophical component in historical judgement as applied to religion. The ground offered so far shows a connection only in regard to rationality and historical judgement. How does this connect, if at all, with showing that some concept of human nature is vital to the enterprise of the history of religions?

One thing that has been urged is the centrality of the concept of reason in the study of human belief and action. Even if this is not necessarily the concept of reason in the same guise or shape as that of the deists, it does vindicate some of their concerns. Consider, for example, Blount's reflections as recorded in Chapter 4 above on the different ways in which we might explain something that corresponded to the foundations of religion and something that merely corresponded to the superstructure of religion. This distinction is inseparably connected in Blount and others with the distinction between what results from genuine attempts on the part of mankind to reflect on God and the moral law, on the one hand, and what results from mere superstition, on the other. The latter forms of religion are imposed upon human individuals by nothing but the weight of custom or the influence of institutions blindly followed. His philosophic question about the rational status of the beliefs he examines is then related to genuine differences in how they may be explained and, with that, to different accounts of how the beliefs stand with respect to human nature. What is the result of custom or the influence of institutions is less close to human nature, but closer to human circumstances, than what is explained as the outcome of reason. These differences in explanation are related to the concept of reason, but connected also to that of human nature. A belief that falls into Blount's class of something that reflects merely 'the modes and circumstances of religion' asks for a different explanation from one that reflects the operation of the essence of our inbuilt religiousness.

Comparison between MacIntyre on the need for philosophical understanding *within* historical and sociological explanation and the thought of a representative deist reveals, then, at least three initial points of interest. First, that the concept of reason is common to both (at least in form – its content will no doubt differ). Second, the practice of relating beliefs and actions under investigation to an understanding of the concept of reason inevitably brings some connection with thoughts about human nature. Third, we see that how we view the relation of religion to human nature could affect our explanation of specific religious phenomena.

The above three points establish the continued relevance of important parts of the deistic legacy, but they do not as yet show conclusively the need for some conception of human religiousness in general as an organizing principle in the history of religion. Further argument for this conclusion must depend upon reflection upon the basic form of historical explanation. There is common agreement that this form resides in the notion of narrative, though less on what exactly a narrative is. A narrative in history is explanatory because it is more than a mere record of events in temporal sequence. It is a record of events related together in significant and relevant ways. The connections between events in a narrative are not merely those of temporal succession, for otherwise there would be no distinction between narrative and the making of lists. It is hard to make the notion of 'significant and relevant' connections between events more precise in general terms, except through the obviously circular notion of connections which provide explanatory links between the events. Under the headings of 'significant' and 'relevant' we will obviously include reference to human motives and goals which link and help to explain events and their outcomes. We will have in mind the links that are provided by the contexts in which two or more events are placed. If we are constructing a narrative in political history, knowledge of the character of political contexts will provide many ways of making significant and relevant connections between events. This knowledge of political contexts will give us rough and ready ideas about what kind of events are to be connected with what. It is important to note that there are not two processes in the construction of explanatory historical narratives: first we establish what the events are that form its substance, then we discover the relevant and significant connections between them to add the missing ingredient of explanation. This is a mistake, for unless one has some idea what are the relevant and significant connections between likely members of a narrative, one will not be able to judge that these events and not others are part of the same 'story' (cf. Danto 1985:ch.VII).

Knowledge of such significant and relevant connections between events comes from the historian's understanding of human affairs. What must be stressed is that much of this understanding is *a priori* with respect to the particular historical narratives the historian constructs. He brings this knowledge to the job of constructing narrative, even if the discovery of the shape of this particular narrative adds to that knowledge. Danto gives an example to illustrate this point. In the task of constructing a narrative to describe some phase of human artistic life, the historian would get nowhere without what Danto names conceptual evidence about the form and character of art as a human institution. That is to say, the historian's prior knowledge of art as an aspect of human life gives him a vocabulary and some rough general expectations which help him reconstruct the narrative of this part of art's history. We cannot begin to make any historical sense, affirms Danto, of materials relevant to the story, unless we have some idea of the narrative which they may support (Danto 1985:122). But the outlines of that narrative cannot be produced unless some conceptual evidence is available to delimit and suggest possible relevant and significant relations between events. Resultant, successful narratives may then be seen as a product of at least two ingredients: material evidence relating to this particular story, and conceptual evidence relating to the general character of the context of the story.

The above may be applied to narrative explanations in the history of religions. When it is so applied we see that here too we need some conceptual knowledge that is at least *a priori* relative to any particular phase of the religious life in history. This conceptual knowledge is a general understanding of religion as an aspect of human life and of the general character of religious systems. It is a knowledge of the human religious condition. It is this which gives us a prior knowledge of the range of descriptions which apply to religious actors, which enables us to classify and connect aspects of the phase of religion we are considering. It is a general familiarity with the context of religious action which we here confront in a fresh form. This human religious condition is a fit object to be denoted by a use of 'religion' in the singular. It is this which can be said to be a 'religion behind the religions' which may evolve in the course of history as its typical features change. All facets of our conceptual evidence about the human religious condition need not be absolutely *a priori*; some may be derived from general and historical knowledge. Yet it can hardly be doubted that some will also be derived from philosophical reflection on the definition of religion and the relation of religion to human nature. Our conceptual evidence that is brought to bear on the construction of narratives in religious history will include a knowledge of the possible as well as the actual (for example, of the *possible* range of human motives in religious action). Knowledge of the possible in the sphere of the human religious condition would appear to be the subject-matter of philosophical reflection.

If we remind ourselves of Max Mueller's views as described in the previous chapter, we have seen a number of grounds for supposing, as he did, that the science of religions should be grounded in a philosophy of religion and that there is a form of religious *a priori* to be employed in the science of religions (an *a priori* describable as a religion behind the religions). But this still leaves some of Rudolph's other main criticisms of attempts to link philosophy and human religiousness to be considered.

The second charge that Rudolph makes against belief in a religiousness that underlies the religions is to the effect that history as a science can know nothing of such things. The only historical realities are the discrete religions of history. There is something correct and something incorrect in this complaint. Its limitations can be seen once we distinguish what is directly present in the study of the human past and what may be inferred from information which may be so directly gathered. The religion behind the religions, when properly understood, is not a mysterious entity which may be guessed at only through abstract speculation. It is the evolving human religious condition – a compound of facts about human nature and human circumstances which jointly help to account for the existence and nature of functional, structural, and substantive similarities in the religions of history. Though some thoughts about the nature of this condition must be *a priori* relative to the study of any particular religion, its character is ultimately a matter of inference from and interpretation of historical and contemporary data about the religions. (There is a paradox in these remarks about the empirical and the *a priori* which will be explored below.) It is not in this respect mysterious, though its precise character may be the subject of competing theories, as the example of the debate between substantive and functionalist definitions of religion in the previous section makes clear.

The respect in which Rudolph's charge is justified can be brought out by admitting, that though religion (in the singular) can be known by inference from historical data, it is not the task of the historian to focus upon it. This point is well brought out in Danto's affirmation of the primacy of the historian's concern to discover 'precisely what happened' (to borrow a famous phrase from the nineteenth-century historian von Ranke; Danto 1985:130). The historian's primary focus is properly the construction of narrative to record and explain precisely what happened in some phase of the human past. This focus imposes upon him a discipline of relevance. Matters not concerned with helping to bring out precisely what happened are extra-historical and of no concern to the historian *qua* historian. What can not or need not enter into significant and explanatory narratives should not be mentioned in the historian's account. But this is not to say that such other, perhaps wider, connections visible in the facts as presented in significant narrative do not exist or are of no importance at all. The focus of the historian of religions should be on precisely what happened in human religious history. For an historian the generalities of the human religious condition will be objects of merely subsidiary, not focal, awareness, to use Polanyian terms (Polanyi 1973:55). This does not deny the reality of these generalities or that they may not become the objects of focal awareness for other disciplines in the study of religion.

Implicit in what has been said already is an answer to the third charge that Rudolph makes against belief in a religion behind the religions. It must be admitted, by anyone concerned with the integrity of historical investigation, that answers to historical questions cannot be dictated in advance by *a priori* visions of how history must go. A concept of religion cannot be allowed to compromise the autonomy of history as a discipline. As David Thompson affirms, the study of history must be

> independent of creed or regime or orthodoxy of any kind. The autonomy of historical investigation – that is, its pursuit and achievement for the sake of truth alone and not in order to serve or support or defend any system of thought or of politics – is indispensable for its vitality.

> (Thompson 1968:104)

While it must be conceded that belief in a religion behind the religions has led to a prior dictation of the pattern to be discovered in the history of religions on the part of theology or philosophy, it does not follow that this need be the case. Two related points show why this conclusion does not always follow.

First, we have seen in the above that, though a case can be made for saying that a general, conceptual, understanding of religion of some sort is presupposed by historical and empirical investigation into religions, this constitutes a religious *a priori* that is only relative. The content of this conception of religion is itself something that is fed by philosophical reflection on the data uncovered in the course of empirical investigations. Some initial concept of religion, produced no doubt by philosophical reflection on the intuitively evident facts about religion in the particular society in which the concept of religion in question originates, may be necessary to provide the initial conceptual evidence that is needed to give shape to historical enquiry. But that conception should itself be capable of being modified and expanded upon, as empirical study provides more material for philosophical reflection on the nature of the human religious condition. The concept of a human religious condition, knowledge of which informs the study of particular religions, is a 'dialectical' one (cf. Bianchi 1987:400) – dialectical, in being ever-evolving and enriched through the creative tension between its character at any one moment and the facts which suggest the necessity of its modification. The call for what was described as 'a philosophical history of religions', which we found in Blount and is in fact displayed by a number of writers considered in this study, need not be interpreted as the demand for a philosophical pre-writing of the shape of the history of religion. It may instead be seen as, first, the demand for some reflective conception of religion to get the study of religion started, and, second, as the call for continued reflection on the general character of the human religious condition to bring out the universal, religious significance of the detail revealed in the history of religion.

The second point which may defeat the fears of *a priori* dictation of historical investigation by philosophical reflection rests on the abandonment of the idea that 'religion' in the singular determines the course of religious history independent of the circumstantial details of religious life. There is a tendency to see in the idea of a universal, underlying religiousness a reference to something in human nature which will act like an engine, driving religious change and development on pre-set, and philosophically discoverable, paths. This bad side to the attempt to see pattern in religious history through philosophical reflection is clearly evident in, for example, the deists and Hegel. But our religiousness – 'religion' in the singular – need not be so conceived. It is that condition of humanity which predisposes individuals and groups to engage in religious life and institutions and gives those forms of life and institutions recognizably similar patterns and structures. But the human religious condition is not something that can be viewed independently of contingent facts about human societies in history. The good side of philosophical attempts to relate contingent facts about religious history to a philosophically reflective account of the human religious condition is displayed when they can be seen to be informed by a knowledge of historical religious facts and to be attempts to discern what those facts mean for our view of human nature, human society, and the relation of religion to each of these. The results of the history of religions properly provoke reflections on these relations because of the apparent universality, or near-universality, of religion, and because of the importance of the questions raised by religion for human life.

R. G. Collingwood gives, as part of his definition of what the study of history is, a statement of the purpose history serves – that of increasing human self-knowledge (Collingwood 1961:10). Human self-knowledge is increased by history on the premiss that it adds to a knowledge of human nature. This is, essentially, the argument for employing the notion of natural religiousness in relation to the history of religion and for asserting the relevance of philosophy of religion to the history of religions. Some conceptions of human religious nature are necessary to give the history of religions a framework for the construction of significant narratives in this area. And philosophy may plead a number of grounds for using the results of historical investigation to inform a continually advancing understanding of the human religious condition. This may all be true without admitting the charges that – there is no difference between the history and the philosophy of religion as disciplines, or that the history of religions is being sent in pursuit of some hidden and mysterious 'religiousness' that lies beneath outer facts about religion, or that historical study will be forced into passively confirming the pattern dictated in advance by philosophical reflection on the meaning of religion.

NATURALISM AND THE HISTORY OF RELIGIONS

The authors influenced by, or reflecting upon, the legacy of natural religion we have surveyed have been found to share agreement on a fundamental naturalism in the history of religions despite the other points which may divide them. In relation to this issue, if nothing else, the pattern laid down by Mueller has been followed. Twentieth-century historians of religion assume no distinction between some religions which are divine or supernatural and others which are merely natural. The explanation of the origin and course of each and every religion is fitted into a broadly naturalistic pattern. That is to say, the standard form of a significant narrative in the history of religions allows reference to only human or other mundane agencies. This point of agreement marks one of the most significant parts of the legacy of deism. However, at least two important questions can be raised about it. The first has already arisen in the context of discussing Hume and Tylor. It relates to how far this naturalism extends to seeking a reductive, external explanation of religion as a whole. The second arises out of contemporary attacks on the belief that historical narratives must be based on naturalistic assumptions, these attacks being combined with corresponding defences of the viability of belief in miracles.

The descent of naturalism into reductionism is not something that is part of the legacy of deism itself. The emphasis of deism on the existence of a natural human religiousness – on there being a religion behind the religions which is one of the distinctive marks of being human – brings with it a non-reductive naturalism. Naturalism, in the sense of an anthropocentric approach to religion, is implied by the very emphasis on the roots of the religions in a human religiousness. But this emphasis encourages the thought that there is a distinct logic to religious thought and practice and, with it, the notion that religion is an irreducible element in human life. These consequences are clearly present in the writings of some of those who wrestle with the legacy of deism, notably in Herder, Schleiermacher, and Mueller. We have already tried to bring out the distinctiveness of Hume's naturalism, with its insistence that there is little sense to be made of religion and its categories. What logic Hume sees in popular religious thought is in the last analysis the logic of illusion. This fits in perfectly with his

241

attempt to show that religion is but the secondary effect of non-religious causes.

If the legacy of deism is followed, then we will accept the thesis that anthropocentrism in the science of religion does not entail a reductive naturalism (cf. Wiebe 1981:79). This thesis does not show that some form of reductive naturalism is false. A Humean picture of religion as an illusion using categories derived from modern psychological and sociological theory may be argued for on a variety of grounds. The point maintained here is that such a picture needs independent argument and does not simply follow from the anthropocentrism implicit in the concept of religion which structures the modern scientific study of religion. The question of how naturalism should proceed, once the anthropocentric bias in the science of religion is accepted, turns out to be a matter of the final philosophical judgement to be made of the status of human religiousness. We have the assumption, derived from the deistic legacy, that the facts of the history of religions can be universally understood in terms of the human religious condition. An understanding of this condition provides the conceptual framework in which all such facts can be made sense of, and the facts of religion wherever and whenever we find it can in turn be used to add to our comprehension of human religiousness. However, different kinds of judgement are possible on the nature and status of the human religious condition. Some may argue that its character shows it to be a reflection of a universal awareness of a real, sacred reality; others that it can be reduced without remainder to the simple effect of non-religious factors in human life (for example, neurotically based fantasies or the ideological expression of class consciousness); yet others may be content to leave the status of human religiousness undecided and undecidable. Which of these options is chosen obviously relates to the kind of philosophical judgement about whether religion is or is not an illusion mentioned in the previous section. There such philosophical judgement was connected via the arguments of Alisdair MacIntyre with further issues concerning the rationality of religious thought and practice. Very roughly speaking, those who choose the reductive approach to the interpretation of the human religious condition are responding to the sense that behind it lurks a monumental illusion signalled by the irrationality of religion. On this ground the family-related categories and structures of human religions can be set aside as masks hiding the true roots of religion in something outside itself.

The adoption of one or other of the competing interpretations of the human religious condition listed above would obviously have important implications for the conduct of the scientific study of religion. The first interpretation, for example, suggests that such a study will have important links with and implications for theology. The second suggests that the science of religions will in the end be an applied version of some other study – that which describes the true forces operating to generate religion. The third implies the possibility of a neutral, agnostic anthropocentric approach to religious explanation. No attempt can be made here to decide in favour of any one of these interpretations. The important implications they bring with them, however, bear out the crucial role of philosophical reflection in shaping the structure of the critical study of religion. As asserted above, we cannot insulate the science of religion from the philosophical question of the ultimate status of human religiousness, and even the study of particular phases of religion will be affected by philosophical reflection on their character as illusions or otherwise.

The common anthropocentric approach to explanation of religious facts in the historical and critical study of religion is the target of those who wish to defend some role for divine agency in the structure of the history of religions. Attacks on the assumption of anthropocentrism in the history of religions come from a number of quarters in the current debate on the nature of the study of religions. For example, a theologian of world religions, Wilfred Cantwell Smith, can be found to complain of the 'unproven naturalism' on which the history of religions currently depends (Smith W. C. 1981:124–5). Smith's protest is made in the interests of gaining a proper appreciation for the claim of religious awareness throughout history to have a focus in a genuine transcendent reality. More relevant to our theme are the strictures of those writers in the Evangelical Christian tradition on the naturalistic approach of modern scholarship toward the Bible and the origins of Christianity. W. J. Abraham's *Divine Revelation and the Limits of Historical Criticism* and W. L. Craig's *The Historical Argument for the Resurrection of Jesus during the Deist Controversy* are good examples of this point of view. The target of such works is the assumption that Scriptural events can be universally treated as the subject-matter of history, meaning by this the study of *human* actions in the past. This assumption we have seen to be at the heart of deistic naturalism (or anthropocentrism as we have come to call it in this chapter). It provides the ground for rejecting the distinction between natural and divine religions and is related to one of the most fundamental elements in the conception of religion to which deism helped to give birth – the belief that all religions are through and through human phenomena. The apparently impressive agreement on this naturalistic assumption among the varied writers we have surveyed here amounts, in the view of contemporary opponents such as Abraham and Craig, to no more than a common acceptance of the dogma that miracles (direct divine acts in history) are impossible. There is no reason why a properly critical study of the past of religions should not be ready to accept that at least some forms of religious development are due to divine action. In this respect, they attempt to reassert Locke's presentation of the nature and origins of Christianity.

Beyond the sheer dogma that direct divine interventions into history are impossible, the naturalistic banishment of the category of miracle from study of religious history can be seen to rest on two linked grounds, which are both prominent in the deistic writings surveyed in Chapter 4 above. One relates to the notion that, when assessed by the canons of probability, miracle-stories are much less likely to be true than are alternatives (such as a misreporting of the events in question or the existence of some mundane but unknown explanation of them). The other, connected, ground rests on the assumption that there are procedures essential to the construction of historical narrative which exclude by their nature the admission of miraculous events into them. An influential, post-deistic account of procedural assumptions behind the construction of historical narratives is contained in Ernst Troeltsch's famous essay 'On Historical and Dogmatic Method in Theology' (Troeltsch 1913:729–53; summarized by Harvey 1967:14 ff.). Troeltsch's argument turns around the belief that history is the critical reconstruction of the human past. To frame any narratives on the basis of evidence from the past the historian must first filter the likely from the unlikely. Critical construction of narrative is only possible if he relies on the principles of analogy and correlation. The first tells him that he must rely on a general agreement between his present experience of the world and its ways and the course of past history. The second principle assures him that each and every event fits into an intelligible pattern of causes and consequences. There is an interdependence between all occurrences which allows any real event to be seen as intelligibly connected with others that precede and succeed it (Troeltsch 1913:732–3). Both these principles suggest the same conclusion – that a miraculous occurrence is one that must be discounted in the critical construction of significant narrative. It would be disanalogous to events experienced in the present and disconnected from its antecedents and consequences to a large degree.

The direct appeal to what may be allowed to be probable and the appeal to analogy and correlation in historiography are ways of insisting that, without stringent standards of critical reflection, the historian would be at a loss in construction of narrative, with no means of distinguishing fact from fiction. Such standards can, moreover, only come from applying what science and the study of human affairs have established about the regular causes of events in the world as we know it (cf. Middleton 1749, as quoted in Chapter 4 above). A knowledge of how the world in general goes yields positive principles in the interpretation of the past of a religion such as Christianity, since it teaches us in general about the background to the formation of new religions and the creation of 'inspired' writings. It is the application of this knowledge, rather than appeal to notions of divine inspiration, which will yield the best means of an historical reconstruction of the Biblical message and the origins of Christianity.

The criticisms from a writer such as Abraham of this contemporary case for an anthropocentric approach to sacred history are in essence no different from those Locke, Leland, and Clarke offered in reply to seventeenth- and eighteenth-century attacks on Christianity's status as a divine religion. This is evident if we consider the manner in which Abraham treats the objection to the admission of miracles in history based on the nature of probability. If we take the case of the resurrection of Jesus, are we not forced to rely on common knowledge of what is possible and impossible and to conclude that the *a priori* improbability of such an event is so great that not even a favourable view of the testimony in its favour could allow it to be a genuine occurrence? Abraham's reply to this standard deistic-Humean approach to the resurrection is to appeal to the notion that events are probable or not only in relation to a context. If the resurrection of Jesus is placed in context of belief in a God who has a record of action stretching through history, and who has ends and purposes which might be served by this particular piece of direct divine agency, then the resurrection might indeed become probable in the light of the positive evidence in its favour. As Abraham puts it:

> What is claimed is not simply that Jesus came back from the dead but rather that God raised him from the dead with certain intentions and purposes. It was an act of God related to His overall purposes for the world.

(Abraham 1982:132)

This is the Locke-Leland-Clarke reply to rationalist dismissal of miracle put in modern terms: an event is probable or not only when considered under a given description or descriptions. Described merely as a 'rising from the dead' Jesus' resurrection is no doubt improbable; described as 'God raising him from the dead' it could be probable, if it is allowed that such a description establishes a relation between the event and a context of plausible considerations which lend it likelihood. Here the context would be belief in an agent-God willing and able to intervene in the course of history and with specific purposes and plans which make intervention in this mode likely. If such beliefs are allowed to be plausible in themselves then they lend probability to miracle-reports such as the resurrection.

Abraham's argument is in effect that only a dogmatic scepticism about the existence of a personal God can rule out the rational option of holding such background beliefs, which in turn can lend credence to at least some miracle-reports in history. (The same point provides the main burden of the apologetic for miracle in Craig 1985.) Abraham also argues that any force the principles of correlation and analogy might have to rule out well-grounded beliefs about divine action in history is dependent on such dogmatic scepticism. His strategy to defeat the use of Troeltsch's principles to rule out divine action from history begins with the argument that analogy is in fact dependent for its force on correlation (Abraham 1982:109). Analogy is an implausible and vague principle if it merely states that the past is only discoverable on the condition that it is like the present. On the one hand, we expect the human past to contain events and actions which are unique in their own ways (an historian who expected the past to be no different from the present would be on a road to nowhere); on the other hand, we need some idea of the relevant respects in which the past might be like or unlike the present to operate with analogy in any clear way. The relevant respect in which the past must be like the present takes us to the principle of correlation. The past should be like the present in exhibiting a close causal interdependence between its events, and thus in providing a basis for applying the principle of correlation. Having established that analogy is more or less equivalent to correlation Abraham goes on to argue that a believer in traditional sacred history has nothing to fear from correlation unless a *material* conception of correlation is forced upon him (Abraham 1982:109–10). A material conception is one which lays down in advance that events can only be interdependent in certain prescribed ways. If these prescribed ways refer only to natural or human forms of causal agency, then of course the person who takes the idea of sacred history seriously will be accused of believing in past events which are not correlated to other events. The events would not then fit into a significant, explanatory narrative. But such a prescription of modes of correlation constitutes a massive begging of the question. The believer in historical miracles does regard such events as correlated with other events in the closest possible way. It is merely that he admits direct divine agency as a causal factor that binds together events in the world's history. Since the purposes and intentions of the God of history are in a measure discernible, miracle-events can be intelligibly correlated by us with their antecedents and consequences. So even sacred history is formally analogous with the present in being an intelligible history of correlated, interdependent events.

Abraham's own way of advancing the argument just given rests on the notion that how we view the possible ways in which events may be correlated and interdependent depends on our background beliefs about the nature of reality. (His treatment of the importance of background beliefs in the formation of historical narrative is confirmation of the points made about conceptual, *a priori* evidence in history and the role of philosophy in historical understanding in the previous section of this chapter.) Given beliefs of the right sort about an agent-God then miracle-events could be seen as correlated with other events (Abraham 1982:109). If these background beliefs are rejected then naturally an attempt to recognize the existence of a miracle-event in the past will appear tantamount to admitting an event which is anomalous and unrelated to its surrounding circumstances. The rise of scientific history has taught us that we must not accept as probable events which cannot be fitted into patterns of interdependence and causality. But it has not taught us that the only patterns of causality are those admitted by the natural sciences. We still operate in ordinary life, and indeed in much if not most of our historical understanding, with the notion that personal agency is real and can explain connections between events. Only a dogmatic atheism smuggled in disguise into the 'presuppositions of history' can rule out relying on well-founded beliefs about the patterns of divine personal agency to correlate some events with others.

Abraham appears to allow that there is a form of methodological atheism that historians of religion can be permitted to operate with. For the fact is that historians rightly steer clear of theological and philosophical controversy, and to base an history of some phase of religion, such as the rise of Christianity, on background assumptions which allowed divine agency to be a correlating factor in history would be to invite endless dispute. So for the purposes of the professional practice of history an anthropocentric, naturalistic stance is assumed. The historian rightly ignores theological considerations which might bear on the character of sacred history so as to focus without controversy on human acts in the past. But this naturalism of method is valid only within the limited context of the usual and agreed practice of the professional historian (Abraham 1982:161–2).

Abraham's limited concession to naturalism is perhaps the point at which to begin the questioning of his latter-day defence of Locke. The historian's desire to avoid needless theological controversy does not appear to be a strong ground on Abraham's own assumptions for ignoring miracle-events in the construction of narrative. For according to Abraham the use of background beliefs about the existence and intentions of an agent-God will be vital if a certain portion of events in religious history is to be correlated properly with antecedents and consequences. The construction of successful narratives will be impossible for a range of events concerning the origins of Christianity (if that is where we think our agent-God has been particularly active), unless the relevant background beliefs are brought to bear which enable the interdependence between these events to be discerned. Craig would appear to be more consistent in arguing that, once a dogmatic belief that divine intervention in history has been abandoned, events such as the resurrection, understood as a full-blown miracle, should be admitted to be probable by the twentieth-century historian (Craig 1985:544–5). To be fair to Abraham, he does suggest that an investigation of the origins of Christianity bound by the constraints of professional history will be a limited one. A full treatment of this phase of religious history will be a matter for 'subtle interaction between theologian and historian' (Abraham 1982:162). Granted the crucial nature of the character of the background beliefs which are needed to flesh out some conception of historical interconnectedness, we must envisage, if Abraham is right, not *a* discipline called 'the history of religions' but *many* such disciplines corresponding to the type of background assumptions about divine/sacred agency that a historian employs. There will be a Christian history of religions, a Jewish, an Islamic, an atheist, and so on, though of course there will be a large measure of overlap between them. (Abraham, for example, admits a large measure of human response and initiative in the sacred history of Christianity, cf. Abraham 1981 *passim*.) This thought of many histories of religion might appear grossly implausible, yet it could be contended that the opposing concept of a unitary discipline is based on an illusion – the illusion inherent in the idea of an uncontroversial yet anthropocentric conception of religion. It may also be urged that those who live in debt to the legacy of deism cannot have both the assertion that the history of religions is intimately connected to the philosophy of religion *and* the notion that there will be just one, unitary discipline corresponding to that title. For there are different philosophies of religion from which to choose.

The ideal for the history of religions that we have seen descend from deism to writers such as Mueller is for dependence on a philosophy of religion committed to a mitigated form of naturalism (anthropocentrism). This does not amount to dogmatic atheism, but it does amount to seeing any form of divine or sacred agency that particular faiths are committed to in their traditional or sacred histories as mediated agency – something that is expressed through natural and human causes. This mitigated form of naturalism is what we have seen emerging in our survey of the deists (in contrast to Hume) and those who succeeded them, and it is the foundation of the anthropocentric concept of religion that results from this passage of thought. A leading Biblical scholar has noted in criticism of Abraham the extent to which mitigated naturalism (as I phrase it) has proved fruitful in exegesis of the Bible. Biblical critics have had insightful things to say about narratives such as those of the nativity because they have pursued suggestions about which human authors might have produced them, how the narratives were related to the mental structures of the ancient world, and so on: in other words, by pursuing anthropocentric principles of correlation (Barr 1982:1422). This points to one means through which the mitigated naturalism descending from deism could be tested – simply by seeing which form of approach to the history of religions results in the most insightful, plausible narrative accounts. Here we have in Barr's remarks an echo of the criticisms of Woolston and others on a supernaturalistic reading of, say, the Gospels: such a reading does not produce coherent, intelligible interpretations of these narratives.

How far testing of the above sort might be possible in anything like a neutral fashion could of course be questioned. Further reflection on Abraham's proposal could do worse than consider the original deistic criticisms of supernaturalism in the history of religions, as recorded in Chapter 4 above.

One of the major points on which the deistic case for naturalism in the history of religions rests is the need for consistency in the patterns of explanation the criticism of religion must use. Consistency in this context has two aspects. First, there is the demand for consistency in the categories of explanation used of *all* the world's religions. If we take it that anthropocentric modes of explanation are to be used in the account we give of the origin and development of non-Christian faiths, should we not consistently apply these modes to Christianity itself? To treat the religions differently in this regard may appear to adopt one way of correlating events in one portion of religious history, but a different and incompatible form of correlation in another portion. There appears then to be a failure in really carrying through the principle of analogy in the historical interpretation and explanation of world religious history. A further failure of analogy might be perceived if we follow out Middleton's point that how we explain religious facts in the present should be reflected in how we explain them in the past. If, in relation to contemporary events, we have no room for the categories of miracle and direct divine action, how can we use them of the past? If we seek and find anthropocentric causes of the events in the religious life of the present, why are we allowed to give up this search when faced with events two thousand years ago? Again there appears to be a failure to apply in a consistent manner the principle of correlation, and a consequent omission to abide by the dictates of analogy.

To such criticisms, derived from the deist attack on miracle, the defender of a non-naturalistic history of religion, or of Christian origins, must reply by arguing that it is perfectly possible to be consistent in the explanation of events throughout the world's religions and across the religious past and present while at the same time coming to different conclusions about the character of various episodes in the religious life of mankind. Consistency is valuable here in so far as it refers to a consistent application of one and the same set of explanatory principles (or body of conceptual evidence about the character of religion). But such principles could initially include a belief in an agent-God as the initiator of some religious events, while making room for the belief that this non-anthropocentric factor in religious history only operated on selected occasions. The non-naturalistic historian of religion would be consistent in operating with one and the same set of material principles of correlation, and consistent in looking for the same types of evidence in past and present and through all religions to establish whether there were good grounds for invoking the 'supernatural' elements in those principles. He would only be inconsistent if it could be shown that he could point to no relevant differences among the events he singles out for non-anthropocentric explanation. Debate would then have to turn to the kind of detailed arguments we saw in Middleton and others in Chapter 4 concerning the presence of important and relevant differences between those events in the life of religion that we were disposed to explain naturalistically and those other events of supposed sacred history which allegedly could not be explained without invoking principles of correlation of a supernatural sort.

So far in considering criticisms of Abraham's defence of non-anthropocentric history we have come across two points which appear to demand debate about the detail of sacred narrative if they are to be settled. (One concerns which approach to narratives tends to produce the most insightful results; the other concerns to the presence or absence of relevant and important differences between religious history explained anthropocentrically and religious history explained through invoking divine agency.) Because they concern the detail of narratives they cannot be further dealt with here. Two further matters of principle need to be considered, relating to the plausibility of the background beliefs which might provide the particular, substantive principles of correlation that an historian working on the lines mapped out by Abraham would require.

The background beliefs in question must include belief in an agent-God willing and able to act/intervene in the course of human history, but only on some, infrequent occasions. (The last clause is required (1) to avoid an implausible threat to belief in a stable natural order required by the success of natural science; and (2) to accommodate the readily accepted way in which the greater part of the historiography of religions is conducted. I am assuming that the intellectual price for abandoning both (1) and (2) is too high.) These background beliefs will, of course, be implausible to one who is an atheist. But no argument of principle against their use in the history of religions could rest on the superiority of atheism to theism as a world-outlook: that would only confirm Abraham's and Craig's hints that naturalism in the historical study of religions rests on nothing other than dogmatic atheism. Independent reasons must be sought for questioning these background beliefs. The deistic legacy contains at least two important ones.

Consider first the final part of the description of the relevant background beliefs we are considering: that the agent-God has reason to intervene in some few selected portions of religious history. Any expansion of such a claim must provide good moral grounds for selective divine intervention – a point rightly insisted upon by Thomas Chubb, as we noted in Chapter 4 above. Abraham offers a detailed case for saying that the work of effecting and attesting revelation could only be accomplished if there is special divine action in history (see e.g. Abraham 1982:91). Implicitly, he is affirming that the ends behind revelation are sufficiently good and important as to justify *selective* divine action in history. Yet we have seen that this case, similar in many respects to that offered by Locke, has to face the problem of the uniqueness of Christianity and the justice of God. In Chubb we saw the direct link made between the apparent injustice of the God of a unique Christian revelation and the implausibility of using belief in a God willing and able to intervene in history as a background belief which might make miracle-stories anything other than inherently unlikely. We cannot propose to adjudicate finally on the possibility of reconciling divine justice with Christianity's uniqueness, but a number of important points require underlining. The particular deistic response to the contextual defence of the probability of miracles shows that a rejection of them need not be based on either dogmatic atheism or dogmatic assertion of the unity of nature and history. What is at issue is the *coherence* of the full description of the context which is supposed to make a non-anthropocentric account of some events in the history of religions plausible. We see also that placing the historical study of Christianity (or any other particular faith) in the context of knowledge of the entire religious life of mankind does make a difference to the approach to the historical account we are disposed to give of this religion. For it is reflection on global religious life which raises the issue of Christianity's alleged uniqueness. Uniqueness is an issue when considering the cost of not having a single concept of religion and a uniform set of conceptual evidence about the character of religion in studying the full range of mankind's religious life.

A further objection to the background beliefs about God before us may also be seen to have its roots in deistic reflections, particularly in those reflections concerning the alleged oddity of using anthropocentric categories to account for the present of religious life, but non-anthropocentric categories to account for at least part of its past. For we may wonder how far we could have any evidence that there was agency in history of a supernatural kind except through well-confirmed miracles in the present: contemporary events which could only be explained by invoking this special type of agency. The problem focuses on how we might reasonably acquire the belief that a God, supposing his reality, was willing and able to intervene in nature and history. The point is well summed up by J. M. Thornton thus: 'How could we have any grounds at all for this prior belief in a personal god apart from evidence provided by a series of miracles is hard to see' (Thornton 1984:228). Thornton's point is that the relevant belief is not simply in a deity but in a special type of *agency* associated with this deity. It would appear that the clearest evidence we could have of the existence of this mode of agency would be evidence provided by actions which evinced it. But we have seen that events which might be instances of this agency – that is, miracles – only lose their taint of *a priori*, inherent unlikelihood once belief that there is the relevant type of agency is brought to bear upon them. Recognition of miracles then appears hopelessly circular: events are plausibly seen as really miraculous in the light of a background belief about divine agency, but this belief is only well founded if instances of the miraculous are admitted.[2]

The force of the charge of circularity in an explanatory scheme for history such as Abraham's could be blunted if it could be argued that the admission of the type of non-anthropocentric agency in history he seeks might stand as a working hypothesis, which in itself requires no prior proof. The possibility of its truth cannot be ruled out in advance of looking at the details of history, and its actual use could be defended if there are indeed a range of historical facts and evidences which can only be properly explained on the assumption that it is true. It requires no prior proof, but is justified in the actual practice of historiography, because for example it provides the simplest explanation of a group of historical facts (cf. Swinburne 1979:225 ff.). The problem with this reply is that it looks implausible to suppose that a range of facts about the past, and particularly the ancient past, could ever be full or clear enough to force us to use a material principle of correlation in history that is otherwise idle. If we have a series of principles accounting for the ways that events, and particularly events in the life of religion, are interconnected and interdependent, and these principles are sufficient to provide successful narrative explanations of the events of the present and recent past, it would be hard to see how events from the remote past for which limited evidence is available could make us add to these principles. We must be alert to the fact that the conceptual evidence used to construct narratives in religious history is only relatively *a priori* and can be added to or modified as the discovery of religious facts dictates (as described above). However, it might appear, as Thornton argues, that, in the absence of a belief in the special mode of agency miracles require, it will always be more economical and reasonable to assume that an event in the religious past can be fitted into the principles of correlation we find sufficient in the present, provided enough were known about the antecedents of the event and the relevant natural connections that might explain it.

If this reply to Abraham is accepted then it would vindicate the deist's concern with consistency both in our accounts of all religions and between our accounts of the religious present and religious past. It would also suggest that Troeltsch's principle of analogy does have some force after all in asking us to make our accounts of the past conform to those we offer of the present.

Consistency in the historical and global conception of religion we employ in the discipline of the history of religions is one of the key elements in the concept of natural religion as it has come down to us from the legacy of deism. To see *all* religions as natural and as expressions of our natural religiousness is the challenge with which the legacy of deism confronts us.

*

NOTES

2 HUMANISM AND RATIONALISM

1. This latter work was published posthumously and attributed to Herbert. For a cogent defence of Herbert's authorship see Hutcheson's introduction to Herbert 1944.

2. A full treatment of the naturalism present in the Lockean account of reason and human nature will be found in Schouls 1980.

3. In *A Second Vindication of the Reasonableness of Christianity* Locke identifies faith in Jesus as the Messiah more fully with 'receiving him for our Lord and King, promised and sent from God' (Locke 1823e:421). It is a way of returning to God, giving our natural allegiance to God and promising to advance the coming of God's kingdom, which in turn has been promised by God to Jesus (1823e:235). Both here and in the first *Vindication*, he is noticeably coy about accepting any interpretation of Messiahship which makes Jesus part of the Godhead.

4. This consequence is not necessarily accepted by Locke. In the ensuing section of the *Essay* he explicitly denies that his argument is meant to 'lessen the credit and use of history'. He implies that history is the sole evidence we have in many cases of truth and praises the value of the 'records of antiquity' (1823c;IV,16,11). His underlying point in this section is perhaps that where we have *original documentary evidence* for an event or truth, the rule of the diminishing value of traditions of testimony does not apply. His affirmation of the certainty of faith that is based directly on the text of Scripture (as in *The Reasonableness of Christianity*) demonstrates his conviction that we can appeal behind the tradition testifying Biblical happenings and truths to the original, documentary evidence for them. In the *Third Letter for Toleration* he implies that the evidence provided by miracles in the New Testament remains beyond reasonable doubt (1823d:443–4). As we shall see in Chapter 4, the deists do not accept this mode of argument, contending that document and tradition cannot be so easily separated, and they therefore read the passage against traditional truths in the sceptical manner I point to.

3   DEISM AND THE CASE FOR NATURAL RELIGION

1. There is no clearer statement of this point than in Thomas Chubb's argument for natural religion: 'Man has a right by the common laws of equity to be invested with such a capacity or power, as is sufficient (when duly exercised) to discover what he is accountable for, and what it is that renders him the proper object of divine favour or displeasure' (Chubb 1734:4).
2. Proponents of natural religion inevitably stressed the moral difficulties in redemption and atonement; that is, the objections that it was wrong to make one individual (Jesus) suffer for the guilt of others and that merit in conduct could not be transferred from one individual to another. See Chubb 1731:16, Morgan 1738:125 ff. and Anon (?Annet) 1746:41.
3. Indeed one of their major points against revealed religion is that, given its foundation, it must be changeable. Thus Morgan: 'Now, this political hierarchical religion, as it never was nor can be built on any other foundation but tradition, history and human authority, has been always different in different ages and countries' (1738:95).
4. For Lessing's views see Lessing 1956:53. Morgan is particularly clear on this point, claiming that all tradition and testimony will inform us of is what our forefathers believed, not whether what they believed is true or not (1738:35). The lack of connection between truths of reason and truths of history is presented in these words: 'the being and moral perfections of God, and the natural relations of man to him, as his reasonable creature and the subject of moral government, cannot depend upon the truth or falsehood of any historical facts' (Morgan 1738:345–6).

4   DEISM AND THE CRITICISM OF RELIGION

1. This account of the Church's descent from paganism is reaffirmed in similar terms in Morgan 1740:108–9 and Middleton 1729:36 and 39.
2. Middleton's argument in *A Letter from Rome* that Papal Christianity repeats in contemporary form the paganism of old is an extremely clear illustration of this point. The people of Rome worship 'in the same temples, at the same altars and always with the same ceremonies as the old Romans' and are therefore involved in 'the same crime of superstition and idolatry with their pagan ancestors' (Middleton 1729:69–70).
3. My presentation of the deists' case against miracles is greatly indebted to R. M. Burns's survey in *Great Debate on Miracles*, though I have tried to offer in my much briefer treatment a distinctive account of their critique.
4. Woolston's addiction to allegory, and in particular the allegories favoured by the Fathers, would seem to disqualify him as a *deistic* critic of the Bible. Yet the criticism of the Bible in the six *Discourses* is presented under the banner of allegiance to natural religion (see for

example 1729e:70 and 1729f:37) and is marked throughout by pleas for free-thinking and against clericalism.

5. A more positive appreciation of Jesus is of course possible from those who normally get the title 'deist'. Morgan for example in vol. 1 (1738) of *The Moral Philosopher* presents Jesus as the great prophet of natural religion (392), as a noble martyr for virtue (167–9) and as the greatest religious teacher to have appeared in the world (358). This picture of Jesus as a superior Socrates is made possible because in vol. 3 he claims that the Apostles are the source of many of the 'bad' sayings and actions in the portrayal of Jesus in the Gospels (1740:203 ff.).

5 THE PROGRESS OF THE CONCEPT OF NATURAL RELIGION

1. R. M. Burns in *The Great Debate on Miracles* demonstrates in detail how the content of Hume's essay was anticipated point by point in deistic thought even though Hume regarded himself as making an original contribution to the debate. See Burns 1981 chs. 4 and 7.

2. See Gaskin 1978:146–9 for a fuller discussion of Hume's references to 'true religion'.

3. This point provides the third striking instance of an echo or borrowing in *The Natural History* of Lockean ideas, even phrases. The assertions that there are some nations without religion and that Christianity was born into a world without monotheism are the others. Hume's reference to monkeys in human shape closely parallels a similar assertion in the *Essay concerning Human Understanding* IV,18,11.

4. Hume does of course allow that religious enthusiasm, as opposed to superstition, plays some role in the advancement of liberty. See Hume 1882a:149–50.

8 THE CONTEMPORARY STUDY OF RELIGIONS

1. Some brief mention should be made here of Stark and Bainbridge's *Future of Religion*. Two notable features of this recent sociological attempt to offer a theory of secularization are: (1) it relies on a definition of religion outwardly similar to Spiro's, but (2) it concludes in favour of religion's universality. The argument employs a familiar recourse to a description of ineradicable human needs which can only be satisfied by belief in 'supernatural' beings or values. The following is typical of their conclusion:

> In the future, as in the past, religion will be shaped by secular forces but not destroyed. There will always be a need for gods and the general compensators they offer.

(1985:527–8)

2. Thornton does argue that the argument from design would offer independent ground for believing in this supposition about divine agency. Recognition of miracle is not therefore the only ground on which the supposition might rest. The problem with this alternative is,

as he sees it, that contemporary philosophy has shown that argument in its various forms to be unsound (Thornton 1984:228). However, even this is perhaps giving too much away to the defender of miracle as a category of explanation. The argument from design will not surely tend to prove the assumption about the possibility and likelihood of divine agency in history unless it too focuses on miracle-like occurrences (such as the special creation of organic species complete with their adaptive features) as the only explantion of facts otherwise inexplicable. Only appeals to design-as-special-creation will lead to the needed conception of divine agency, but it is just this kind of appeal to design which is most open to question by the discoveries of science. As the deists themselves show, belief in design and order is perfectly possible without the relevant assumption about divine agency but with a belief in general providence only. See the discussion of Wollaston in Chapter 3 above. If this is correct then design is not an escape from Thornton's charge of circularity.

WORKS CITED

Abraham, W. J. (1981) *The Divine Inspiration of Holy Scripture*, Oxford: Oxford University Press.

(1982) *Divine Revelation and the Limits of Historical Criticism*, Oxford: Oxford University Press.

Annet, p. (1743) *The Resurrection of Jesus Considered*, London.

Anon (?P. Annet) (1746) *Deism Fairly Stated and Vindicated*, London.

Aquinas (1924) *Summa contra Gentiles*, tr. Dominican Fathers, London: Burns Oates.

(1974) *Summa Theologiae*, tr. Dominican Fathers, London: Eyre & Spottiswood.

Athanasius (1971) *Contra Gentes*, tr. R. W. Thompson, Oxford: Oxford University Press.

Augustine (1925) *On the Spirit and the Letter*, tr. W. Sparrow, Simpson Library of Christian Classics, London: SCM Press.

(1943) *Of True Religion*, tr. J. H. S. Burleigh, Library of Christian Classics, London: SCM Press.

(1979) *The City of God*, tr. H. Bettenson, Harmondsworth: Penguin.

Barnard, F. M. (1965) *Herder's Social and Political Thought*, Oxford: Oxford University Press.

Barr, J. (1982) 'Allowing for divine intervention'. *Times Literary Supplement* (24 Dec. 1982), 1422.

Bedford, R. D. (1979) *The Defence of Truth*, Manchester: Manchester University Press.

Bellah, R. N. (1970) 'Religious evolution'. In *Beyond Belief*, ed. R. N. Bellah, New York: Harper & Row.

Berlin, I. (1976) *Vico and Herder*, London: Hogarth Press.

Bianchi, U. (1987) 'History of religions'. In *The Encyclopedia of Religion*, ed. M. Eliade, New York: Macmillan, vol. 6:399–408.

Blount, C. (1695a) *The Oracles of Reason: Miscellaneous Works* Part 1, London.

(1695b) *Great is Diana of the Ephesians: Miscellaneous Works* Part 3.

Bolingbroke, Henry St John (1754) *The Philosophical Works* vol. 2, London.

(1776) *The Philosophical Works* vol. 3, London.

Brandt, R. B. (1941) *The Philosophy of Schleiermacher*, New York: Harper.

Burns, R. M. (1981) *The Great Debate on Miracles*, London: Associated University Presses.

Byrne, P. A. (1988) 'Religion and the religions'. In *The World's Religions* ed. S. R. Sutherland *et al*, London: Routledge, 3–28.

Chantepie de la Saussay, C. P. (1891) *Manual of the Science of Religion*, London: Longman.

Chubb, T. (1731) *A Discourse concerning Reason with Regard to Divine Revelation*, London.

 (1734) *An Enquiry concerning the Books of the New Testament*, in *Four Tracts*, London.

 (1741) *A Discourse of Miracles*, London.

 (1748) 'Concerning Miracles'. In *The Author's Farewell to His Readers*, in *Posthumous Works* vol. 2, London.

Clarke, S. (1738) *A Discourse concerning the Unchangeable Obligations of Natural Religion and the Truth and Certainty of the Christian Revelation*, in *Works* vol. 2, London.

Collingwood, R. G. (1961) *The Idea of History*, Oxford: Oxford University Press.

Collins, A. (1713) *A Discourse of Free-Thinking*, London.

 (1717) *A Philosophical Enquiry into Human Liberty*, London.

 (1724) *A Discourse of the Grounds and Reasons of the Christian Religion*, London.

Craig, W. L. (1985) *The Historical Argument for the Resurrection of Jesus during the Deist Controversy*, Lewiston, NY and Queenston, Ont.: Edwin Mellen Press.

Danto, A. (1985) *Narration and Knowledge*, New York: Columbia University Press.

Durkheim, E. (1976) *The Elementary Forms of the Religious Life*, tr. J. N. Swain, London: Allen & Unwin.

Evans Pritchard, E. (1965) *Theories of Primitive Religion*, Oxford: Oxford University Press.

Forbes, D. (1975) *Hume's Philosophical Politics*, Cambridge: Cambridge University Press.

 (1982) 'Natural Law and the Scottish Enlightenment'. In *The Origins and Nature of the Scottish Enlightenment*, eds. R. H. Campbell and A. S. Skinner, Edinburgh: Donald, 186–204.

Forstman, J. (1977) *A Romantic Triangle: Schleiermacher and Early German Romanticism*, Missoula: Scholars Press.

Frazer, J. (1926) *The Worship of Nature* vol. 1, London: Macmillan.

Gaskin, G. C. A. (1978) *Hume's Philosophy of Religion*, London: Macmillan.

Gay, P. (1967) *The Enlightenment: An Interpretation* vol. 1, *The Rise of Modern Paganism*, London: Weidenfeld & Nicolson.

Geach, P. T. (1969) 'On worshipping the right god'. In *God and the Soul*, London: Routledge, 101–16.

Hardin, B. and Kehrer, G. (1984) 'Sociological approaches'. In *Contemporary Approaches to the Study of Religion* vol. 2, ed. F. Whaling, The Hague: Mouton.

Harvey, V. (1967) *The Historian and the Believer*, London: SCM Press.

Hegel, G. W. F. (1942) *The Philosophy of Right*, tr. T. M. Knox, Oxford: Oxford University Press.

(1956) *Lectures on the Philosophy of History*, tr. J. Sibree, New York: Dover.

(1977) *The Phenomenology of Spirit*, tr. A. V. Miller, Oxford: Oxford University Press.

(1984) *Lectures on the Philosophy of Religion* vol. 1, tr. P. C. Hodgson, Berkeley: University of California Press.

Herbert, E. (1705) *De Religione Gentilium*, tr. W. Lewis as *The Antient Religion of the Gentiles*, London.

(1768) *A Dialogue between a Pupil and his Tutor*, London.

(1936) *De Veritate*, tr. H. Carre, Bristol: Bristol University Press.

(1944) *De Religione Laici*, tr. H. R. Hutcheson, New Haven: Yale University Press.

Herder, J. G. (1879) *On the Spirit of Hebrew Poetry* 1st Part, *Sämmtliche Werke* vol. 11, ed. B. Suphan, Berlin: Weidmansche.

(1880a) *On the Spirit of Hebrew Poetry* 2nd Part, *Werke* vol. 12.

(1880b) *Christian Writings*, *Werke* vol. 20.

(1881) *Meta-critique of the Critique of Pure Reason*, *Werke* vol. 21.

(1887a) *Ideas for the Philosophy of the History of Mankind* Books 1–10, *Werke* vol. 13.

(1887b) *God: Some Conversations*, *Werke* vol. 16.

(1891) *Treatise on the Origin of Language* and *Yet another Philosophy of History*, *Werke* vol. 5.

(1892) *Perception and Experience in the Human Soul*, *Werke* vol. 8.

(1909) *Ideas for the Philosophy of the History of Mankind* Books 11–20, *Werke* vol. 14.

Hume, D. (1882a) *Essays Moral, Political and Literary* vol. 1, eds. T. H. Greene and T. H. Grose, London: Longman.

(1882b) *Essays* vol. 2.

(1975) *Enquiry concerning Human Understanding*, eds. L. A. Selby-Bigge and P. H. Nidditch, Oxford: Oxford University Press.

(1976) *The Natural History of Religion* and *Dialogues concerning Natural Religion*, eds. A. W. Colver and J. V. Price, Oxford: Oxford University Press.

Johnson, S. (1755) *A Dictionary of the English Language*, London.

Justin the Martyr (1943) *The First Apology*, tr. E. R. Hardy, Library of Christian Classics, London: SCM Press.

Kant, I. (1930) *Lectures on Ethics*, tr. L. Infield, London: Methuen.

(1960) *Religion within the Limits of Reason Alone*, eds. T. M. Greene and H. H. Hudson, New York: Harper.

(1963a) 'Conjectural beginnings of human history'. In *Kant on History*, tr. L. Beck, Indianapolis: Bobbs-Merrill, 53–68.

(1963b) 'The end of all things'. In *Kant on History*, 69–84.

(1971a) 'Idea for a universal history with a cosmopolitan purpose'. In *Kant's Political Writings*, tr. H. Nisbet, Cambridge: Cambridge University Press, 41–53.

(1971b) 'Perpetual peace: A philosophical sketch'. In *Kant's Political Writings*, 93–130.

Katz, S. T. (1978) 'Language, epistemology and mysticism'. In *Mysticism and Philosophical Analysis*, ed. Katz, London: Sheldon Press, 22–74.

King, W. L. (1987) 'Religion'. In *The Encyclopedia of Religion*, ed. M. Eliade, New York: Macmillan, vol. 12:282–92.

Leland, J. (1757a) *A View of the Principal Deistic Writers* vol. 1, 3rd edn., London.

(1757b) *A View of the Principal Deistic Writers* vol. 2.

Lessing, G. E. (1956) *Theological Writings*, ed. H. Chadwick, London: A. & C. Black.

Locke, J. (1823a) *An Essay concerning Human Understanding* Books I-II ch.22, *Works* vol. 1, New Edition, London.

(1823b) *Essay concerning Human Understanding* Books II ch.23–IV ch.4, *Works* vol. 2.

(1823c) *Essay concerning Human Understanding* Book IV chs 5 ff., *Works* vol. 3.

(1823d) *A Third Letter for Toleration*, *Works* vol. 6.

(1823e) *The Reasonableness of Christianity* with *A Vindication of the Reasonableness of Christianity* and *A Second Vindication of the Reasonableness of Christianity*, *Works* vol. 7.

(1823f) *A Paraphrase and Notes on the Epistles of St Paul*, *Works* vol. 8.

(1823g) *A Discourse of Miracles*, *Works* vol. 9.

(1954) *Essays on Human Nature*. ed. W. von Leyden, Oxford: Oxford University Press.

Luther, M. (1961) *Lectures on Romans*, tr. W. Pauck, Library of Christian Classics, London: SCM Press.

(1975) *The Bondage of the Will*, tr. J. J. Packer and O. R. Johnston, London: James Clarke.

MacIntyre, A. (1971) 'Rationality and the explanation of action'. In A. MacIntyre, *Against the Self-Images of the Age*, London: Duckworth, 244–59.

Middleton, C. (1729) *A Letter from Rome*, London.

(1749) *A Free Enquiry into the Miraculous Powers*, London.

Montouri, M. (1983) *John Locke on Toleration and the Unity of God*, Amsterdam: J.C. Geiben.

Morgan, T. (1738) *The Moral Philosopher* vol. 1, London.

(1739) *The Moral Philosopher* vol. 2.

(1740) *The Moral Philosopher* vol. 3.

Mueller, F. M. (1861) *Lectures on the Science of Language*, London: Longman.

(1867a) *Chips from a German Workshop* vol. 1, London: Longman.

(1867b) *Chips from a German Workshop* vol. 2.

(1888) *Lectures on the Origin and Growth of Religion*, London: Longman.

(1889) *Natural Religion*, London: Longman.

(1891) *Physical Religion*, London: Longman.

(1892) *Anthropological Religion*, London: Longman.

(1893a) *Introduction to the Science of Religion*, London: Longman.

263

(1893*b*) *Theosophy or Psychological Religion*, London: Longman.

Polyani, M. (1973) *Personal Knowledge*, London: Routledge & Kegan Paul.

Popkin, R. H. (1979) *The History of Scepticism from Erasmus to Spinoza*, Berkeley: University of California Press.

Redwood, J. (1976) *Reason, Ridicule and Religion*, London: Thames & Hudson.

Rudolph, K. (1985) *Historical Fundamentals and the Study of Religions*, New York: Macmillan.

Schleiermacher, F. D. E. (1928) *The Christian Faith*, tr. H. R. Mackintosh and J. Stewart, Edinburgh: T. & T. Clark.

(1958) *On Religion: Speeches to its Cultured Despisers*, tr. J. Oman, New York: Harper.

Schouls, P. (1980) *The Imposition of Method*, Oxford: Oxford University Press.

Sharpe, E. (1975) *Comparative Religion: A History*, London: Duckworth.

Smart, N. (1973) *The Science of Religion and the Sociology of Knowledge*, Princeton: Princeton University Press.

Smith, W. C. (1978) *The Meaning and End of Religion*, London: SPCK.

(1981) *Toward a World Theology*, London: Macmillan.

Smith, W. R. (1923) *Lectures on the Religion of the Semites*, 3rd edn., London: A. & C. Black.

Southwold, M. (1978) 'Buddhism and the definition of religion'. *Man* NS 13:362–79.

Spiro, M. E. (1966) 'Religion: Problems of definition and explanation'. In *Anthropological Approaches to the Study of Religion*, ed M. Banton, London: Tavistock Publications, 85–126.

Stark, R. S. and Bainbridge, W. S. (1985) *The Future of Religion*, Berkeley: University of California Press.

Stephen, L. (1881) *A History of English Thought in the 18th Century* vol. 1, London: Smith & Elder.

Sullivan, R. E. (1982) *John Toland and the Deist Controversy*, Cambridge, Mass.: Harvard University Press.

Swinburne, R. G. (1979) *The Existence of God*, Oxford: Oxford University Press.

Thompson, D. (1968) *The Aims of History*, London: Thames & Hudson.

Thornton, J. M. (1984) 'Miracles and God's existence'. *Philosophy*, 59 ccxxviii 219–29.

Tiele, C. P. (1877) *Outlines of the History of Religion*, London: Trübner.

Tindal, M. (1730) *Christianity as Old as the Creation*, London.

Toland, J. (1696) *Christianity not Mysterious*, London.

(1704) *Letters to Serena*, London.

(1751) *Pantheisticon*, London.

Troeltsch, E. (1913) 'Historische und Dogmatische Methode in der Theologie', *Gesammelte Schriften*, vol. 2, Tübingen: Mohr, 729–53.

Tylor, E. B. (1865) *Researches into the Early History of Mankind*, London: Murray.

(1903*a*) *Primitive Culture* vol. 1, 4th edn., London: Murray.

(1903*b*) *Primitive Culture* vol. 2.

Wach, O. (1958) *The Comparative Study of Religions*, ed. J. M. Kitagawa, New York: Columbia University Press.

Walker, D. P. (1972) *The Ancient Theology*, London: Duckworth.

Webb, C. C. J.(1915) *Studies in the History of Natural Theology*, Oxford: Oxford University Press.

Wiebe, D. (1979) 'The role of belief in the study of religion', *Numen* 26 ii 234–9.

(1981) *Religion and Truth*, The Hague: Mouton.

Wollaston, W. (1724) *The Religion of Nature Delineated*, London.

Woolston, T. (1729*a*) *A Discourse on the Miracles of Our Saviour*, 6th edn., London.

(1729*b*) *A Second Discourse on the Miracles of Our Saviour*, 4th edn., London.

(1729*c*) *A Third Discourse on the Miracles of Our Saviour*, 4th edn., London.

(1729*d*) *A Fourth Discourse on the Miracles of Our Saviour*, 4th edn., London.

(1729*e*) *A Fifth Discourse on the Miracles of Our Saviour*, 3rd edn., London,

(1729*f*) *A Sixth Discourse on the Miracles of Our Saviour*, 2nd edn., London.

Yinger, J. M. (1970) *The Scientific Study of Religion*, New York: Macmillan.

INDEX

above reason 45–9 *passim*
Abraham, W. J. 243–55 *passim*
absolute dependence, feeling of 159
Adam 44, 86
allegory 104, 109
analogy, principle of 244–6, 250–3
Analogy of Religion, The 121
ancestor worship 84
animism 126, 199
Annet, Peter (1693–1729) xiv, 75
anthropological religion 188
anthropology and study of religion 196–203, 229–39 *passim*
Apostles 91, 92
a priori in religion 185, 187, 195, 208, 229, 235–9
Aquinas (c.1224–74) xv, 1–6, 13, 41, 62, 63, 210
Archbishop Whately 196
Athanasius 14
Augustine (354–430) xv, 5–6, 8, 11–17 *passim*, 85
authenticity 162
autonomy of history 209, 238
autonomy of religion 158–66 *passim*

Barnard, F. M. 152
Besonneheit 147–8
Bible, The 91, 92, 93, 137; deists on 93–101; humanity of 106, 110; and presuppositions of history 243–55 *passim*
Blount, C. (1654–93) xiv, 53–6, 66–7, 75, 82–7 *passim*, 90, 124, 226, 227, 234, 239
Bondage of the Will, The 18
Buddhism 210, 213

Burns, R. M. 79

Chantepie de la Saussaye, P. D. (1848–1920) 182, 183, 196
Christ 8, 11, 12, 15, 16, 18–20, 25, 27, 42–7, 75, 81, 83, 89, 92, 93, 104, 108, 110, 125, 152, 165, 192, 193; and miracles 101, 102; and prophecy 103, 104
Christianity 4, 7, 8, 9, 11, 14, 21, 43, 52, 53, 64, 65, 67, 71, 79–82, 88, 92, 93, 94–9 *passim*, 112, 115, 190, 191, 193; as continuation of paganism 89; moral interpretation of 136–9; origins of 104–6, 244, 245, 248, 249; uniqueness of 1, 16, 19, 21, 22–4, 27, 29, 38, 40, 43, 67, 79, 93, 192–4
Christianity not Mysterious xiv, 71, 89
Christianity as Old as the Creation xii, xiv, 54, 59, 66, 105
Christian Writings 132
Chubb, T. (1679–1746) xiv, 92, 94, 95, 100, 102, 116, 252
Church, the 81, 88–93 *passim*, 99; fathers of 82, 91, 92; Kantian idea of 137; in patristic age 90–3
Cicero 63
City of God, The 5
civil theology 1, 5, 29, 79, 85, 119, 120
civilization, origins of 198, 199
Clarke, S. (1675–1729) xiii, 58, 59, 81, 98, 99, 108, 245, 246
Collingwood, R. G. 240
Collins, A. (1676–1729) xiv, 65, 73, 90, 103–5, 109
common notions (catholic articles) 26–37 *passim*, 46, 48

comparability of religions 70, 139
comparative theology 184, 185, 191
concept of development 229
concept of religion ix–xv, 11, 36, 52, 63, 64, 111, 117, 128, 129, 140, 143, 181, 207, 209–26, 239; Western origins of 210–19 passim
conceptual evidence 236–9, 251, 253, 254
Conjectural Beginning of Human History, The 134
consistency in history of religions 250–5
Constantine 91
contemporary study of religion 207–55
correlation, principle of 244–54 passim
Craig, W. J. 243, 244, 249, 252
cumulative tradition 214, 215, 223, 224

Darwin, C. 199
Darwinism 198, 203
De Religione Gentilium 26, 29, 37
De Religione Laici 30
De Veritate 31, 32, 34, 36
definition of religion 63, 64, 153, 154, 185, 186, 210–22 passim
deism, deists 6, 8–10, 17, 22, 52, 53, 71, 76, 79–82, 111, 112, 131, 134, 156, 161–3, 173, 178, 181, 205, 209, 211, 216, 219, 221, 226, 234, 240, 241, 244, 249, 255; and the Bible 93–111; and the Church 88–93; defined xiii–xiv; and doctrine of God 53–61; and doctrine of man 61–9; and Herder 152–6; and history of religion 82–8; and Hume 114–18, 122–4, 128; legacy of ix, xii, 69, 112, 140, 196–200 passim, 207–9, 213, 215, 224, 229, 233, 235, 241, 242, 249, 252, 255; and Mueller 189, 190; and religious certainty 70–8
dialectic (in history) 171
Dialogue between a Pupil and his Tutor, A 24
Dialogues concerning Natural Religion 1, 2, 119
Dictionary of the English Language, A 3
Discourse concerning the Unchangeable Obligations of Natural Religion and the Truth and Certainty of the Christian Revelation, A xiii, 58
Discourse of Free-Thinking, A 73
Discourse of the Grounds and Reasons of the Christian Religion, A 103
Discourse of Miracles, A 48, 51

Discourses on the Miracles of our Saviour 102
discursive reason 33–5
divine agency 252–4
divine goodness 23, 25, 27
divine immutability 58–60
divine justice 12, 13, 16, 17, 18–21, 25, 35, 38, 43–8 passim, 54–8, 62, 73, 74, 98, 116, 253
divine law 59
divine perfection 57, 74
divine religion see supernatural religion
Divine Revelation and the Limits of Historical Criticism 243
divine–human relationship 17, 20, 21, 23, 26, 33, 34, 37, 163, 177
Durkheim, E. 206, 217

Elementary Forms of the Religious Life, The 206
enlightenment xi–xiii, xv, 13, 44, 85, 113, 129, 140, 165, 172, 214, 215
Enquiry concerning Human Understanding, An 114, 120
enthusiasm 76, 103
Essay concerning Human Understanding, An xv, 37, 39, 48–51, 71, 72, 77, 96, 108, 122
Essays on the Law of Nature 41, 47
Essays Moral, Political and Literary 127
ethical commonwealth 134, 135, 137
Evangelists 102
Eve 85
evolution of religion 126, 180
evolutionism 197–203 passim
explanation, nature of 231–5
expressionism 149, 153–6, 167, 168, 171, 173, 177
external apprehension 33, 34

faculty of faith 186–8, 192
faith 43, 44, 48, 49, 72, 85, 214, 215, 225
fall, the 14, 45, 54, 59, 61, 65
family resemblance definitions of religion 221, 222
feeling 159, 160, 170
Forbes, D. 117, 127
Forstman, J. 166
foundations and superstructure of religion 88, 234
Frazer, J. 198
Free Enquiry into the Miraculous Powers, A 90–3, 99
free thinking 73

freedom, free will 18, 147, 167–8, 171, 173
functionalism in definition and explanation of religion 212–20 *passim*

Geist 166–71 *passim*
generic religious experience 216, 225
Genesis 155
God: Some Conversations 145
Goethe, J. W. von 184
Gospel(s) 19, 42, 44, 81

Hegel, G. W. F. (1770–1831) 113, 142, 143, 166–80 *passim*, 181, 182, 184, 205, 226, 240; conception of God 171, 172, 175–8; on human nature 166–78
Herbert, E. (Lord Herbert of Cherbury) (1583–1648) xiv, 22–37 *passim*, 40, 43, 48, 52, 53, 56, 61, 70, 73, 118, 122, 136, 157, 209, 211
Herder, J. G. (1744–1803) xv, 113, 142–56 *passim*, 159, 161, 182, 184, 192, 205, 241; and deism 152; and Hegel 166, 167, 169, 172, 178, 179
Hinduism 223
Historical Argument for the Resurrection of Jesus during the Deist Controversy, The 243
historical-comparative study of religions 184–6
historical-critical method 94, 95, 101, 105, 108–10, 241–55 *passim*
historical-ecclesiastical faiths 137, 138, 140
Historical Fundamentals and the Study of Religion 228
historical perspective on religion 130, 131, 135
historical religions 190, 191
history 12, 17, 21, 26, 35, 37, 40, 41, 57, 70, 100, 181; of culture 197; and human nature 147, 148, 150; humanist 87; naturalism in 241–55; philosophical 87, 124, 125, 140, 239; progress (pattern) in 139, 140, 167–9, 171, 177; religion in 129, 130, 138, 140, 230–40; of religions 10, 64, 67, 69, 80, 82–9, 106, 122, 128, 129, 133, 169, 179, 180, 196; as revelation 151, 192, 193, 194; sense of 143, 147
Hobbes, T. xiv
human nature 3, 4, 9, 12, 15, 20, 21, 44, 45, 47, 133, 142, 208; and culture 205;

evolution in 134, 136; Herbert on 25, 27, 34, 35, 36, 37, 85, 87; Herder on 143, 146–9; Hume on 114–28 *passim*; immutability of 61, 65; uniformity of 35, 66, 67, 69
human religious condition 236–40, 242, 243
humanism 20, 21, 22, 23, 26, 35, 47, 51, 52, 56, 64, 65, 129
humanity of religion 111, 112, 114, 175
Hume, D. (1711–76) xiv, 1, 2, 113–28 *passim*, 129, 130, 139, 140, 142, 153, 154, 182, 209, 219, 241, 250; naturalism in 117, 124; and Tylor 196, 199, 202

Idea for a Universal History with a Cosmopolitan Purpose 134, 139
idealism 141, 143, 178, 195, 208, 209, 228
Ideas for the Philosophy of the History of Mankind 144
idolatry 13–15, 18, 27–9, 84, 86, 88, 89
imagination: and Herder 154; and Kant 130, 131, 136, 140
immortality 44, 61–3, 74, 121
individualism 51
infinite, the 211; in Mueller 187, 188, 192; and Schleiermacher 160, 164
inscription (innate ideas): and deists 76–8, 118; in Herbert 26, 30, 33, 34, 36, 37; and Hume 122, 123; and Locke 37, 39, 40, 47, 49
inspiration of scripture 245, 247; and deists 93–101, 103, 106, 107, 109; and Herder 144–6
intentionality of religious experience 225, 226
internal apprehension 33–5
Introduction to the Science of Religion 190
Islam 43, 90, 223

Jainism 210
Johnson, S. 3
Judaism 7, 8, 27, 125, 133, 138, 139, 190

Kant, I. (1724–1804) 23, 68, 113, 128–31 *passim*, 142, 147, 150, 172, 182, 196, 209; and Mueller 183, 185, 186, 189
Kingdom of God, Kant on 135
knowledge, naturalistic views of 38–40, 44, 76, 77

Koran 135
Kraft 145–6, 154

language 148, 162, 185
law and constitution 173–5
Lectures on Ethics 131
Lectures on the Philosophy of History 166, 167, 171
Lectures on the Philosophy of Religion 170, 171, 176
Lectures on the Religion of the Semites 205
Lectures on Romans 17, 18
Leland, J. xiii, xiv, 98, 245, 246
Lessing, G. E. 75
Letter from Rome, A. 91
Locke, J. (1632–1704) xv, 8, 37–51 *passim*, 52, 57, 61, 62, 81, 86, 89, 209, 244–8; and deists 71–4, 76, 96–8, 106–8; and Hume 116, 122, 125
Luther, M. (1483–1546) 17, 18, 52, 55

MacIntyre, A. 32, 234, 242
master–slave relation 168, 172
Meaning and End of Religion, The 213, 223, 224
methodological atheism 248
Middleton, C. (1683–1750) xiv, 90–2, 99, 250, 251
mind 146, 149
miracle 163, 191, 193, 244–54 *passim*; deists on 90–103, 106; Hume on 114–17; Locke on 44, 49–51
modes and circumstances of religion 88
monotheism 15, 133, 159; Hume on 124–8 *passim*; Locke on 42, 43, 49
Montaigne, M. de 32
morality 4, 9, 13, 15, 74, 80; deists on 61–4; Herder on 152, 153; Kant on 132, 133, 136; Locke on 40–3, 47; Schleiermacher on 157–60; *see also* natural law
Morgan, T. (d.1734) 4, 9, 64, 83, 84, 125
Moses 8, 24, 81
Mueller, F. M. (1823–1900) 7, 8, 143, 144, 183–96, 200–4, 208–9, 228, 237; and universality of religion 209–13, 216, 225, 241, 249
mystery 46, 71, 72
myth 131; Mueller on 133
mythic theology 1, 5, 29, 79, 85, 119, 120

narrative 235–40 *passim*
Natural History of Religion, The 114–28 *passim*, 130, 140, 153, 154, 199
natural human religiousness 1, 69, 87, 118, 122–5, 133, 143, 144, 159, 166, 175, 181–3, 187, 189, 195, 196, 201, 202, 204–6, 208, 209, 226–42 *passim*, 255
natural instinct 33–5, 39
natural law 4, 8, 9; in deism 58–60; and Hume 121, 122
Natural Religion 7
natural religion xii–xiv, 112, 113, 204, 255; and Christianity 11, 12, 15–17; defined 1–10 *passim*; and deists 52–3, 56, 63–80 *passim*, 86–9, 93–5, 105, 108, 109; and Hegel 166, 169, 172, 174, 175, 178, 179; and Herbert 32, 34–6; and Herder 143, 144, 146, 151, 152; and Hume 114, 118–21, 125, 126; and Kant 129–40 *passim*; and Locke 38, 43, 44, 49, 51; and Mueller 186–91; as original religion 10, 82–4, 112; and Schleiermacher 156–9, 161, 164, 198, 199 202
natural religions (as opposed to supernatural) 7, 8
natural rights 173–5
natural theology xii, 1–4, 5, 7, 8, 12, 13, 28, 29, 119
naturalism 23, 32, 36, 165, 166, 182, 208; as anthropocentrism 241–55 *passim*; in contemporary study of religions 214–15, 241–55 *passim*; in deists 52–3, 76, 77, 95, 98, 100, 106; in Locke 39, 40, 44, 45, 51; mitigated 249, 250; and reductionism 241–2; in Tylor 196, 198
nature 28–31, 36, 59, 159, 160
nature mysticism 186
neo-platonism 43
New Testament 8, 49, 50, 82, 92, 145
non-theistic religions 210–17

'Of Commerce' 127
'Of the Immortality of the Soul' 119, 120
'Of National Characters' 119
'Of Refinement in the Arts' 127
'Of Religion, Doctrine and Rites' 152
'Of the Rise and Progress of the Arts and Sciences' 127
Of True Religion 15

Old Testament 8, 24, 49, 50, 82, 103, 104, 108, 144, 155, 156; relations with New Testament 109
'On Historical and Dogmatic Method in Theology' 244
On Religion: Speeches to its Cultured Despisers 156–66 *passim*, 176
On the Spirit of Christianity 144
On the Spirit of Hebrew Poetry 144, 155
On the Spirit and the Letter 15, 17
Oracles of Reason, The 53, 59, 75, 87
original truths 108
origins of religion 82–3, 125, 126, 129; *see also* natural religion

pagan (-ism) 5–7, 10, 13–18, 27–9, 42, 43, 80, 81, 84, 88, 89, 92, 125, 136
pantheism 145, 146
Paraphrase and Notes on the Epistles of St Paul, A 51
passions 123, 124
permanence of religion 201–3
Phenomenology of Spirit, The 166, 168, 171
Philosophical Enquiry into Human Liberty, A xiv
philosophy of history 209
philosophy of religion 208, 209, 243, 249
Philosophy of Right, The 173
physical religion 188
Plato 14, 15
platonism 6, 13, 14, 118
poetry 155, 156
Polanyi, M. 238
politics and religion 172–5
polytheism 28, 29, 42, 136
popular religion 131–3, 136
positive religion 67, 124, 157, 158, 162, 163
postulates of practical reason 133
priestcraft 29, 42, 67, 69, 80, 81, 84, 86
primal spirituality 187, 189
Primitive Culture 7, 196, 202
primitive religion 8, 153–5, 197
probability in history 96–100, 103, 116, 244–6, 248
problem of evil 121
progress (evolution) in religion 130, 133, 140, 163, 195, 208, 209
prophecy 103, 104, 165
Protestant (-ism) 82, 90, 91, 99
providence 12, 129, 150, 151; and deists 54, 60–2; general 60; Herbert on 24–37 *passim*; Hume on 118, 120–3,

126; and Locke 38–40, 43; special 60
psychological religion 188

rationalism 60, 61, 64, 88, 135, 228
'Rationality and the explanation of action' 232
reason 1–4, 7, 132, 189, 199, 203, 233, 234; and deists 63, 65, 66, 68, 70–8, 83–5, 89; Herbert on 32–7; and Hume 120–3; and Locke 38–51
Reasonableness of Christianity, The 41–8, 51, 62, 71
Redemption 26, 35, 44
Redwood, J. 79
reflection 39, 40, 45
religion–faiths distinction 135–8
religion as illusion 231–3, 242
Religion within the Limits of Reason Alone 131–40 *passim*
religion of nature *see* natural religion
Religion of Nature Delineated, The 61
'Religion: Problems of Definition and Explanation' 211
religion of reason 8, 64, 65, 79, 172; Hume on 120–8 *passim*; Kant on 129–40 *passim*; *see also* natural religion
religion (in general) and the religions 161, 181–3, 186, 200, 226–9, 236–9
religious certainty (knowledge): deists on 70–8, 100; Herbert on 23, 30–6 *passim*; and Locke 38–51 *passim*
religious diversity 31, 190
religious radicals 189, 190
repentance 44, 46, 47, 57
Republic, The 14
Researches into the Early History of Mankind 198
resurrection, the 75, 101, 193, 245, 246
revealed religion xiii, xiv, 1–4, 31, 44, 51, 53, 54, 70, 75, 76, 79, 132, 137, 139
revealed theology 1–4, 5
revelation 9, 111, 112, 118, 121, 132, 188, 191, 198, 252; and deists 55, 57, 60, 70–4, 98, 103, 108; domestication of 143, 144, 165, 192, 193; general 10, 118, 181, 192, 229; and Herbert 30, 31, 35; and Locke 39–51; as primeval 187; progressive 151, 162, 163; special 10, 192
ritual 131
Roman Catholicism 81, 82, 91, 92
Roman Empire 89

Romans 13, 18
romanticism 141–3, 166, 178, 184, 189, 190, 195, 208, 209, 214; perspective on religion 178–80, 228
Rudolph, K. 228, 229, 231, 237

sacred 217
sacrifice 84
St Paul 13, 14, 20, 41, 55, 103
salvation 3, 4, 11–13, 16–20, 24–6, 29, 30; deists on 53, 62, 63, 74; Locke on 40, 43, 45–7
salvation (sacred) history 103, 104, 247, 248, 251
scepticism 32
Schleiermacher, F. D. E. (1768–1834) 113, 142, 143, 156–66 *passim*, 169, 175–9, 181, 182, 203, 241; and Mueller 186, 189, 192; and universality of religion 211–13, 216, 225
science (study) of religion 124, 192, 204; Mueller on 184, 190, 191, 194–6; *see also* history of religions
sensation 39, 40, 45
Sensus numinis 186
sin, sinfulness 14, 15, 18–20, 25, 54, 55
Smith, W. C. 213, 215, 222–6, 243
Smith, W. R. 205, 206
social anthropology 205
social character of religion 205, 206, 208, 227; Kant on 130–1, 135–7, 140
Socrates 14, 65
Southwold, M. 221, 222
Spinoza, B. 145, 159
Spirit, Holy 76
Spiro, M. E. 211–13, 217, 221
state of nature 173, 174
Stephen, L. 79
Stoicism 77
Summa Contra Gentiles xv, 2
'Summary Account of the Deists' Religion, A' 56
Summa Theologiae xv, 2, 5
superhuman beings, belief in 212
supernatural religion 1, 7, 8, 79, 111, 187–91
superstition 42, 71, 88, 89
survivals 203

testimony 50
theoretic theology 184, 185
Third Letter for Toleration, A 48
Thompson, D. 238
Thornton, J. M. 253, 254
Tiele, C. P. 182, 228
Tindal, M. (?1657–1733) xii, 86, 113, 125, 143, 152, 155; on the Bible 99, 105–11; on God 54, 55, 57, 59; on human nature 61, 64–7; on religious certainty 74–7
Toland, J. (1670–1722) xiv, 71–6, 81, 83–5, 89–91, 125
totemism 206
Toward a World Theology 214
tradition 49, 73, 75, 76
traditional religion 68, 69, 80
traditional truth 50, 108
Treatise on the Origin of Language 148
Troeltsch, E. 244, 246, 255
truth 32, 141, 193; and rationality 231–4; and universality 131, 132
Tylor, E. B. (1832–1917) 7, 196–204, 241

ultimate concerns 217–19
uniformity of religion 65, 80, 143, 200
universality of religion 9, 10, 27, 122, 135, 155, 195, 200–2, 227; in contemporary thought 209–26 *passim*; deists and 52, 53, 63, 64, 69; Locke on 38–43 *passim*

Varro, M. 6, 8, 9, 28, 29
Vedas 135
View of the Principal Deistic Writers, A xii–xiv

Way of Ideas 49, 50, 76, 107, 108
Wiebe, D. 223, 231, 233
Wollaston, W. (1660–1724) xiv, 54, 58, 60–2, 66, 100, 121
Woolston, T. (1670–1731) xiv, 101, 102

Yet Another Philosophy of History 150, 151, 154
Yinger, J. M. 227

Zend-Avesta 135

DATE DUE

HIGHSMITH   # 45220